THE Bewitched BOOK

HERBIE J PILATO

THE Bewitched BOOK

THE COSMIC COMPANION TO TV'S MOST MAGICAL SUPERNATURAL SITUATION COMEDY

Delta

A Delta Book
Published by
Dell Publishing
a division of
Bantam Doubleday Dell Publishing Group, Inc.
666 Fifth Avenue
New York, New York 10103

The author conducted interviews with Dick York, Harry Ackerman, Jerry Davis, and David White before their untimely deaths. This book is dedicated to their memory.

Permissions have been granted for all *Bewitched* photos, illustrations, memorabilia, and cover animation courtesy of Columbia Pictures Television and Don De Mesquita, Senior Vice-President, Corporate Communications/Publicity of Columbia Pictures Television.

Library of Congress Cataloging in Publication Data

Pilato, Herbie J
The Bewitched book : the cosmic companion to TV's most magical supernatural situation comedy / by Herbie J Pilato.
p. cm.
ISBN 0-385-30699-7 (pbk)
1. Bewitched (Television program) I. Title.
PN1992.77.B48P5 1992
791.45′72—dc20 92-9080 CIP

Manufactured in the United States of America
Published simultaneously in Canada

October 1992

10 9 8 7 6 5 4 3 2 1

RRH

Dedicated to the
silent magic
named "Peace"

CONTENTS

COSMIC CODEX

INTRODUCTION

Consider this treatment for a prospective television show for the postmodern, postfeminist era:

A young woman comes from a tight-knit ethnically exotic family that still observes religious orthodoxy. This woman, in fact, is the family's shining hope, a true believer in the ways of the old world, and the most spiritually vibrant practitioner of the family's religious customs.

The woman shocks her family when she chooses to marry outside the faith. In fact, she falls in love with a man with no faith of his own but the good old American work ethic. He is the consummate American corporate man, and he insists that his betrothed give up the traditional practices of her faith and become a nice corporate wife.

For the good of the relationship, but with misgivings, the woman agrees. Of course, her family is outraged. More than that, they are deeply hurt that the woman would discard her natural-born talents, especially because they hold the husband in such low regard. He is the embodiment of secular humanism, and they are among the last torchbearers of their increasingly archaic religion. The family has no choice, since the woman is determined to please her new husband. But they vow to make life difficult for the newlyweds and try to get the husband to lighten up on his position, if not actually convert.

Therein is the premise underlying each episode of this prospective comedy series. Week after week, the husband will try to succeed in business without the help of his wife's direct connection to the greater Spirit. He will be unsuccessful because his wife's family messes things up. As much as the wife tries to keep her word not to let her natural talents save the day, eventually she must do just that.

Every program's moral is the same: No matter how much one tries to suppress one's natural idiosyncracies in order to fit into modern society, it will not work. Spirituality must always prevail over matters of commerce. And love conquers all.

Sound familiar?

Of course, since you are reading this book, you must already realize what a special show *Bewitched* really was. Debuting in the fall of 1964, *Bewitched* was progressive without being moralistic. It boasted a brilliant cast of regulars who were augmented by a repertory company of supporting players. The men and women who worked behind the scenes knew very early on that they were blessed with a great premise, and they made the most of it.

The Bewitched *Book* was created to honor the cast and crew who created this most heaven-blessed series, and to remind readers, with pictures and text, of what made *Bewitched* television's most magical, supernatural situation comedy.

THE *Bewitched* BOOK

WELCOME TO THE MAGIC SHOW

I belong to the greatest minority of them all . . . I'm a witch.
—Samantha, Episode No. 164, "The Battle of Burning Oak"

What would happen if a pretty little witch with a twitch named Samantha married a nice young mortal named Darrin? That question was successfully answered for eight highly rated television seasons on *Bewitched*.

A triumph of storytelling, special effects, and gimmickery, this magic sitcom originally aired on ABC–TV from September 17, 1964, to July 1, 1972.

The cast was charismatic, as Elizabeth Montgomery portrayed Samantha; Dick York and Dick Sargent offered a dual turn as Darrin (York left in 1969 because of a serious back ailment); the late David White was Larry Tate, Darrin's greedy boss and vice-president of McMann and Tate Advertising, and the late Agnes Moorehead played Samantha's feisty mother, Endora.

While on ABC, the series collected twenty-two Emmy nominations (five alone for Elizabeth), winning awards for director William Asher in 1966 (he also produced and was at the time Montgomery's husband), and posthumously for both Alice Pearce as nosy mortal neighbor Gladys Kravitz, also in 1966, and Marion Lorne as the bumbling witch, Aunt Clara, in 1968.

Darrin and Samantha's first meeting. (Columbia Pictures Television.)

Other performers included Sandra Gould (who stepped in as Gladys Kravitz when Pearce passed away in 1966), George Tobias

(Abner Kravitz), Paul Lynde (the practical joker and warlock, Uncle Arthur), Alice Ghostley (the inept magic maid, Esmeralda), Bernard Fox (Dr. Bombay, the witch doctor), Irene Vernon and Kasey Rogers (as Larry Tate's supportive wife, Louise, 1964–66 and 1966–72, respectively), Mabel Albertson (as Darrin's nerve-wracked mother, Phyllis Stephens), Robert F. Simon and Roy Roberts (sharing the role of Frank Stephens, Phyllis's husband), and Maurice Evans (as Samantha's regal father, also named Maurice), among several more.

The sitcom's debut met a superreceptive audience that was quickly won over by Samantha's magic. In its first season the series ran second in the ratings only to NBC's *Bonanza* and received a 31.0 Nielson rating, meaning that 31 percent of the television population tuned in to *Bewitched* in its initial year.

In 1969 the sitcom's combined prime-time and daytime audience (ABC ran it daily from January 1968 to September 1973) totaled 55 million viewers—a record for a program in its sixth season. That same year *Good Housekeeping* magazine named the half-hour comedy "the most agreeable show on the air."

Samantha's series averaged a 22.6 rating and 35 percent audience share for its entire eight-year run on ABC, and it was the number one show on that network for four of those years. Until 1977 (and the surpassing popularity of *Happy Days*), *Bewitched* was the highest rated half-hour prime-time program ever to air on ABC.

Today, in reruns the world over (England, Australia, Germany, and Egypt, just to name a few), Darrin and Samantha continue the trials and tribulations that arise when witch meets mortal, a mixed marriage follows, and they try to live happily ever after.

In the show's pilot segment, "I, Darrin, Take This Witch, Samantha," she informs him of her supernatural persuasion—after the wedding and during the honeymoon. Each episode that follows is a new misadventure, as Sam (as she's affectionately known to Darrin) tries to adapt her unique ways to the life of the average suburban woman.

Learning to live with witchcraft is one thing, but Endora's petulant dislike of her son-in-law (due to his eagerness to succeed without witchcraft) is the story conflict that carried the sitcom through its extensive run. This dissension, coupled with the fact that Samantha and Darrin love each other in spite of their differences, is the core of the show's appeal.

Satirically, *Bewitched* promotes a positive outlook on an all-American—albeit all-witch-American—way of life. Samantha and Darrin are not presented simply as witch and mortal, but rather as caring wife and faithful husband, who as parental figures (they have two supernatural offspring, Tabitha and Adam, played by twins Erin and Diane Murphy and David and Greg Lawrence), take pleasure in the family unit.

Bewitched proves to be enduring escapist fare augmented by a humanist outlook.

As in contemporary times, the 1960s had their share of turbulence and political tensions. The *Bewitched* pilot began production on November 22, 1963—the day President John F. Kennedy was assassinated—and premiered less than one year later.

Bill Asher had produced Kennedy's televised birthday bash, featuring Marilyn Monroe singing a breathy "Happy Birthday," and he recalls the President's passing on the pilot's first day of rehearsal: "It was a tough day because both Liz and I were friends with Kennedy. But we knew we had to go on."

Elizabeth remembers being in her bedroom, getting ready to go the studio for the pilot's production, and hearing Asher scream from the parlor, "No! It can't be true!" "For some reason," she says, "I felt it had nothing to do with the family, but it's as if I inherently knew what had happened.

"The whole thing was very strange, but to keep on working did seem to be the right thing to do, to go ahead and have the first reading of the script. And it was very interesting because there wasn't one person who didn't show up, and there weren't any phone calls made. It was like everyone on the set just needed to talk to each other."

During the years *Bewitched* was aired, America also lost Senator Robert Kennedy and the Reverend Martin Luther King to assassins. In an era of these losses, the Vietnamese War, and race rioting, many might have thought that only a magical intervention could have put an end to the turbulence of the times.

These were not "wonder years" at all, but wonderless, save for *Bewitched*. Samantha offered her world of sane fantasy to the insane reality of the television audience. She was beautiful, smart, and filled with magic . . . everything our world wasn't. As the

Bill Asher and Elizabeth check a shot during the filming of the pilot. (Columbia Pictures Television.)

American people viewed the weekly escapades of a witch, they could daydream about how much simpler their war-torn lives might be if they had Samantha's magical finesse.

As a result of its popularity, *Bewitched* inspired several replicas. *I Dream of Jeannie* began on NBC–TV in 1965. This fun show, starring Barbara Eden as a genie to Larry Hagman's frantic astronaut master, was most similar to *Bewitched*—right down to the animated opening credit sequence.

While Samantha would manifest her magic with the twitch of her nose, Jeannie would do the same with the blink of her eyes. On *Bewitched,* Samantha had a mischievous cousin named Serena, played by Elizabeth in makeup and a brunette wig. Likewise, Jeannie acquired a look-alike sister of a Serena-sinister nature, acted by Eden in a black coiffure.

Jeannie's genesis was assuredly inspired by Samantha.

Screen Gems (known today as Columbia Pictures Television), which produced *Bewitched,* and rival network NBC were quite anxious to cash in on the success of ABC's witch-comedy format. So anxious, in fact, that they tried to acquire the services of *Bewitched*'s pilot scripter, Sol Saks, who declined. "I had already created one witch," he said recently. "I did not wish to do another."

The studio then commissioned novelist and now miniseries king Sidney Sheldon to create *I Dream of Jeannie.* Ironically, *Bewitched* executive producer Harry Ackerman (who passed away in December of 1990) had introduced Sheldon to Screen Gems's executives some years before, and he held himself partly responsible for delivering Jeannie to her master viewership.

Moreover, Bill Asher and Sheldon were close friends who had worked together on *The Patty Duke Show.* "Sidney was very polite about the whole situation," says Asher. "He came to me and said, 'How do you feel if I do a show about a genie?' And I told him I didn't care."

Asher's confidence rested with Elizabeth's aforementioned and now-famous unique ability to wriggle her upper lip. Referring to the birth of Samantha's coveted, quick-twisting nose, Asher says, "I knew it had to be something that no one else could do. And the witch-twitch was the answer. It was a little nervous thing Liz did without her being aware of it."

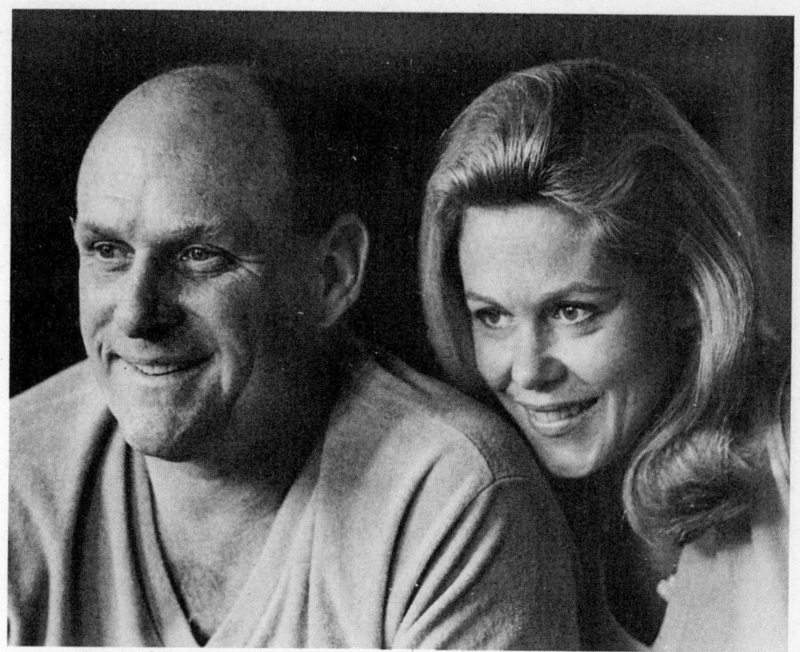

Bill Asher and Elizabeth Montgomery. (Dan Weaver collection.)

When first approached about employing her facial expertise, Elizabeth told Asher, "I don't know what you're talking about. I don't do anything like that." "It became quite an issue between us," says Asher. "I couldn't believe that she didn't know what I meant. I thought she was trying to avoid doing it. And it wasn't until the night before we filmed the pilot that she did it and I said, 'That's it!'"

Sheldon then wondered with what distinguishing gesture would Eden's Jeannie exercise *her* magic? Asher told him: "I don't know. Maybe you have to marry Barbara to find out!"

CBS jumped on the magic bandwagon and introduced *Sabrina, the Teen-Age Witch* to Saturday mornings. Sabrina had first appeared in the comic book *Archie's Madhouse No. 22* (October 10, 1962). She had blond hair just like Samantha, and while Samantha twitched, Sabrina—of all things—tugged her ear to make magic. And the closeness to Samantha's cousin's name is obvious.

Other charming color copies include Samantha and Darrin themselves, as they made an animated appearance in episode No.

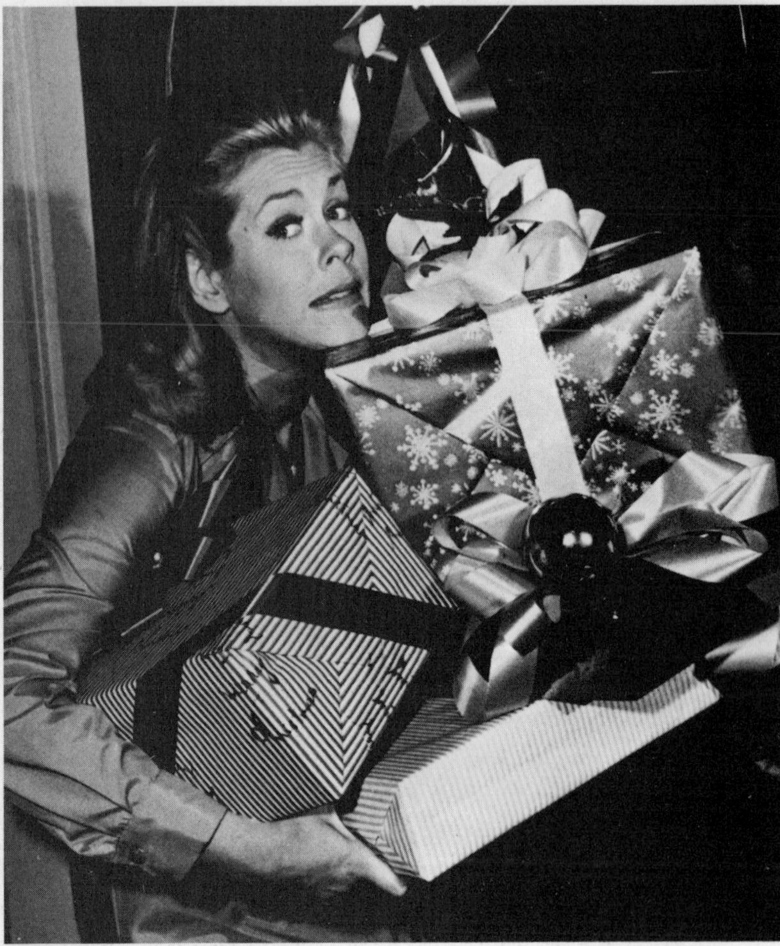

Samantha as a gift-bearing witch. (Columbia Pictures Television/Milton T. Moore, Jr.)

146 of *The Flintstones* entitled "Samantha." This segment, which was recently released by Hanna-Barbera on video as part of the six-tape *Flintstones' 30th Anniversary Collection*, even featured the voices of Elizabeth Montgomery and Dick York.

How did this all come about?

"The network and the studio made us do that," says Bill Asher. *Bewitched* and *The Flintstones* were both on ABC, and Columbia had a contract with Hanna-Barbera.

Of her experience in working with Fred and Wilma Flintstone, Elizabeth recalls little. "I just remember going into the voice-over studio," she says, "and having fun with the script." "It was the 'in thing' to do at the time," adds Dick York. "Everyone guested on that show, so Liz and I just decided to go in there and have a great time with it."

York distinctly remembers not getting paid for the job. "Instead of a check," he says, laughing, "I got a TV."

The "Samantha" *Flintstones* episode, which can also still be seen in reruns, involved the Stephenses in caveman garb temporarily moving next door to Bedrock's favorite Stone Age family.

Needless to say, Wilma makes a mild Mrs. Kravitz.

As many times as television has tried to repeat the magic formula of *Bewitched*, it rarely manages to duplicate its success.

For example, NBC aired a supernatural sitcom pilot in May 1989 called *A Little Bit Strange*. This was a combination of *Bewitched* and *The Munsters* with a black cast. There was a mom with ESP, a Frankenstein-like son, a cousin who was a vampire, and a little boy warlock who rapped incantations. But the entertainment trade magazine *Daily Variety* explained why *A Little Bit Strange* was even too strange for the fantasy comedy market. "It's a takeoff on the old *Bewitched* series," said the publication, ". . . but the producers seem intent on playing up the gimmickery."

Elizabeth explains what distinguishes *Bewitched* from *A Little Bit Strange* and other fantasy comedies and tryouts: "*Bewitched* is not about cleaning up the house with a magic wave . . . or zapping up the toast . . . or flying around the living room. It's about a very difficult relationship. And I think people pick up on this. They know there's something else going on besides the magic. If the show is watched carefully, its other elements can be seen."

Elizabeth points out that one of these other elements is the sitcom's central hidden theme, which is, in fact, the same as the general story conflict of the entire program. In a word, it's "prejudice," she says, "and how it can get people off on the wrong track at times." She continues to explain that Samantha, being a witch, "is an outsider trying to belong . . . always looking for Darrin's or the mortal world's approval in some indirect way, if not directly. Actually," she says after a pause, "one of the few things that Endora and Samantha agreed on was that witches were an ousted minority group."

The self-effacing actress, who is active in such groups as AIDS Project L.A., Amnesty International, and the peace movement, says she's not labeling *Bewitched* the "message show of the century, but I always felt that there is something in it for everybody. As much fun as I know it is for little kids to watch, I also know adults enjoy it as well. And if the audience is looking for a message, they'll find it."

Bewitched speaks to the patriot in the audience as well as the socially conscious viewer. Many episodes celebrate freedom and equality and condemn prejudice. When great historical figures such as Benjamin Franklin and George Washington visit the Stephenses through the magical mishaps of either Marion Lorne's bumbling Aunt Clara or Alice Ghostley's nervous witch-maid Esmeralda, they leave behind profound wisdom for Samantha, Darrin, *and* the audience to relish.

"I think the show strikes some real chords with the viewers," states Bill Asher. "It's concerned with an individual's expression of liberty . . . people's rights in general, and the restrictions that are placed on those rights."

One episode protesting prejudice and hailing human unity was among the show's initial episodes from 1964, No. 7, "The Witches Are Out." Here Samantha, Aunt Clara, and other immortals persuade Darrin's client to change the trademark of his Halloween candy from the stereotyped wicked-old-crone-with-warts look to a more flattering guise.

In a similar premise Endora turns Darrin into a werewolf because of his antiwitch comments in No. 43, "Trick or Treat," from the second season. But here Samantha really lets her mother have it: "For years you've complained about how they [mortals] make fun of witches," she scolds Endora, ". . . dressed up as ugly old crones . . . cackling and pretending to turn people into toads. 'We're not like that,' you said; 'we're civilized, nice people,' you said. But now you're acting just like those ignorant people think a witch acts. Don't you *see*? You're behaving like all the stereotypes of witches you hate so much! And you've done it to the one person who was willing to believe we were different!"

Endora apologizes to Darrin and Samantha in this episode (she actually says "I'm sorry"), but she never seems to learn her lesson thoroughly as she continues to "change" him throughout the series. In fact, in No. 177, "To Trick or Treat or Not to Trick or Treat" (another Halloween outing), she turns Darrin into one of

A *publicity shot of Samantha and Endora over a witches' brew. (Columbia Pictures Television.)*

the old crones her daughter had earlier referred to. Yet in each of these segments, prejudice was properly displaced.

Another episode blasting bias is No. 119, "Samantha's Thanksgiving to Remember." Here, Aunt Clara's dysfunctional magic finds herself, Sam, Darrin, Tabitha, and Mrs. Kravitz (who thinks the whole thing is a dream) in seventeenth-century Salem, where Darrin is quick to point out, "They burn witches . . . !"

To his surprise, it is he who is accused of witchery, as he lights the fire for turkey dinner with a twentieth-century match.

Samantha delivers a rousing speech on ethnocentrism in the dialect of the day (which Darrin termed "Pilgrim talk") at her husband's trial.

She defends him in this way:

> "Art thou clumsy, 'tis not thy own fault; cry witch. Art thou forgetful, blame not thyself; cry witch. Whatever thy failings, take not the fault upon thyself. 'Tis more a comfort to place it on another. And how do we know we decide who is the witch? 'Tis simple. . . . Does someone speak differently from thee? A sign of witchery? Does he show different mannerisms? Witchery, of course. And should we not find differences in speech and mannerisms to support a charge of witchery, be of good cheer. There are other differences.
>
> "What of him who looketh different," she continues. "What of her whose name has a different sound? If one examineth one's neighbors closely, he will find differences enough so that no one is safe from the charge of witchery. But is that what we seek in this new world? Methinks not. The hope of this world lyeth in our acceptence of all differences and a recognition of our common humanity."

An encounter with bigotry closer to home may be found in No. 164, "The Battle of Burning Oak," in which Sam and Darrin have a slight brush with the arrogant members of a pretentious private club, and Endora pickets the witch-horror film *Rosemary's Baby* (which Uncle Arthur does as well at the Cannes Film Festival in No. 169, "Samantha's Shopping Spree").

One *Bewitched* episode, which also happens to be one of Elizabeth's personal favorites, is No. 213, "Sisters at Heart," a Christmas story in which Darrin is removed from an important toy account because a bigoted client mistakes a little girl who happens to be black for the Stephenses' daughter. The child, Lisa, is the daughter of McMann and Tate's Keith Wilson, and she becomes close friends with Tabitha—so close that Tabitha wishes they could be sisters.

Unfortunately, while in the park, a playmate tells the two young girls that this is impossible because they are of different colors. Upset, Tabitha uses her "wishcraft" (anything she wishes comes true) and turns herself and Lisa into sisters . . . of sorts. White polka dots appear on Lisa and black spots on Tabitha.

Samantha acquires an antidote from Dr. Bombay and tells Lisa and Tabitha, "You can be sisters without looking alike. . . . Sisters are girls who share something. Actually, 'all' men are brothers . . . even if they're girls."

"When we did that one," says Elizabeth of "Heart," "I thought, 'Yeah . . . this is what I want *Bewitched* to be all about.'"

Apparently, "Sisters at Heart" was a special episode for many reasons. The story was written by students of the fifth period English class at Thomas Jefferson High School in Los Angeles, and that year (1970), an article appeared in *TV Guide* profiling the occasion.

Bewitched writer Barbara Avedon, who had assisted the students with certain aspects of the story, states, "That was my favorite script of all time." Avedon, a veteran of *The Donna Reed Show,* and more recently *Cagney and Lacey,* recalls: "I had stopped writing for *Bewitched* and everything else when Bill Asher phoned me and explained how these kids had written this great script, but that it needed a slight rewrite.

"So I went down to Jefferson High," she continues, "which was an inner-city school, and I was horrified. Locker doors were hanging off their hinges, and there wasn't a blade of grass in sight. And what was worse is that these kids had been reading on a third-grade level. It was awful.

"But I walked into their classroom, and their teacher, Marcella Saunders, had asked them who had watched *Bewitched* the night before. And every hand in the room went up. And then she asked them why they liked it. 'Well,' said one young man, 'it's a mixed marriage. She's a witch and he's human . . . and she could have anything she wants but doesn't use her powers for selfish reasons . . . only once in a while to help her husband.' It was really a wonderful moment," she says.

Avedon then read the story the class had written and "was amazed!" "That script," she states, "was as good as any that I had seen from established writers. It just had to be polished up a little. So I was honest with the kids. I said, 'I don't like to be rewritten and I don't want to rewrite you, but maybe if we work together, I think we can really create something beautiful.'

"I told them I wouldn't make any changes that they wouldn't approve of because I loved the basic idea. The one major change I suggested was that we make it a Christmas show because it was so infested with the spirit."

After Avedon finished talking with the class, "they all kind of just sat there stone silent for a minute," she says. "Then one of them stood up and introduced himself. Almost immediately, the other students rose one by one, and the class and I became friends."

Marcella Saunders, who's still teaching today, could not say enough good things about this unique *Bewitched* experience. "We were writing a Christmas story and we were experiencing a Christmas story. Everyone on the show was so pleasant and supportive."

Dick Sargent, however, credits Saunders with being the motivating force behind her students' creativity. "She was the inspiration," he says. "She was interested in innovative forms of teaching. And these kids, who might have been stuck in the ghetto for the rest of their lives, loved *Bewitched*, and with just a little approval and motivation, came alive on the set.

"One of them," says Sargent, "was the assistant director, who had the chance to scream, 'Quiet on the set!' . . . and it was marvelous. . . . Doing the show gave them—at least for a brief time—a change of pace and scenery. And they just reveled in it."

In 1971 "Sisters at Heart" won the Governor's Award at the Emmy ceremony.

"Sisters" and other episodes negated prejudice and celebrated freedom. One segment campaigned for UNICEF (No. 166, "Samantha Twitches for UNICEF"); others had Samantha fight city hall to have the proper city councilman elected (No. 23, "Red Light, Green Light") or to save a neighborhood park (No. 149, "Samantha Fights City Hall"). Obviously, *Bewitched* spoke to patriots and socially aware viewers.

Bewitched came to us in the sixties at a time when social upheavals were common and attitudes about marriage and family were being redefined. The fantasy element of the show offered an escape from everyday life, and the humor of absurd situations delighted us over and over again. On many occasions *Bewitched* effectively wove moral and social values into its illusory tales. It gave us a lovable witch, a happy and committed marriage, and it created wonder in our living rooms.

BORN IN THE SPARKLE OF A STAR

We are quicksilver, a fleeting shadow, a distant sound.
Our home has no boundaries beyond which we cannot pass—
we live in music—in a flash of color.
We live on the wind and in the sparkle of a star.
—Endora, Episode No. 2, "Be It Ever So Mortgaged"

A TV sitcom is usually created with a particular star in mind for the lead role. With *Bewitched*, stage and film actress Tammy Grimes was originally chosen to play Samantha.

"Tammy was approached about doing the show," said Harry Ackerman, "but before we went into production, she informed me that [playwright] Noel Coward had asked her to star in *High Spirits* (a Broadway musical directed by Coward based on his *Blithe Spirit*), so we let her out of the contract. And it's funny," he said, because he ran into her every two or three years and she was "still kicking herself for not having done the show."

Enter Elizabeth Montgomery and William Asher. The couple had recently been married, and after completing the film *Johnny Cool* (1963—she starred, he directed), Asher recalls, "Liz didn't want to work [anymore], mostly because it meant separation and shooting locations. But I felt that would have been a great loss because I knew she had a lot to offer the industry . . . and that she should be working—for herself as well as for her contribution to the business."

Asher suggested the possibility of doing a television series with his wife—then there wouldn't be any periods of separation.

According to Asher, "Liz was all for that." The producer/director then thought of developing his idea for a series about "the richest girl in the world . . . a real Getty's-daughter type thing," he says.

This project, entitled *The Fun Couple*, centered around a young married surfer twosome named Bob and Ellen. He worked at a gas station and was a very independent person, and she was wealthy, which proved most intimidating for her spouse.

Asher took *The Fun Couple* to Columbia Studios and executive William Dozier (who brought *Batman* to television in 1966). Dozier told him, "I think you should talk to Harry Ackerman. He's got something in mind that's very similar and that you might like better."

That "something" was *Bewitched*. Asher and Montgomery flipped over it and signed to do the show.

Regarding Tammy Grimes as the original choice for the series lead, Elizabeth says, "I got the role because Tammy turned it down, and I will always be eternally grateful to her for that. I didn't get the part because I beat out hundreds of women in some huge casting call which was painstakingly narrowed down to me. Tammy said 'no,' and I said 'yes,' and I was simply at the right place at the right time."

Who actually gave birth to *Bewitched*? The line of creativity stretches far and wide. According to Harry Ackerman, he "created *Bewitched* through the instigation of Bill Dozier who was my superior at Screen Gems at the time," and that together, they hired Sol Saks (who received screen credit) to write the *Bewitched* pilot.

"He [Dozier] took me to breakfast one morning," said Ackerman, "and asked me if I'd be interested in developing a show about a man who married a witch. I was immediately taken with the idea, and I began typing a treatment that ran eight or nine pages and that I called *The Witch of Westport*." Ackerman outlined the characters who would eventually become Samantha, Darrin, and Endora, and he brought it to Dozier, who was enthusiastic about the project. They started to look for writers.

The first person they talked to was George Axelrod (who cowrote the screenplay for *The Manchurian Candidate* [1962] with Richard Condon from Condon's novel), whom Ackerman had known from his radio years at CBS in New York. "George was as excited as Bill and I were about the idea," said Ackerman, "but he contacted us after he agreed to do the show, and said he was much too busy with feature films to do *Bewitched*."

This led Ackerman to meet with another well-known screenwriter named Charles Lederer, who had cowritten the Broadway musical *Kismet*. Unfortunately, when Lederer was approached about doing *Bewitched*, cancer had left him in poor health, so the search continued.

Then Ackerman and Dozier ventured into television land and hooked up with Sol Saks (who had previously written for Ackerman and CBS on *My Favorite Husband*, 1953–55). And as Ackerman stated, "Sol ended up writing the pilot."

Though Saks agrees that he wrote the *Bewitched* pilot, he remembers the story differently. "I met with Harry Ackerman and Bill Dozier and we talked about different ideas for a comedy series. I then suggested the premise of a witch who lives as a mortal. I wrote the pilot and went on to teach a writers' workshop."

In Saks's *The Craft of Comedy Writing* (Writer's Digest Books, 1985), he says, "There has been much published and public controversy about who of several were initially responsible for the [*Bewitched*] idea, a contretemps that I carefully stayed out of. I felt the entire question was academic . . . because I was already receiving contractual and screen credit."

Ackerman's response? "The Writers' Guild rules," he said, "state that whoever writes the pilot episode [of a particular series] will be credited as its creator. Yes, Sol Saks did write and develop the *Bewitched* pilot, but it was I who had initially introduced the basic concept and story many months before my first meeting with Sol."

Furthermore, the individual who writes the pilot episode of a given series continues to benefit monetarily for his efforts throughout the life of the series, even from episodes that were scripted by other writers.

Ackerman confirmed this: "I never had any ownership of *Bewitched*, because I was salaried at Screen Gems. But I must say that years later, my agent raised hell (with the studio) for not remunerating me properly for having created the idea. Afterward we worked out a new deal which paid me $50,000 over and above my salary each year the show was on ABC."

The creator's spot on *Bewitched* was not the show's only hot seat, however. Though William Asher was with the series from the start as its main director, he was essentially a silent producer and was credited as a production assistant in the show's initial years.

Danny Arnold, Jerry Davis (who passed away in January 1991), and William Froug were credited as producers for the first, second, and third seasons, respectively.

Asher was heavily committed to films (including, in 1965, *How to Stuff a Wild Bikini,* which featured Elizabeth in a cameo role doing the "twitch"), so he was unable to produce the TV show. He credits the three producers: "Each made major contributions to the show . . . particularly Danny with regard to writing."

Bewitched story editor Bernard Slade, who also wrote seventeen scripts for the show, confirms Asher's assessment of Arnold's input on the program: "Danny set the tone of the show, and his casting was brilliant. . . . It certainly wasn't by accident that he went on to produce *Barney Miller* (ABC, 1975 to 1982), which had impeccable casting. He's just very imaginative and one of the best story people I know."

As the show evolved, a creative conflict developed when Harry Ackerman suggested that Samantha should become mortal after her first year of marriage to Darrin. Arnold was opposed to the idea. "I felt we would have hit a brick wall with that angle," he says. "It bypassed the main conflict of the show."

Bill Asher agreed with Arnold; he felt this "would have been a major drawback" in the series.

Ackerman's suggestion was that each time Samantha twitched, she'd move closer to a permanent mortal transformation because she was practicing witchcraft in a human environment. He felt this would add an element of suspense to the series.

From Arnold's perspective, the show's conflict was divided into two main sections: (1) the power of a woman versus the ego of a man, and (2) a mother's objection to her daughter's marrying an unsophisticated man.

These conflicts were sustained on *Bewitched* without direct recourse to Samantha's witchcraft and supernatural premise of the series. Consequently, the show was allowed to concentrate more closely on the characters' relationships. Samantha remained a witch and was never granted free use of her powers (on a regular basis) by Darrin.

There were still other decisions to be made in creating *Be-*

witched, such as who would play Darrin (whose last name was originally Douglas in the pilot script).

Before Dick York won the role, Richard Crenna (a good friend of Bill Asher's) and Dick Sargent (years before he replaced York in 1969) were distinct possibilities.

"By the time they got back to me," recalls Sargent, "I had signed with Universal to do a [television] show called *Broadside.*" This program aired on ABC from 1964 to 1965 and also featured Kathleen Nolan and Edward Andrews.

Sargent doesn't mean to denigrate York, but he says, "I was the first person they saw, read, and liked for the role." Ironically, before he finally did appear on *Bewitched,* Sargent portrayed the twin brother to initial *Bewitched* lead choice Tammy Grimes in her series, *The Tammy Grimes Show.* Her name on the show was "Tamantha."

Nevertheless, Dick York won the role. "I went in and met with Elizabeth," York recalled, "and then someone handed us a script, and we did a quick run-through [reading]. We went through it again in front of Bill [Asher] and Harry [Ackerman], and when we finished, I hopped on Liz's lap, turned to them and said, 'Hey . . . aren't we cute together? You have to hire us!' And I got the job. And that's how I got all my acting jobs. I figured they'd either hire me or they wouldn't, so I would never pull any stops and just go for it."

After the pilot was completed, Sol Saks remembers, there was serious speculation as to whether or not York was good-looking enough, even though he thought York's average looks were a plus. But Bill Asher doesn't remember thinking that York wasn't right for the role. "He was just too good," Asher states.

"What made it work," adds Elizabeth, "is that you didn't have Cary Grant, which—don't get me wrong—would have been lovely, but Darrin didn't need to be exquisite-looking for Samantha to have married him. That was the whole point. She could have zapped up the most gorgeous guy in the world—right out of *GQ*—but she didn't because she loved Darrin in particular and in spite of the way he looked, talked, or thought. There was so much more going on between them besides any physical attraction they had for each other."

Once Darrin was cast, the next question was who would play Endora, who was referred to as just plain Mother in the original pilot script.

"I suggested Agnes Moorehead," said Harry Ackerman. "Everyone in Hollywood had thought of her as a highly dramatic actress, but I had worked with her in radio days on *The Phil Baker Show,* where I was assistant director. Phil used her regularly as a stooge [a comedian positioned in the audience] and she was quite funny."

A*gnes Moorehead publicity shot. (Columbia Pictures Television.)*

Elizabeth remembers meeting Moorehead in a New York department store and offering her the Endora role. "We [she and Bill Asher] were in Bloomingdales," says Liz, "and I heard this voice. I turned around, and there—in the ribbon department—was this incredible redheaded lady. She looked like a serving of cotton candy because she had this rather large hat on her head that was made of pink tulle. I had never seen anything like it.

"So I said out loud, 'Oh, my God—who is that woman? She's absolutely marvelous!' And someone said, 'Oh, that's Agnes Moorehead.' And I said, 'The actress?' And they said, 'yes.'

"So I went up to Aggie and introduced myself and asked her right off the bat if she was working in anything. And she said, 'Well . . . no.' And then I asked her if she would ever consider doing a television series. And she said, 'Probably . . . probably not.' *Sounds good to me,* I thought, and I ran up to Bill and said, 'I found Mother.' And he said, 'Oh, that's nice. Where is she and why didn't you invite her to dinner? We haven't seen her in a while.'"

"No, not *my* mother," Elizabeth told Asher. "Mother! . . . as in Samantha."

It didn't take too much to persuade Asher to hire Agnes as Endora. He remembered working with the famed redheaded star in the NBC–TV remake of *The Wizard of Oz,* in which Agnes played—what else?—the Wicked Witch of the West.

Moorehead, however, reluctantly agreed to do the *Bewitched* pilot. "It was absolutely ridiculous the way it happened," she told a reporter in 1965. "First they offered me an enormous amount of money to make the pilot of the series. I read the script and said to myself, 'Why not? This series is so way-out, so totally devoid of commercial possibilities, it couldn't possibly sell.' So I did the pilot, pocketed the money, and went on the road to do a one-woman show.

"I completely forgot about it until I got back to California. Then I received a call from the producer. '*Bewitched,*' he said, 'has been sold.'" Agnes shuddered at the recollection. "All I could think of was, 'Oh, how dreadful!'"

"She confessed to me once," admits Elizabeth, "that she was hoping *Bewitched* was going to be a terrible flop so that she wouldn't have to be stuck in it. And I joked with her and said, 'Oh, that's a wonderful attitude.'"

Of course, despite Moorehead's protestations, she did a marvelous job in the role of Endora.

Grounded Pilot Concepts

There were several characters created by Sol Saks, Bill Asher, and Danny Arnold who did not appear in the pilot.

For example, Darrin's sister and Samantha's father were written out of the pilot because of lack of time. And according to Sol Saks, who created each of these characters, this was unfortunate. Even though Samantha's father was finally written into the show, Saks says, "Darrin's sister was not . . . and she would have been a good character. Someone on his side."

Fortunately, more members of Darrin's family who were also created during the pilot's formation *did* appear as the show continued, in particular, Darrin's parents, Phyllis and Frank Stephens. "We always knew we'd use them," says Bill Asher of the elder Mr. and Mrs. Stephens, "so we just kept them on the back burner until it was the right time for them to show up."

According to technically oriented production notes, many people were responsible for creating the sitcom's theme and general music content, as well as its opening credit sequence.

Don Kirshner was the show's musical consultant (and later host and producer of *Don Kirshner's Rock Concert* on NBC in the 1970s—a precursor to MTV), while Warren Barker, Van Alexander, Pete Carpenter, and Jimmie Haskell all coordinated the general music on the series. Of major musical note, Howard Greenfield and Jack Keller wrote the opening theme.

At one point the Broadway tune "Bewitched, Bothered and Bewildered," from the classic stage musical *Pal Joey* (1940), was to be used in the initial sequence on *Bewitched*. And as Danny Arnold recalls, "Everybody was really excited about that, but the studio wanted to use an original theme."

Though Columbia did own the right to *Joey*, they opted for the

Greenfield/Keller title, though Elizabeth was a little disappointed that "Bewildered" was not thematically employed. "I thought the one we used served its purpose," she says. "It was lilty and nice, but 'Bewitched, Bothered and Bewildered' is so pretty. I really wish we could have used it. . . . Also because the lyrics were so good."

There were also lyrics to the Greenfield/Keller theme, but they were not used on the show. Why not? "I just thought it would have been too much activity for the audience to follow," said Harry Ackerman. "I wanted them to be able to read the credits and see the animation. And listening to the theme's words might have almost become a chore."

Ah, yes, the animation, which Ackerman "was quite thrilled with. . . . It was a different way to go," he said, "and it kind of tipped off the fact that Samantha had supernatural powers."

Elizabeth was never fully satisfied with the cartoon image of Samantha and Darrin. "I thought it was cute," she says, "but it was too simple. I wanted something snappier. I always looked at it as a great animated storyboard that could have been developed into something more sophisticated. I just thought it never looked as good as it could have."

What would she have preferred? "Well," she says, smiling, "something along the lines of *Who Framed Roger Rabbit*. If not, then at least *Bambi* or *Snow White*."

There was still one last conceptual adjustment to make. Elizabeth and Bill were expecting their first child, William, Jr. Would Samantha and Darrin be expecting as well?

Asher had experienced a similar predicament on *I Love Lucy* (which he also directed) when Lucille Ball was pregnant with Desi Arnaz, Jr. This situation was remedied by having both Lucys deliver Desi, Jr., and Little Ricky. On *Bewitched*, the decision was made to shoot around Elizabeth's pregnant condition. That is, only close-ups, over-the-shoulder angles, and long shots with Liz were used.

So, in 1964 *Bewitched* was created. It was the first TV show to use fantasy in a modern, suburban world. It was a test, an unconventional stab at entertaining America. Each carefully cast actor worked with writers, directors, and producers to create a convincing picture of an unreal world. Happily, the cooperative effort proved to delight us over and over for eight years.

THIS WITCH FOR HIRE, ON FIRE

When we had Samantha in bed with Larry, and Darrin in bed with Louise . . . that was about as racy as we got on the show.
—*Bewitched* director/associate producer Richard Michaels, commenting on Episode No. 221, "Mixed Doubles," in which a spell causes Darrin and Larry each to mistake his own wife for the other's

***B**ewitched* was not without its controversies on the way from the finished pilot to full sponsorship and a place on ABC's schedule. Even today, network executives would probably be leery of programming a series with themes of witchcraft or satanism, so imagine how cautious they were in the early sixties!

It may come as some surprise, then, that it was a sponsor that finally prodded ABC executives to add *Bewitched* to the schedule. Quaker Oats sought to promote its products on ABC and chose *Bewitched* for sponsorship. Yet ABC President Tom Moore was concerned that the show's supernatural themes would offend viewers in the Bible Belt. "My network will lose all the South and the Midwest," he told Bill Asher. "Tom, this is all made up," Asher says he replied. "It's only a TV show." Moore replied that "if it's only a TV show, then the audience won't believe it or watch it anyway."

Because ABC waffled on picking up *Bewitched*, the show was offered to CBS executive James Aubrey, who wanted the series for his network. Ultimately, Tom Moore was pressured into picking up the series despite his own discomfort, and ultimately the show enjoyed the shared sponsorship of Quaker Oats and Chevrolet.

Samantha and Endora. (Columbia Pictures Television.)

It is clear that when it comes to controversy, network executives haven't changed much in the past thirty years. Yet the creators of *Bewitched* were always careful not to interject the darker elements of the supernatural into the show.

"We were very conscious," explains Jerry Davis, "not to cross those lines." And Richard Michaels, the show's associate producer, who also directed fifty-four episodes, adds, "There were never any intentional evil elements to *Bewitched*. We were all having too much fun to concern ourselves with such an angle. If people drew such conclusions, they did so on their own accord. I mean, we're talking about a comedy here. . . . We had people like Marion Lorne and Paul Lynde, for Pete's sake."

"The only objections I've come across," says writer Sol Saks, "was through a radio show I did promoting my book. Before I did this one show, the station manager asked me not to mention anything about *Bewitched* because the station was very family-oriented." Saks thought this was "a little silly," as *Bewitched* has been the most financially successful work of his career, and he also included the series pilot script in his publication.

"I found out later," he says, "that it's the belief of some very conservative people that witches are considered very evil creatures. Now, the truth of the matter," continues Saks, "is that there have always been bad witches . . . *and* good witches, such as Cinderella's godmother. And I just couldn't understand how they were picking on little innocent Samantha."

Dick York also recently experienced some flack about Samantha's allegedly "bad" attitude, by a wave of static receptions through the radio. "I was doing a show for the homeless," says York, "and someone called in and explained how they wouldn't let their children watch the show because they thought it was sacrilegious."

York also says that he "receives about one or two letters a year stating, 'I know you didn't mean to imply any evil association, but I can't allow my children to watch your show.'"

York respects these responses, but feels they are wrong assumptions. "I never thought of Samantha or any of the other witches as really evil. . . . The show was about how much two people really loved each other, no matter how different they were."

When a show is as popular as *Bewitched*, there is bound to be a wide range of viewer contact, with varying perspectives and opinions to debate. However, labeling the show as unfit for family viewing seems a bit off the mark—especially since there was never any conscious intent to stir up controversy, and its high entertainment value has brought television viewers the world over many hours of laughter.

Samantha and Darrin displayed many traditional beliefs. The Stephenses honored Sunday as a day of rest in many episodes. In No. 106, "Nobody but a Frog Knows How to Live," Sam says a silent prayer that two opposing characters not run into each other. In another example, No. 111, "Double, Double Toil and Trouble," she helps out at a church function, and she's actually in church in No. 13, "Love Is Blind."

In addition to the show's most conscientious path of dispelling prejudice and other ignorance, the series spoke heartwarmingly in several holiday outings.

In No. 15, "A Vision of Sugar Plums," the Stephenses take an orphan who hates Christmas to see Santa Claus at the North Pole, and the bearded one tells the child, "We all grow older and our

Elizabeth Montgomery and Ronald Long as Santa in "Santa Comes to Visit and Stays and Stays." (Columbia Pictures Television/Dan Weaver collection.)

eyes get weaker, but what we've seen with our hearts remains forever a thing of joy and beauty." And then good ol' St. Nick states, "Remember, Michael, the real happiness of Christmas isn't found in what we get, but what we give."

Agnes of God

If *Bewitched* had ever intended to slur any church or religion, Agnes Moorehead—a strong-willed, opinionated Christian woman—would have put a stop to it. She was the daughter of a Presbyterian minister, and as author James Robert Parish reported in his book, *Good Dames* (A. S. Barnes and Company, 1974), Agnes once said, "My life has been ruled by my beliefs

Agnes Moorehead. (Herbie J Pilato collection).

('working for the glory of God') and in matters of belief I am a Fundamentalist."

"She was *very* religious," noted David White. "We never got into an actual debate over the matter, but if I would say something she didn't like, she'd tell me, 'You better be careful, David. God is watching.'" To which White would jokingly reply, "Then may I be struck by lightning." And just in case such a bolt of fate transpired, "a couple of people who may have been standing around me at the time," he said, "would move away."

"Agnes did quote God a lot," adds Irene Vernon, "but there were so many other aspects of her personality that she made you feel that you could talk to her about anything. On occasion, I would be invited to her dressing room, and that's when I came to realize that she was a deeply religious woman. Very nice, and obviously talented, but most spiritual."

Vernon believes this spiritual energy enforced Moorehead's theatrical talents and allowed her to play Endora with "such flare."

What may be of additional interest to some is that Agnes appeared in the films *The Left Hand of God* (1955), *All That Heaven Allows* (1956), and *The Singing Nun* (1966). And she also tutored the late Jeffrey Hunter (Captain Pike in the first *Star Trek* pilot, entitled "The Cage") as Jesus in the 1961 version of *King of Kings*.

So Let It Be Written, So Let It Not Be Done

There were some restrictions put upon the show that were met with integrity by the show's creators.

For instance, McMann and Tate had every possible kind of advertising account, from Tinker Bell Diapers to Halloween candy to truck transmissions. However, *Bewitched* wasn't allowed to use certain names as clients of the firm.

"If a writer created a particular name," says Richard Baer, who wrote twenty-three episodes for the show, "and that name turned out to be a real person in the advertising business, we would have to change it." How would anyone know? "We had a very good research department," says Baer. He adds, "It was unfortunate in this case, because one of the best ways for a writer to think up a good-sounding name is to reference real people they know, or at least know of."

Baer's predicament was minor compared to what Bill Asher was confronted with regarding the show's censorship blues. There was one *Bewitched* script having to do with greed and the auto industry, which Asher says, "they wouldn't let us do" because Chevrolet was a sponsor.

Asher himself was surprised that "we got away with as much as we did" regarding the advertising business. As an example, Asher points to Endora's consistently negative opinion of Darrin's profession. "She thought he was always making false claims about products that he never used," says Asher.

What exactly was the problem with the auto industry story?

In the script, Darrin was promoting a new car and Endora

explained that this was another example of how insincere he was as an ad man. She felt there was not any real necessity for people to buy *new* cars. One line of Endora's particularly stands out in Asher's memory. She said to Darrin: "You make people buy things that they don't really want or need."

She subtly stated a similar opinion in many episodes that did make it to the air, but never as directly, nor was there a chance of offending an actual *Bewitched* sponsor. Bill was disappointed not to be able to complete the "auto" episode. "I thought it was a good idea," he says, "and that it taught a great lesson. People don't really have to buy new cars every year. They only do it because their neighbors up the street do and because they're overloaded with commercials that are very convincing.

"If no one bought a new car for, say, a year," Asher states, "it wouldn't affect anyone's life. People who would buy cars for their kids coming of age would just buy a used car—that may be a couple of years old. There's nothing wrong with that . . . it shouldn't have to be a new one."

Further developments in this unproduced *Bewitched* story almost blew a spark plug at Chevrolet. In the script, Endora puts a spell on the entire country, prohibiting anyone from buying a new car for an entire year. As a result, the economy begins to deteriorate. Understandably, Chevrolet was, as Asher recalls, "not too happy."

In spite of Asher's experience with this "lost" *Bewitched* script, the producers actually did air episodes that were controversial. For example, in No. 110, "Business, Italian Style," Darrin needs to learn Italian for proper client negotiations with Chef Romani Foods. Endora casts a spell on her son-in-law and basically turns him into an Italian. This prompts Samantha to say things like *"Oh, Mamma!"* and *"Mamma mia!"*

Through the course of the segment, Darrin understands the Italian language so well that he has forgotten English, and he has to relearn it with Samantha's help. Consequently, one of the first lines he speaks upon relearning his native tongue is broken English, heavily accented with Italian. When he meets Mr. Romani, he says, "I am-a hoppy to-a mak-a your-a acquainten-ence."

Samantha reacts to this with embarrassment and Darrin replies, "I'm-a doin' the best I-a can." Furthermore, when Sam insists Endora take the spell off her afflicted husband, it's a slow

Darrin and Gene Blakely as his friend Dave. (Columbia Pictures Television/Milton T. Moore, Jr.)

Elizabeth and writer Richard Michaels on the set in 1964. (Courtesy of Richard Michaels/E. Ben Emerson.)

road, as Endora offers a sarcastic excuse: "I'm-a doin' the best I-a can."

Elizabeth defends the funny and innocent dialogue of this and other *Bewitched* episodes, "We were always careful not to overstep the bounds of bad taste . . . or not to get anyone too upset." And then she adds, "I guess it would have had to depend on who we were offending, but it would have to have been something really terrible."

For example, she points out, "If we received letters from Italians saying, 'How dare you make fun of our race,' it would have been one thing, but we never received anything like that."

Of his role in "Business, Italian Style," Dick York says firmly, "I loved saying 'I am-a hoppy to-a mak-a your acquainten-ence,' and I don't think it offended anybody."

From the writers' perspective on the show's censorship situation, Bernard Slade, who was story editor for *Bewitched* during its first two seasons, explains: "At the staff meetings, if someone ever objected to a story, it really wasn't because of censorship, but rather because they did not like the idea itself.

"When writers would come in," Slade continues, "they would generally pitch [offer] maybe six or seven plots. And sometimes we would use them, and sometimes we wouldn't . . . or maybe we had already used them before. But if someone came in with a risqué idea"—which, Slade professes, never happened—"the network wouldn't have objected anyway because they had much less control over their television shows in the days of *Bewitched*."

In fact, when the *Bewitched* pilot was made, it was sold to ABC as a finished product, so they had very little editorial impact. In spite of the lack of censorship on the show's issues, the writers of *Bewitched* stayed well within the bounds of mainstream American standards of good taste. The show presented a broad array of characters, none of whom were used as stereotypes. Although the cast occasionally received negative feedback from viewers who took the witchcraft seriously, overall they were delighted at the wide audience they were able to please.

A publicity shot of Samantha and Endora in witches' garb. (Columbia Pictures Television.)

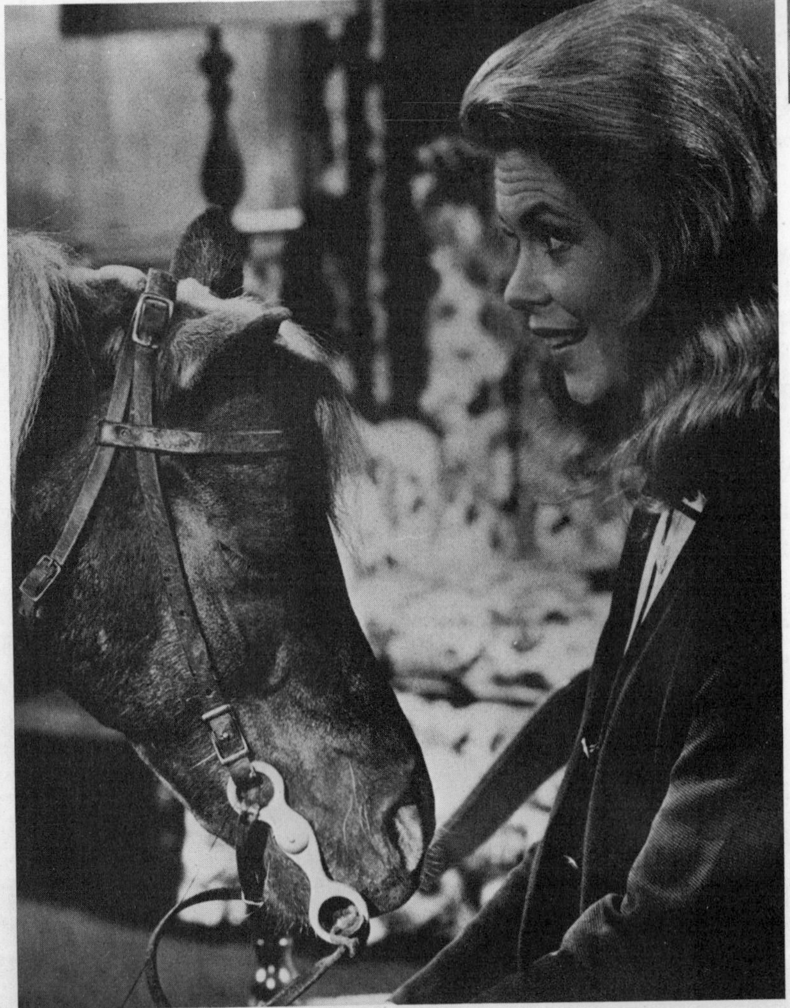

Samantha talking to a horse. (Columbia Pictures Television/Milton T. Moore, Jr.)

THE TWITCH DIMENSION

I happen to think cooking on a stove is a lot more fun than using witchcraft . . . and I also enjoy taking care of my husband and children in the everyday mortal way.

—Samantha, Episode No. 181, "Darrin the Warlock"

Several *Bewitched* episodes deal with Samantha's loss or lack of powers. This was instigated by some rare witches' disease or metaphysical presence such as Endora or the Witches' Council, both of whom strongly objected to Samantha's mortal bonding.

These story lines contributed to the show's substance. Often, Samantha's being left without witchcraft to function as a mortal was the result of a miscast spell. There were times, too, when Samantha chose to forfeit her powers. In such cases, the mortal audience related more easily to her on a human level, and further endeared her to them.

Bill Asher explains: "I knew that the magical aspects of *Bewitched* would not hold up on their own. In the beginning, the audience would think it was cute and funny that Samantha could twitch her nose, but if it was done too often, the gimmickery would lose appeal.

"At first," says Bill, "Liz was having trouble holding back Samantha's 'witch-twitch'. . . . I think she was a little put off by the fact that Sam would always wait to zap or hex some obnoxious character. She'd say, 'Samantha's a wimp!' And I'd tell her, 'No, she's not—she's a hero—she's Shane.'"

Asher was referring to the 1953 film starring Alan Ladd as a retired gunslinger who hangs up his guns. He goes through much humiliation and insult as his townspeople taunt and challenge him to draw his weapons.

Asher screened the movie for Elizabeth and told her, "Sam doesn't twitch her nose until the audience wants her to."

Says Elizabeth of the Shane interpretation, "It made absolutely perfect sense. If you have a weapon, be it a gun, witchcraft, or a sharp-tongued wit, you recognize it as something that you can rely on. But your principles are such that you do not pull out the big guns unless you really have to.

"There's a certain dignity to Samantha's decision to hold back on her power just as there was for Shane to control his fast draw. It had to do with Samantha's promise to herself and to Darrin of not using witchcraft . . . her own self-expectations and living up to them.

"A kind of exaggerated promises-you-can't-quite-keep-except-only-sometimes type thing," says Liz. "And the feeling that maybe if Samantha does help, then getting caught at something she wasn't supposed to do wasn't so bad after all because the end result was positive. . . . The guns shouldn't be pulled off the wall indiscriminately, because someone could get hurt. . . . And also, it just implies good manners. Something we're all brought up with . . . that you don't take advantage of other people."

A perfect example of Samantha's heroic Shane-like ethic occurs in an episode from the third season, No. 88, "Samantha for the Defense," which is the conclusion of a two-part story involving a surprise visit from Benjamin Franklin, compliments of Aunt Clara's bumbling witchery.

In the course of this segment, Franklin is accused of stealing a classic fire engine from the town's firehouse and is brought to court on charges of grand theft. Assistant D.A. Chuck Hawkins feels Franklin is a publicity stunt planted by McMann and Tate, and he insults Franklin, thinking he is just an actor. This prompts Samantha to whisper to Darrin, "I wish I could put a hex on him." But Darrin holds her back.

Finally Samantha is called to the bench by Hawkins as a witness, and she has had enough of his inconsiderate behavior, as has the audience. With a long-held twitch, she immobilizes the D.A.'s jaw and presents a plaque to the court that she had earlier removed from the engine. It reads: BENJAMIN FRANKLIN MEMORIAL FIRE ENGINE. The courtroom then hails her as she states, "A man can't be accused of stealing his own property."

Samantha properly withheld her powers in "Defense" (as well as in several other episodes involving confrontations with repugnant characters—for example, No. 65, "Disappearing Samantha"), as would any average person when pushed to the limit. But as an actress, after Elizabeth understood Samantha's affinity with Shane, she felt more comfortable with her TV counterpart's apprehensive manifestations of witchcraft. Accordingly, Samantha retained her self-respect, which in turn endeared her to the audience, as the witch-twitch became something eagerly anticipated by the television viewer.

Bewitched was the sum of its parts and never relied on any one specific element of its premise, but rather on the rigid structure and format from which it was initially conceived. Bill Asher expands on the program's original idea as he explains the boundaries in which it remained: "The story I was after all the time—and the one we usually would use—would be one that would work without witchcraft. There was always the danger of ruining the

The Bewitched *cast and crew in 1967. (Columbia Pictures Television.)*

premise and characterizations with too much magic. I always felt that the audience really didn't care about the magic, but rather the relationships and interactions between the characters.

"Darrin loved Samantha enough to stay with her regardless of how bad the situation was . . . it would have been worse without her. And Samantha's love for Darrin was so potent, she was willing to give up her heritage to be his wife.

"It's important to remember," says Asher, "that Samantha could have had anything she wanted, but she chose not to take that path. And I think, on a subconscious level, the audience picked up on this. They'd look at Darrin and Sam and say, 'Hey, they're not going for the easy way out, they want to earn their way. If Samantha doesn't think life as a mortal is so horrendous, I guess I don't have it so bad after all.' "

"I always felt," adds Montgomery, "that Samantha and Darrin's marriage was the one thing that witchcraft couldn't do anything about, one way or the other. Sam's feelings for Darrin were so real and honest that even though she could have gone and zapped him into being madly in love with her, it would have been a hollow victory, because he would have been under a spell.

"So when it came to her love for Darrin, she knew exactly where she was coming from. And if she ever had any questions as to how he felt about her, there would only be that same doubt as with anyone. She would ask herself, 'Has he found someone else? Have I done something wrong? Is there anything I could do right?' All of the things that would go through the average mortal woman's head."

Samantha–Darrin dialogue from two episodes illustrates perfectly their mutual love: No. 99, "Charlie Harper, Winner" and No. 157, "One Touch of Midas."

In "Winner," Samantha conjures up a fur coat to impress the snobbish wife of Darrin's overachieving college chum, Charlie Harper. After Darrin gets wind of this, he confronts Samantha.

> Sam: Well, Darrin, what was I to do? Daphne was being so patronizing. She practically called you a loser.
> Darrin: So to prove what a winner I was, you gave yourself a mink coat!
> Sam: Well—I'm sorry, darling. Well, she could have said anything in the world about me, but I didn't want her to knock you . . . don't you understand?
> Darrin: Perfectly. I'm enough of a breadwinner to pro-

vide you with the necessities, but when it comes to the luxuries I want to give you, I can't compete with your witchcraft. I can't give you anything you can't zap up yourself.
Sam: Darrin, please let me explain—
Darrin: Explain what? I think everything is all too clear.

Later, however, Samantha ends up giving the coat to Daphne, who so fell in love with the fur that she offered to buy it from the Stephenses.

Sam: Daphne, you don't understand . . . I want you to have the coat.
Daphne: You're *giving* it to me?
Sam: Charlie told me how much you admired it, so I want you to have it.
Charlie: Well, that's a marvelous coat, Samantha. This is worth a great deal of money . . . you can't do that.
Daphne: Oh, you can't give away anything this valuable.
Sam: Oh, yes, you can, Daphne. When you value something else a great deal more.
Daphne: More than this. Oh, you're kidding.
Sam: No, I'm not. I don't think I've been as serious or meant anything as much in my life.

In the meantime, Darrin is watching from the side, and on hearing these last lines from Samantha, he walks over and hugs her, speaking her name softly.

In "Midas," Endora enchants a toy doll to be manufactured, which will make Darrin a rich man. Unaware of this, Darrin confesses to Samantha that he'll now be able to give her the things he's always wanted to, but couldn't afford.

Darrin: Honey, it's just that I've always wanted the best for you and Tabitha. When we were married, you made a big sacrifice for me. . . . [he tickles her nose]
Sam: But—
Darrin: Now, you did. You gave up . . . you know what. And I realize I'm probably overdoing it, but this money is my chance to give you all the things you could have had.
Sam: Darrin, all the money in the world couldn't buy what we already have.
Darrin: I know that, Sam. Just let me have the joy of overdoing it for a little while.
Sam: Uhm? That may be the nicest thing you ever said to me.

Of both No. 99 and No. 157, Dick York says: "When these moments occurred, the show was no longer just a sitcom." Samantha and Darrin endured trials and tribulations that were universal. In these episodes and many others they were a young married couple struggling to get the hang of marriage. They occasionally doubted each other but always reaffirmed their love and commitment. It was the power of Samantha's human qualities that made *Bewitched* transcend its time and made her the most adored witch in television history.

Actress Nancy Kovack played Darrin's ex-fiance, Sheila Sommers, who wanted Samantha out of the picture as much as Endora wanted to get rid of Darrin. Ironically, Kovack feels that "Samantha lovingly touched everyone in the audience by giving her love to Darrin. . . . And she was forgiven the slight use of her witchcraft because she was supportive of him.

"And I used to watch the episodes for that very same reason. I was unmarried [today she's the wife of orchestra maestro Zubin Mehta] and probably wanted to be, and I liked to watch how different couples got along. That may sound awfully simplistic, but I think everyone is looking for a promise in the world, and by giving up her extravagant powers to be with Darrin, Samantha bespeaks that promise."

It is this unconditional, mutual support between Darrin and Samantha and between the show itself and its audience that invariably defines *Bewitched* as a love story. For this reason, in perspective, it can be seen how important it was to minimize the witchcraft on the show, particularly where Samantha was concerned.

Bill Asher sensed the viewer would hold Samantha in higher regard when she regulated her powers. "We were dealing with witchcraft," says Asher, "with someone who could do anything, and get out of any situation. That's such a powerful weapon that you can only respect the person if they don't use it. And that's how Samantha gained respect—by not using her powers in the face of all kinds of embarrassing situations."

Samantha, of course, would twitch the eggs sunny-side up or "fly" to her husband's side in dire need, but she was just too nice a witch to hurt anyone's feelings or to use her powers for personal gain. To maintain the balance and appeal of the show's fantasy element, the majority of the witchcraft was saved for other supernatural characters such as Endora and Aunt Clara. Yet even their metaphysical manifestations were carefully monitored.

"There were certain things," states Asher, "that I would never allow to happen on the show." One such occurrence was the ability to bring someone back from the past. This would happen only in extreme emergencies or by mistake. For example, the magic of the inept Aunt Clara and Esmeralda conjured up historical figures like Leonardo da Vinci and Julias Caesar.

"If they were able to have used that power correctly," Asher explains, "then we would have had to do a show in which President Kennedy or Martin Luther King would be brought back."

The witches and warlocks on the show also had the power to see the future and read minds, but Asher chose not to have these supernatural characteristics developed. "These are things," he says, "that I thought the witches didn't care about because they didn't have those kinds of needs—or that kind of ego. Why would they develop a skill they wouldn't use? It's as if someone had the talent to be a great pianist but they never developed their ability. What good would it be?"

It would seem, then, that just as the average mortal is able to pick up the phone and dial any number he chooses, Aunt Clara or Esmeralda would try to make historic figures materialize, and would "dial a wrong number."

Of the witches' ability to read minds and the future, Asher states, "Reading someone's mind is like opening their mail. You don't intrude upon their privacy . . . that's just rude behavior."

Adds Elizabeth, "If there was any dialogue such as 'I know what you're thinking,' it would have taken away from the mystery of the show and the relationship between Darrin and Samantha. It's like knowing what sex your baby is going to be before it's born. You go through nine months of labor, anticipating the birth, and it happens, and you say, 'Oh, I knew it was going to be a boy.'"

After Asher explained each of the witchy provisions to himself, he did so with the rest of the cast and crew. But he still had his own "quiet little fun" on the show. Like making sure most of the witches' names ended in *a* or its phonic sound, such as with Samanth*a*, Endor*a*, Aunt Clar*a*, Esmerald*a*, and Hepzib*ah*, and Ticheb*a*. He thought, "I'll just keep this one to myself."

If Bill were to pick a favorite episode from the show, it would be No. 17, "A Is for Aardvark," from the first year. He considers

"A" the quintessential *Bewitched* story "because it had to do with what the show was all about. . . . Darrin sprains his ankle, and Sam gives him the powers of witchcraft to make his life easier while he recuperates. He goes wild with the power, but then realizes that if you can have things without working for them, they're not worth having."

And as Bill continues to explain, "We repeated this theme on the show many times. That's why I would allow Endora to ridicule Samantha for scrubbing the floor, or cooking dinner . . . because Sam would defend herself by saying, 'Oh, Mother, you just don't know what it's like to set the table, or prepare a meal for your husband, and have him appreciate it.'"

Bill never wanted to get "too sticky on the show, so we would sugarcoat it by having Darrin come home and say something like 'What's for dinner? Pork chops? I hate pork chops!' But the sense of morality was still there."

From the beginning, Samantha promised love, honor, and no witchcraft to Darrin; she vowed never to defy, doubt, or betray him in any serious manner; and to be faithful always. She consistently offered him love, support, and devotion, unless through circumstances beyond her control one of her spells backfired or she fell ill with some personality-changing witch disease.

She was well aware of her near-unlimited powers, and she could have rid herself of any annoyance or problematic situation at will. Yet she chose first to deal with whatever came her way on a mortal basis, using witchcraft only as a last resort.

SOME ENCHANTING WOMAN

Hers was a remarkable performance. I've never seen an actress more suited to a role. She was to Bewitched *what Jean Stapleton was to* All in the Family . . . *perfect for the part. As an actress, she lent credibility, warmth, energy, and a great positive view of life.*

—*Bewitched* writer Lila Garrett speaking about Elizabeth Montgomery

In spite of the above praise, Elizabeth doesn't feel her being cast as Samantha either helped or hindered the show's popularity. "Whether or not it was I or someone else from the beginning really doesn't matter," she says, "because *Bewitched* told too wonderful a story for it not to succeed."

Born in Los Angeles, Elizabeth is the daughter of the late famed actor Robert Montgomery and Broadway and film actress Elizabeth Allen. She enjoyed a privileged childhood and upbringing, as her parents were rich, well established, and heavily respected in the entertainment industry.

Her school vacations were usually spent with her parents in England, where her father produced films. She was educated at several highly esteemed schools, including the Westlake School for Girls in Beverly Hills, California, the Spence School in New York, and the American Academy of Dramatic Arts in New York (which Agnes Moorehead also attended).

Elizabeth brought a well-adjusted and level-headed personality to the show, not to mention a great deal of charm. Had Elizabeth developed an arrogant personality, that insolence would have filtered into Samantha and *Bewitched* would have bombed.

Instead, she made everyone like and believe in witches, because she made witches so likable and believable.

"There are not many actresses," says E. W. Swackhamer (who directed eight *Bewitched* segments), "who can get away with playing a witch week after week, and bring to it the sense of realism that Elizabeth did. She's extremely professional and has a lot of talent. She'd make scenes work that I thought were impossible."

"In many of the animal shows we did," adds writer Richard Baer, "she'd talk and react as if she was really communicating with them. This, I believe, is a very difficult thing to do. Yet there wasn't any question as to whether she could pull it off."

Baer remembers asking Elizabeth if she ever grew tired of her *Bewitched* character. "Oh, no," she told him, "I just loved it. I found new things to do with the role and professional challenges every week."

Today she adds, "I always felt that doing comedy was more of a challenge than drama. I mean, if you have ten people in a room, and somebody comes in and says, 'I just saw a dog get hit by a car,' those ten people—hopefully—are going to respond in the exact same way with 'Oh, no! That's horrible!'

"But if someone comes into that same room and tells those same ten people a joke, that person will receive ten different reactions. Some may think it's moderately funny, some may think it's very funny, and others may not think it's funny at all.

"So with humor, you're not always hitting the same emotional chords with people as you might with drama . . . therein lies the challenge. And that's why I love acting . . . and why I loved doing *Bewitched.* I enjoyed playing Samantha because I liked her sense of humor . . . her incredible discipline . . . she certainly had more than I ever did."

She then adds, "And besides the magic on the show, I knew audiences would love the humor of the situation, and allow themselves to be affected by it any way they chose to perceive it."

Does she have any personal favorite episodes (besides "Sisters at Heart," which was discussed in Chapter 1)? "I liked the two we did with Henry VIII [Nos. 229 and 230]," she says. "I liked most of the ones we did with Serena . . . they were fun, especially when she sang [Nos. 128 and 192]. I *loved* all the shows we did with Aunt Clara, mainly because of Marion Lorne. She was really so special. And she used to prove such a challenge to get from one place to another.

"I also loved all the 'double' shows we did [Nos. 24, 59, 78, and several others]," she continues. "I think the audience enjoyed that kind of thing, to see how other people behave as they shouldn't behave. . . ."

Elizabeth's other favorites include: No. 101, "The Crone of Cawdor" ("That one was really different," she says); No. 241, "Three Men and a Witch on a Horse" (she enjoys the race track); No. 174, "Samantha's Curious Cravings" ("I love it when she [Samantha] is standing there eating the head of lettuce"); No. 142, "Samantha Goes South for a Spell" ("Isabel Sanford was wonderful") and No. 152, "Weep No More, My Willow," where Samantha was bewitched from crying to laughing constantly ("That was challenging").

Elizabeth also is fond of No. 108, "Long Live the Queen" ("I got to play dress-up"), and No. 121, "My, What Big Ears You Have," among several others.

You Two, Serena

Elizabeth as her zany cousin, Serena. (Elizabeth Montgomery/William Asher collection.)

If Elizabeth was ever compelled to try other theatrics on *Bewitched*, she would don a black wig, raise her skirt a tad higher, and *voilà!* Samantha's man-crazy cousin, Serena, would appear. "I was always a little bogged down that Samantha was so nice all the time," Liz admits, "so Serena just kind of became my alter ego, I guess. I could have a smidgen more fun with her."

As opposed to Samantha, Serena was a whole new ball of crystal. She was a free spirit with a quick temper who wouldn't think twice about turning Darrin into a gorilla or his mother into a cat.

"Serena was also somewhat of a chameleon," says Bill Asher. "She changed over the years from a deep-voiced sultress into a hippie, and in the last three seasons, kind of kooky. . . . But we really tried to give her the attitude of the times—whatever was hot at the moment—that's how she would show up—but she was always a flirt."

The Serena idea was first generated in No. 24, "Which Witch Is Which," and No. 31, "That Was My Wife" from the first season. In "Wife" Larry thinks that Darrin is fooling around with another woman, but Larry is unaware that it's really Samantha in a black wig. And in "Which" Endora transforms herself into a Samantha clone.

Bill Asher explains the true origin of Serena: "When Liz was growing up, she had a cousin named Panda who was always playfully starting trouble, but Liz would get blamed." "It was just kid stuff," adds Elizabeth. "We'd wear the same clothes and have a great time confusing adults. I would walk up to somebody and start a conversation, leave, and then Panda would show up and continue talking. It was a real ESP type of thing."

In the credits Pandora Spocks was listed as playing Serena, starting with Episode No. 192, but this did not have anything to do with Elizabeth's cousin Panda. Instead, this play on words alludes to the ancient Greek myth of Pandora, the evil being created by Hephaestus out of clay at Zeus' command. The gods made her beautiful, but when she opened her jar (or box, in some versions), she loosed all the ills and failings of mankind on the world.

Elizabeth says, "At one point somebody said, 'Why don't you use the name Pandora Box?' And I said, 'I don't think so. Pandora Spocks is subtler and funnier.'" Surprisingly, though, the credits' listing of Pandora Spocks led many fans to believe that Serena was played by a different actress. The fans were not the only ones fooled, as Elizabeth enjoyed playing Serena on—and off—the screen.

Producer Jerry Davis recalls a most humorous incident on the set of Serena's first episode, No. 54, "And Then There Were Three." "I noticed this rather hot-looking brunette and walked over and started to flirt with her. I remember wondering, 'Now, how am I going to get this lady to go to dinner with me?' But before I had a chance to ask her, she picked the time, the place, and the day we were going to go out. And then it dawned on me who this woman was. Elizabeth had the time of her life putting me on for twenty minutes."

It seems Elizabeth was as mischievous as Serena. "Lizzie was like a little kid," says Marvin Miller, who was assistant director on *Bewitched* for its first five seasons. "I remember shooting one episode where she was pregnant," says Miller, "and we needed her for a particular scene, but she wasn't anywhere to be found."

Miller searched the entire set. "I even went to the ladies' room," he says, "and screamed 'Lizzie! Lizzie!' from outside the door . . . and still nothing. So I was just about to ask Melody [Melody Thomas, Elizabeth's stand-in] to go inside, when I heard this little giggle coming from inside Lizzie's dressing room. And there she was, underneath the makeup table, covered with a blanket, hardly able to come out from under there because she was so pregnant."

"I wasn't just pregnant," says Liz, confirming Miller's account, "I was pre-e-e-e-egnant. I had to look twelve months on . . . So no one could believe that I was able to fit under that table, because the space was no larger than two feet wide, and all I could see were Marvin's legs."

Providing an interesting perception on that day, Elizabeth says, "But while I was under that table, I flashed back to when I was a little girl, hiding from my parents in my dad's bathroom. . . . They were yelling all over the place just like Marvin was." And Liz remembers thinking, "Ha, ha . . . they can't find me."

When her father came into the room all she could see were his legs, as she was hiding behind the toilet. So when Marvin came looking for her years later and she was under the makeup table, she laughed to herself, "My, my . . . things change, but remain the same."

As much laughter as Elizabeth caused on the set, Dick Sargent notes, "it was almost impossible to break *her* up." Though he did succeed, finally. He explains: "Each time my back would be toward the camera, I would lip-synch, 'Oh, shit, Samantha,' and she'd always laugh."

Liz herself remembers the heartiest laugh she ever had as a result of *Bewitched*. It happened one cold day at the races. "I was at Santa Anita [the popular race track in Southern California] and it was freezing out. So I went into the ladies' room to freshen up, and then these two women walked in, and one turned to the other and said, 'Boy . . . it's colder than a witch's ti-,' and then noticed me and said, 'Oh, excuse me.'

"Well, I laughed so hard that I just couldn't believe it. And when I left the ladies' room I was still laughing, and I started to tell everyone I saw, what this one lady said. I told the headwaiter and maître d' at the track restaurant, and then I went around the entire room—I even told the bartender. And I'm sure that poor woman was just chagrined about the whole thing, but everybody else, including me, was just hysterical."

Bad Vibrations

Of all her *Bewitched*-related, general public encounters, Elizabeth says, "Most of the time, people are nice. . . . Different generations of little kids watch the show, so it's really neat."

The only time she feels uncomfortable is when some parent forces a child, against the youngster's will, to "say hello to Elizabeth Montgomery."

"And this," says Liz, "inevitably happens at least once a year, and it's heartbreaking."

She recounts one such incident. "I was shopping, and this woman brought her little girl up to me—in tow—telling her, 'Well, come on! You come over here and say 'hi' to Miss Montgomery.' And the little girl is screaming, 'No, no! I don't want to!' And the whole time, the mother is telling me, 'Miss Montgomery, my little girl wants to meet you.'"

"If that's true," Liz asked the mother, "then why is she yelling to the contrary?"

"She's just shy," the mother replied, "and I told her that if she didn't say 'hello' to you, you'd turn her into a toad." On hearing this, Elizabeth was furious and said, "You told her *what*? How dare you say such a thing? No wonder she's scared to death!" The woman grew angry and, according to Liz, "scuffed away." There have been other oppositions.

The Academy of Television Arts and Sciences has nominated Elizabeth Montgomery nine times for the Emmy award: five times for *Bewitched*, once for an episode of *The Untouchables* (entitled "The Rusty Heller Story," which also featured David White), and three times for her various TV movies, including *A Case of Rape* (one of the ten highest-rated small-screen films ever aired). Still, she has never won.

Is she disappointed?

"I think it's funny," she says. "I mean, if Susan Lucci [Erica Kane on the daytime serial *All My Children*, who has been nominated more than twelve times], who I think is wonderful, has never won, then I'd say I'm in pretty good company. Maybe the two of us should work together, do something really brilliant, and then both lose. That would be hysterical."

Actually, other television performers who have never won Emmys for their work include such veterans as Jackie Gleason, Bob Newhart, and Leonard Nimoy. So Liz is indeed in good company.

Richard Michaels comments: "Even though the Emmy is a major form of acknowledgment in the industry, it's not the only form of acknowledgment in the world. Audiences adore Elizabeth just as much as they did in the 1960s, and no one will ever forget her or the show. When people find out that I worked on the show—especially little kids, who weren't even born when the show first aired, the first question I hear is, 'What is Elizabeth Montgomery really like?' or 'How did she twitch her nose?'

"Now this," Michaels firmly suggests, "more than anything, is a definite form of acknowledgment—and it proves her a mainstay in television history. She knows she's not an actress solely by definition. She's a person, and a very complete person at that.

"She was the darling of the crew on *Bewitched,* and she still is on every picture she makes. She takes care of everyone on the set, and makes sure each person has everything he needs. And she's just as friendly with the gofer as she is with the director. She immediately disarms people, and not everyone is like that. She's a dream."

"Elizabeth was a very caring person on the set," adds *Bewitched* director R. Robert Rosenbaum. "She was probably the most-loved actor in our business. It was fun working on the show, and she helped make that happen. ab01he whole crew really adored her. She was sincerely interested in everybody—and everybody's family, as the show itself grew to become a family. We all had wonderful relationships, professionally and socially. It was a love company, and she and Bill enhanced that.

"I feel very pleased with my years on *Bewitched.* I enjoyed doing the show and going to work. It was probably one of the best jobs I ever had because Liz and everyone made it fun."

Wasn't there *any* pressure in working on a popular sitcom?

"Yes, of course," he replies, "but everyone helped to alleviate that stress with a real mutual support system. Today," continues Rosenbaum (who is the head of production for Lorimar Television, which cranks out such hit sitcoms as *Full House* and *Perfect Strangers* for ABC), "you're in a different business. There's more of a corporate structure and different patterns and routines are followed. The industry is much larger than it was during *Bewitched*, and today's television stars are rarely as modest as Elizabeth."

Speaking for all those associated with the show, Harry Ackerman stated, "I think we were the luckiest people in the world to have someone as warmhearted and appealing as Elizabeth Montgomery—and no one could twitch her nose like she did . . . believe me, we all tried."

However, of Elizabeth's charms, Bernard Slade says it best: "Elizabeth was and is the main ingredient for the success of *Bewitched*. She has never been an overgregarious lady to be around, but most enchanting—and that transfers to the screen."

DARRIN'S DOUBLE FEATURES

I could zap up mink coats all day long, but I could never zap up another Darrin Stephens.
—Samantha, Episode No. 99, "Charlie Harper, Winner"

So why two Darrins?

When Dick York was filming *They Came to Cordura* with Gary Cooper in 1959, York and several other actors were doing a scene that required them to lift a railroad handcar. At one point, the director yelled "Cut!" and everyone but York let go. The car fell on him, wrenching his spine and tearing the muscles around it. His pain continued on *Bewitched*, later escalating, and he had to be replaced by Dick Sargent as Darrin in 1969.

"We toyed with the idea of having Endora change Darrin's looks," says Bill Asher, "but then we'd have a wall between Endora and Samantha." And as Elizabeth adds, "Samantha would never have put up with that. It wouldn't have been fair to the characters or the actors—and the audience would have hated it."

Of the York-Sargent exchange, she notes, "This kind of thing [replacing actors] happens all the the time . . . on soap operas . . . in theater, and the audiences aren't stupid. They're certainly smarter than any network executives ever give them credit for. We presented our case as if to say, 'Look, guys, we know you're out there watching . . . so bear with us. We're going through some changes, but hang in there, because it's gonna work.' And it did.

Dick York and Elizabeth Montgomery as Darrin and Samantha. (Columbia Pictures Television.)

We were just fortunate enough to have Dick Sargent . . . and that he was available."

Dick York, however, feels "they should have changed the character completely . . . Darrin should have been killed off or he and Samantha should have gotten a divorce." Yet Bill Asher argues differently.

"It was so contrary to what the show was all about," he says. "How could you break up a love story, and start it with somebody else? It just wouldn't work. Darrin had to be so special that he'd be the only mortal that any witch, specifically Samantha, could be involved with. We just couldn't mess that up."

Obviously, Dick Sargent is "happy they went the route they did." Harry Ackerman said of Sargent's initial audition for the pilot: "We were very interested in pursuing him for the part, but his contract with Universal prohibited him from being cast."

Before the Sargent era did finally begin on *Bewitched,* Dick York feels he "could have finished the run of the series," had he been given time to recuperate. "All I wanted," he says, referring to the end of the 1968–69 season, "was that summer to rest up."

York missed fourteen episodes of *Bewitched,* twelve of which were due to his back ailment. "The other two," he says, "I missed because my father had passed away, and Bill [Asher] was gracious enough to allow me some time off."

When Darrin wasn't in the show, Larry would end up speaking or reacting to the magic as Darrin would have.

"We compensated," says Elizabeth. "It was an adjustment. But I think that at the same time it brought in an additional element for Samantha . . . to have her play off someone other than Darrin, in a very safe, platonic, and nonthreatening way."

One unique aspect of this transition was that it allowed the cast and crew to remake Dick York episodes with Dick Sargent. For example, No. 46, "Junior Executive," had York's Darrin shrunk to adolescence, while a similar spell was put upon Sargent's Darrin in No. 224, "Out of the Mouths of Babes."

Bill Asher explains: "When you produce two hundred fifty-four scripts, you're going to remake episodes no matter what you're doing. You can't help but dig back and rework old scripts. There's a limit to the situations you can come up with and still be able to maintain your premise. Without developing a whole new way to go, you're bound to travel the same ground."

Concerning York's health and the show's future at the time, Bill Asher says, "He was heroic in the way he was able to hang on through the back injuries. But it became a real tough problem." In the third year "he began to miss shows. . . . At first, we were ahead enough in shooting to afford to take off a couple of weeks if Dick couldn't do the show, but then it got pretty consistent. . . . So we would always keep one script without Darrin, so we could keep on going.

"We would shoot a tag [designated final scene] with him just so his presence was there, or have him be on a trip to Chicago, or have somebody make him disappear. The show's premise allowed us that luxury."

Dick York as Darrin the Bold, a great ancestor. (Elizabeth Montgomery/ William Asher collection.)

Conversely, Richard Michaels feels that the non-Darrin episodes weren't as conceptual as the rest. "The show was about Samantha *and* Darrin," he stresses, "and their marriage. Without Darrin, the main conflict was gone." Michaels feels the show would still have worked with just Elizabeth, but the formats would have had to be changed.

Of Samantha's life without Darrin, writer Bernie Kahn comments, "The main protagonist who served as a counterpoint character to the witches was Darrin. Once you removed him, you removed the show's central discord, and you'd just have a show about witches and warlocks."

Dick York as Darrin

How does Dick York feel about being tagged the neurotic, hyperactive Darrin?

"I wanted him to stop being so damned mad at Samantha all the time," he replies. "I thought, why should he come home and start raising hell every day? I was finding that very difficult to justify as an actor, and as a human being.

"I knew when I would come home from a long day's shooting on the show, I wouldn't want to start ragging on my wife about, 'Oh, boy, honey . . . what a day I had today,' proceed to tell her all about my job, and then condemn her because she didn't follow my prescription for life. So I thought it was terribly selfish of Darrin to do that to Samantha. If I were Samantha," York says, "I would have told Darrin to 'lay off, or I'll turn you into a toad!' "

Though York disagreed with Darrin's overly contrary behavior, he still feels the character had his moments. "I remember when Tabitha was born ["And Then There Were Three"]," he explains, "Aggie and I both had tears in our eyes. And that's when I felt that Endora had to feel some kind of love and pride about Darrin, and that there was some faint form of mutual respect between them.

"That made me think that Endora thought that no matter what she did to Darrin, he would always jump right back on his feet . . . and that Endora knew how much he really loved her daughter."

York applied many guidelines and subtexts to his interpretation of Darrin. For example, he explains what he feels were the character's motivations and thoughts in relation to Samantha: (1) "I don't care *what* your mother does to me, I just want to be with you." (2) "I don't expect you to be perfect, I just want you to be yourself." (3) "I love you and I want you to know how much I care."

York further explains that as he sees it, "Darrin had to work hard for everything he got in life. . . . He had witches and neighbors and even his own parents to deal with, but he didn't care because all he wanted was to be with Samantha."

When writer Richard Baer is asked how he saw the Darrin character, he replies: "As a conventional husband trying to succeed. And he was a square. He didn't want his wife to use her witchcraft because he didn't want to be embarrassed."

Many viewers may have had the same perception, although York disagrees. "That wasn't it at all," he says. "Darrin didn't want Sam to use her powers because he didn't want anyone else to find out about her and anyone else to have her. He wanted her all to himself."

A perfect example of how fearful Darrin was of anyone's finding out about Samantha is found in No. 135, "I Confess," from the fourth season. In this episode, after Darrin is displeased when Samantha discourages a drunk with witchcraft, he declares his wife should disclose to the whole world that she is a witch. Knowing Darrin doesn't mean what he says, Sam shows him with a dream spell what life would be like if everyone knew her secret.

In the dream, the government wants to employ Sam's magic as the country's main defense weapon, and Larry wishes to use her powers to control the world. Fortunately for him, Darrin wakes up and changes his mind about revealing his wife's secret. On the sly, Sam wonders what made him change his mind. "I slept on it," he replies.

According to York, "'I Confess' says it all . . . and the comedy of that episode was brought out in a dramatic way."

Of York's personal comedic and dramatic talents, he firmly believes timing is of the essence if a scene is to work. "I do believe it can be taught," he says, "but at the same time, I don't. I can always explain how I did it—*after* I did it—but not during." He does admit, however, that "it's easier to cry on cue than it is to laugh." York explains this analogy by referring to one particular scene from "Weep No More, My Willow" from the fifth year. Here Samantha comes under a healing spell that Dr. Bombay had intended for her ailing willow tree on the front lawn. Whenever the wind blows, Sam cries, and the more Dr. Bombay tries to right his wrong, the worse things get. Whenever the breeze misses the trees, Sam weeps . . . hysterically.

Later in the episode, when Darrin comes home from work, he finds Sam laughing out of control in the living room with Larry, who's there because he thinks his two best friends are having marital difficulties. Darrin is confused because when he called earlier, Sam was crying and now he sees her laughing. And it's contagious, as Larry's laughing now as well. Darrin doesn't know what to think, but he laughs along with them, because now he can't help it either.

How was all that handled on the set?

"It was ludicrous," York says with a laugh. "And it got way out of hand. We were laughing about something we were told not to laugh about, and that made it funnier. And we also shot that scene at the end of the day, when we were all beat. So that made it worse, but it also made the scene work."

David White recalled the scene as well, and credited York's professionalism and strong theatrical background for this and other *Bewitched* episodes. White remembered another scene from an episode entitled "Dangerous Diaper Dan" [No. 82] from the third season, which he thought worked rather well between York and him.

In "Diaper," speculation arises as to whether or not McMann and Tate's advertising ideas are being stolen by another agency. White said of one moment from the segment: "Larry and Darrin are at their favorite bar, and they think this martini is bugged with a microphoned pimiento. Well, I decided, while filming, that I would take the pimiento out of the glass and flatten it on the bar. Now, this wasn't written into the scene, but Dick just went right along with me. . . . He was just marvelous to work with."

White added, "Most of the scenes we did at the office were a lot of fun to do. That was like . . . our environment. We were the most comfortable there, so whatever techniques we tried always worked."

Of his general *Bewitched* experience playing Darrin, Dick York explains: "There were days when I had to memorize five and a half pages of a client's presentation, and every single line had to be recited word for word. And if it wasn't, we'd keep shooting until it was. It *was* work, but that's the kind of stuff actors are made of. I was always prepared to do a scene a thousand times until we got it right."

York grew up in poverty in Chicago; he lost his baby brother to malnutrition and continues to suffer from numerous health problems himself. "I think actors who experience a deep sense of loss," he says, "find it easier to relate to the dramatic or comedic aspects of their craft."

He adds, "One of the toughest things to do [during a dramatic scene] is to know just how far to take the tears. . . . It's important not to go overboard and have the character feel sorry for himself. As an actor," he explains, "you can't fall to pieces . . . you're supposed to make the audience do that. Where to draw the line is the actor's job.

"I believe I played Darrin as hard and as best as I could, and when the pain became too great, I went as far as I could. And when I wasn't able to give one hundred percent, I left." And even though he felt that had he been given more time to recuperate, he would have finished the run of the series, he wants everyone to know that "I was happy to do the show, and I couldn't have played Darrin unless I loved the role."

Dick Sargent as Darrin

How does Dick Sargent feel about being labeled the "kinder, gentler" Darrin? "To tell you the truth," he says, "I think there was more of a sense of warmth between Samantha and Darrin when I did the show. . . . And I think Liz and I were more 'kissy-kissy.' "

Did Sargent ever object to any of *his* Darrin's behavior? "Of course," he states firmly. "Darrin was a pain in the neck, and he could really be unlikable. He was the 'no man' on the show." And as much as Darrin said "no" to the witchcraft, Sargent says: "He was still unable to put his foot down completely and prohibit Samantha from using her powers. But he had to at least try and stop her, however unlikable that would have made him to the audience. If Darrin didn't object to Samantha's witchcraft, then the show would have been about people who can get anything they want [as in Bill Asher's initial *Fun Couple* idea]. So in a strange way, Darrin was almost the moral backbone for the show."

Elizabeth Montgomery and Dick Sargent. (Columbia Pictures Television.)

Though many feel Sargent's Darrin was lighter than York's, his comedic prowess was equally as distinguished. In No. 187, "The Phrase Is Familiar," from his first season in the role, Endora tries to help Darrin in advertising by casting a spell that has him talking in clichés. After Larry hears a few of these phrases, he becomes infuriated with Darrin and threatens trouble if Darrin isn't more clever in dealing with an upcoming account.

Endora later changes the spell so that Darrin's clichés are fewer, but those he does say, he acts out. For example, at a dinner meeting, Darrin says, "I wish I could see eye to eye with you" (his eyes cross), and "I'm keeping my ear to the ground" (he throws himself to the floor and puts his ear on the carpet). Finally Darrin excuses himself from dinner, saying, "I'd better shake a leg," and of course his leg shakes, and then he says, "I'll just bow out," and he exits bowing.

This genuinely hilarious show features some of Sargent's most wonderful moments of physical comedy. In fact, the whole cast glimmers in support of him, producing a truly memorable show.

How did Sargent approach these scenes? "That comedy was based on the truth in the writing," he says. "That's the way it was written, and that's the way I acted it out."

He goes on to say, "I've always described comedy as 'having a third eye.' Because you can see it, and feel if it's right while you're doing it. You can even hear the timing and sense the look of the scene's physicality, checking on . . . what body postures work." He then states rhetorically, "Is it funnier to sit halfway down, all the way down, or just fall down?"

Sargent then explains that "*Bewitched* was so well written, Darrin remained consistent whether it was Dick York or myself in the role. Most of what I did as an actor," he points out, "was in the scripts. . . . They were just so dam good." Of his character's interpretation, Sargent says: "Darrin's motivations were already put there by the writers. I just had to find reasons *why* Darrin would do the things he'd do.

"It's like the old cliché, 'Why does an actor open a door? Because it's in the script.' But the actor has to find a way, and a reason, to open the door.

"Sometimes," he points out, "actors go beyond that into 'method acting' [exploring real-life experiences of people similar to an actor's role], but the basic explanation of what a character should be doing is in the script. . . . Then all the actor has to worry about is personally interpreting that meaning. And on *Bewitched*, that was very easy to do because Darrin was so well defined. It wasn't long before I realized that he would be either angry, furious, dismayed, or horrified when it came to Samantha and her magic."

David White commented on Sargent's performance. "There was an incredible amount of dry humor that Dick brought to the role. He created a persona that was his and his alone, and he played that type of arid comedy very well. The way he would deliver a line with a certain subtlety—knowing when to hold back—and then knowing exactly when to zing it to Endora with the right amount of punch."

Sargent explains that he has performed dramatic parts as well. "Drama is really only the dark side of comedy," he says, "and I think maybe mostly because I am a comedic actor, I am also able to do drama. But I don't think dramatic actors can always turn around and do comedy as well. I don't think it always works the other way around. But I also think that as you get older, actors generally get better—or at least more versatile."

Does Sargent ever view any of his own performances? "Usually, just once," he replies. "And that's enough, only because I hate watching myself. It's always painful. I ask myself, *Now, why did I walk like that?* or *Why did I turn like that?* or *Why did I just say that?*"

He goes on to say that "filming *Bewitched* was probably one of the happiest times in my life. If not the happiest. I've done pictures that I've enjoyed working on for months at a time, but *Bewitched* was three straight years of pure delight. There was never a moment when I woke up and thought, *Oh, no . . . I have to go to work today.*" Still, he admits to being "a little nervous" during his first few appearances on the show.

In fact, the first episode he filmed, No. 185, "Samantha's Better Halves," contained dialogue that both he and Elizabeth thought was inappropriate. In the segment Endora splits Darrin into two people—one half, business; the other, all fun and games. And when Sam begs her mother to put Darrin back together, she exclaims, "I want only *one* Darrin!"

"I was kind of uncomfortable with that," says Sargent, "but I never thought it was a good episode anyway."

Consequently, "Better Halves" was shelved as Sargent's premiere outing (it was replaced with No. 171, "Samantha and the Beanstalk"), and aired later as a flashback segment at a time when viewers had become more familiar with Sargent.

Sargent admits there were certain aspects of the series he as an actor had to figure out. Specifically—and critically—the relationship between Darrin and Endora. "He couldn't really have acted superior to her in any way. And one time," he says, grinning, "I behaved in a most un-Darrin-like manner. Bill Asher almost took me by the hand and walked me around the set and said, 'No, Dick . . . now Darrin wouldn't act like that.' I felt like I was five years old."

After his initial outings as Darrin, Dick Sargent understood the bottom line of the character. "I knew that Darrin truly loved Samantha, and that he would always be by her side—no matter what happened."

York's and Sargent's respective Darrin interpretations suggest the question: Was there a change in the direction of the series, or in the chemistry of the Darrin character, or between any of the *Bewitched* actors when Samantha changed husbands?

Marvin Miller, the show's assistant director, doesn't feel the series or the Darrin character changed direction, but he does feel York's interpretation was "more neurotic" than Sargent's. Ed Jurist, who took over as story editor after Bernard Slade left, agrees that both actors were funny in the role, but that Dick Sargent "had a lighter air about him."

Elizabeth, on the other hand, doesn't think the situation was "all that black and white . . . I think they overlapped fairly well," she says, "and when Darrin needed to be strong willed or strong tempered, Dick Sargent compared equally to Dick York. . . . They were both fantastic on the show . . . each bringing his own uniqueness to Darrin."

To those who perceive Sargent as a more tranquil Darrin, she says, "By the time Dick Sargent came on the show, Darrin and Samantha's relationship was five years old. . . . And Darrin's objections to witchcraft would have mellowed anyway, whether it was Dick Sargent or Dick York.

"Darrin," she continues, "was becoming a more easygoing presence, and I think the show's situation almost became funnier as he would lapse into this kind of complacency. . . . And maybe into something that he just might enjoy for a minute or two.

"It was almost as if Darrin grew as the relationship developed. He felt he didn't have to be on his guard as much. So that when he was suddenly confronted by witchcraft, the newness of the marriage was gone. And it wasn't as shocking an experience as it was in the show's first season.

"By the final year, he wasn't quite the nervous wreck he was when he first found out about Samantha. He was still against her using her powers, but the objection may not have been as harsh as it was in the past."

If there was a change in the series, than Richard Michaels thinks "it was very subtle . . . because Darrin was insulted and manipulated in exactly the same way by Endora, and was loved

D*ick Sargent as Darrin. (Columbia Pictures Television.)*

equally by Samantha," whether York or Sargent was in the role.

"The truth of the matter," explains Michaels, "is that one day Liz as Samantha came on the set and said, 'Hi, sweetheart,' to Dick York's Darrin, and the next day came on the set and said, 'Hi, sweetheart,' to Dick Sargent's Darrin. As long as we all kept that straight, we were fine."

In either case, Liz felt it was a difficult marriage for both Darrins. "It was tough," she says. "I mean, who would have gone through or put up with the stuff that Darrin did? It had to be a very laborious thing for him to be married to this woman who could have anything she wanted." Yet Liz points out that "the marriage lasted eight years, and how many of those do you find—especially with a mother-in-law like Endora?"

It may be comforting for *Bewitched* viewers to know that there is little competition and only mutual praise between Dick York and Dick Sargent. "Dick's a marvelous actor," says York. "He had a job to do, and he did it well." Says Sargent of York: "He was excellent as Darrin!"

And if Elizabeth is the main attraction of *Bewitched*, then York and Sargent are indeed the double feature.

MOTHER AND THE SON OF A GUN

Larry: "Hello, Endora." Endora: "Mr. Tate."
—A generic greeting between the two

If it had not been for the theatrical expertise of Agnes Moorehead, perhaps Endora would have been considered too severe a TV character and labeled "unlikable" by the audience. As the series continued, however, she evolved gradually from Darrin's central nemesis to a mischievous prankster with just a touch of evil. And whenever she incorporeally interfered with Darrin's personality, or his looks, or his life in general—and she wasn't anywhere to be found—Samantha would simply shout for "Mother!" to appear.

David White's parody of the credit-grabbing, mildly neurotic Larry Tate, who constantly put the client's wishes ahead of Darrin's (or whoever was in the room at the time), might have proved just as off-putting if it had not been for White's ace acting. Larry would heartily approve of Darrin's latest campaign slogan by affectionately calling him a "son of a gun" and giving a soft punch on the shoulder, but he was really describing himself. It was typical of Larry to fire Darrin over the most easily forgivable mistake.

Both Moorehead and White raised their TV personas beyond their basic natures and added dimensions that were amiable and comedic. They were always welcomed by the audience.

Following are discussions of these highly trained actors (both of whom have passed away, Moorehead in 1974 and White in December 1990) and their interpretations of their *Bewitched* characters.

What Moorehead Knew Best

"I think Agnes's interpretation of Endora," says *Bewitched* writer Lila Garrett, "really did speak to—and for—all the mothers in the audience who wanted their daughters to marry the perfect man. And I think they were a little annoyed at times to see a woman like Samantha—who was that capable—insisting on staying home all the time."

"She was everyman's mother-in-law," adds Richard Michaels. "Every man in the world has a certain mother-in-law image in his mind, and where Samantha was concerned, Endora came with the marriage. It was a package deal."

Of Moorehead's portrayal of Endora, producer Jerry Davis said, "She was an especially gifted actress . . . a queen mother in her social life. I remember elegant parties she gave, and a sort of . . . very elite theater group from which she sprang. She was very kind, and I loved her, but she had that nice 'bitchy' exterior that worked brilliantly for the show."

Active in all entertainment media, Moorehead gained the largest audience of her forty-five-year, four-time Oscar-nominated career, on *Bewitched*. She was gratified that the show was loved by an audience of both fans and advertisers, even though she could not confess to complete satisfaction with it and the Endora character in the beginning. "There are so many things I'd like to do with the role," she once said, "but there isn't time to polish in television."

"That was Aggie's big debate on the set," says Dick York. "When do we get time to act?" he remembers her asking constantly. "She was trained in the theater," York explains, "so the fast pace of television acting would get to her at times."

When a reporter from Moorehead's hometown newspaper, *The Cleveland Plain Dealer*, asked her if it was fun to do *Bewitched*, she replied, "No, I can't say that. In TV, there simply isn't time to have fun; people have the impression that actors in television, particularly on comic shows, sit around having a ball. Nonsense. It's the hardest medium an actor can work in."

Still, writer Richard Baer believes Moorehead "*was* having fun, but she'd never admit it. I think she really enjoyed sitting on the mantelpiece in chiffon gowns."

"But she was humorless in a strange way," adds director E. W. Swackhamer. "You'd tell her a joke, and three days later, she'd laugh. Yet she had a sense of humor about herself, which was nice. She didn't mind making fun of herself if it was somehow flattering."

Of her Endora interpretation, Swackhamer says: "I think she said to herself, 'Listen, this is nonsense, but I know what I'm doing. I'm a witch, and so's my daughter, and this is the way it is.' She never fooled around with the part. It was more like 'Boom! . . . I'm Endora!'"

Fellow *Bewitched* director R. Robert Rosenbaum had tremendous respect for Agnes. "She took direction better than anyone," says Rosenbaum, "and she was fabulous. For her to listen to a little nudnick like me [an assistant director turned director], I thought, was a fantastic thing. But she would just do it—exactly the way I explained it.

"She was one of the great ladies of our business," continues Rosenbaum. "She took two to three hours in makeup every morning, and was never, never late. She was always ready on the set, and she always knew her lines. She was very prepared and did not respect someone else who didn't come as well prepared as she." Rosenbaum then concludes: "The show survived due to her talents, and due to the chemistry between her and Elizabeth."

Contrary to the speculations of many in the press, Elizabeth and Agnes were very close friends who had a strong mutual respect for each another. "She knew I loved her dearly," says Elizabeth, "and there really was so much communication between us. It's like we actually had a mother-daughter relationship."

One particular scene from the fourth-season opener, "Long Live the Queen" [No. 108], is most representative of Elizabeth's kinship with Agnes and the bond between everyone on the *Bewitched* set. In "Queen," Endora glows with glory as her daughter is crowned Queen of the Witches. Simultaneously, Samantha smiles back, knowing how happy she has made her mother.

Elizabeth explains: "Since there always seemed to be this animosity between Endora and Samantha because of Darrin, we tried to establish, at times, how much the two of them really felt about each other, and how close they really were." She states that this scene also displayed "how close Aggie and I were.

"It's funny," she continues, "because Aggie told me one day, 'You know . . . I really am very proud of you.' And I just looked at her and gave her this big ol' hug." Furthermore, Liz says, "there'd be times when I would look at Aggie in the very same way that Samantha looked at Endora [in "Queen"]. And it may not have been for more than a second's time, but it somehow confirmed that something had mutually gone right for the two of us . . . on a professional and personal level, as well.

"It's like whenever Aggie and I would complete a scene together, and the director would yell 'Cut and print,' we'd kind of look at each other and go, 'Yeah, that went well.' And it's nice when that kind of communication takes place between the actors on the set.

"So that look that Samantha gave Endora was very significant as to how Aggie and I felt about each other, and to how we all felt toward one another on the show."

One of those "others" was Marvin Miller, who recalls his first meeting with Agnes: "I'll never forget it. It was my first day on the set, and I had to meet her at five thirty A.M. in makeup. I arrived there at about five twenty and she was already in the chair.

"And when I introduced myself and asked if she would like to have some breakfast, she replied with this kind of stony 'No . . . no, thank you.' And then she got all made up and we went down to her stage dressing room." Moorehead had two, one on and another above the set.

"Then it got to be about four thirty in the afternoon—and we were filming all day—and we hadn't used Aggie. And Bobby Rosenbaum [then assistant director; Miller was second assistant] walked over to me and said, 'Would you please go and tell Aggie that we won't be able to use her today?'" On hearing this, Miller panicked. "I can't express the fear that instilled in me," he says.

"Here I was, having to tell this great actress—that after two hours in makeup, and after all day of not using her one bit—we wouldn't be needing her at all!"

He found the courage to knock on her door, timidly, and as he remembers it, "I heard this deep voice reply, 'Yeeeesss?' And when I opened the door, she was sitting down, and I just stood there . . . looking at her . . . speechless for a second or two. And then I thought, *Let me try to be funny.* But I was still at a loss for words.

"Finally, I said, 'You know, it's a terrible shame to have been all made up and let it go to waste. So why don't you go upstairs and we'll go over your lines, because they won't . . . they won't . . . they won't be able to use you today.'

"And she looked at me with that famous Moorehead glare, and I started to shake a little as her face became kind of expressionless. And then all of a sudden, I saw this twinkle in her eye, and she said, 'Oh . . . it's going to be another one of *those* days.' And with an 'I guess so,' I left."

Miller does say that he and Agnes became very good friends, and that beyond her stony demeanor, she was a very warm and wonderful lady. "But that first day," he says, "I must have lost five pounds before I got to her dressing room."

When Irene Vernon is reminded of Moorehead, she recalls what Agnes would tell her about acting . . . and life. "No matter what happens in life," she'd say, "feel it and live it to the fullest—and continue working. Be it good, bad, or indifferent . . . work. You will get some good out of it and you will learn and grow as a person and as an actress."

"And you know something," says Vernon, "she was right."

Bewitched guest star Bernie Kopell, best known for his role as Doc on *The Love Boat*, relates his acting experience with Agnes.

"She was very complimentary of my work on *Bewitched*, and I was thrilled. I remembered seeing her in *Don Juan in Hell* on Broadway and being blown away by her performance. She was the only female in the cast, and in one scene, everybody was formally dressed. The men in black tie, and there was Agnes—with her stunning red hair—in this beautiful gown.

"That picture of her stuck in my mind every time I did *Bewitched*. She was such an overwhelming presence on that stage. And then to have someone with that much charisma and talent praise your work is just a very wonderful thing."

Agnes Moorehead was many things to many people, but all impressions of her were positive. There is no denying her talent and charisma.

The White in Larry's Eyes

How did David White first come to play Larry? "I met Danny Arnold in New York," he recalled, "and we hit it off immediately. And when he went to Florida to shoot a pilot, he asked if I would be interested in acting in it."

Arnold cowrote the pilot for this project, which was entitled *Beachfront*, with Sam Rolfe, who also created *Have Gun, Will Travel* for TV. The Arnold-Rolfe partnership gave birth to the Florida-based small-screen venture. This unsold program starred Keefe Brasselle, best known for his performance in *The Eddie Cantor Story* (1953), and White played a heavy.

While viewing the dailies during the filming of *Beachfront*, Arnold asked White for his opinion of the show, and according to David, "it wasn't much . . . and I told him so. But I also told him," White continued, "that he didn't need to hear my opinion. Even though I think he just wanted to see if I was an honest person [to work with]."

Arnold remembered White's performance on screen in *Beachfront* and the integrity he displayed in viewing it in the screening room, and this led to David's being cast as Larry Tate on *Bewitched*. However, David commented, "I got the part because I was an honest man . . . and that's where Larry and I were completely different. I'm not two-faced and he was. I always knew I had more integrity than Larry ever had, and that I was smarter—with a deeper sense of values. But I had to diminish who *I* was when I was playing him.

"I always saw Larry," explained White, "as a very insecure person who did have a certain brilliance in certain areas. For one, he was smart enough to hire people who possessed the skills he did not . . . like Darrin.

"But he really wasn't a creative man at all . . . he was a businessman—and a reasonably good one—under Darrin's guidance. Which is why, whenever Larry fired Darrin [which was often], he would always say to himself, 'Oh, brother . . . why did I do that?' He knew he was cutting off his nose to spite his face, and that he would only have to think again and hire Darrin back.

"But Larry was no dummy. He was quick and sharp, and was the ultimate chameleon. One who could whiz back and forth and contradict himself in the same sentence if he thought he was about to lose a client . . . or even just notice a frown on the client's face."

White pointed out that if Larry had been "really brilliant, he would have expanded his employees at McMann and Tate. And though his ego was tremendously large, his self-esteem wasn't great enough to push him further, or he would have his own advertising agency, instead of being just partners with McMann."

White felt Larry was a very interesting character to play and he didn't stand in judgment of him, though he did pay attention to how Larry was written.

"I was very protective of Larry," he said, "and I always made sure that he remained consistent throughout the entire eight years. Every once in a while I would tell the writers, 'I don't think Larry would do this or say that,' because I knew more about Larry than anyone else did. I knew his speech patterns exactly. I knew what he would say, how he would say it, and when."

Overall, White concluded: "I wasn't born to play Larry . . . I had to create him. He was a make-believe character of his own truth slated in a comedy series. And when playing comedy—and farce—you take that truth and stretch it as far as it will go—but not any further.

"And when I was playing Larry, though he was a funny character, *I* never tried to be funny, because to me, acting has to do with fulfilling the needs of the character you're playing, not the actor who's playing him." White explained that "the one thing the actor and the character have in common is that both have needs."

Therefore, whereas some may label Larry a heavy, White maintained that Larry was "just a man who showed how far he would go to protect his needs. And a real heavy is a man who truly doesn't have any moral structure whatsoever . . . where he ends up cheating or even killing someone. Now, Larry was selfish, but he was never that extreme. If anything, he was still a little kid who never really matured."

That statement may remind some viewers of episode No. 247, "Serena's Youth Pill," in which Sam's cousin reverses Larry's aging process. As a result, he returns to his youth—red hair and all. During the filming of this segment, there was some discussion of whether or not Larry's hair should remain white—just for laughs.

Fortunately, in keeping with the show's integrity, this decision was vetoed. However, David's white locks caused some laughter, and this involved Serena.

Whenever Elizabeth played Serena in a scene with White, she would refer to him as "cotton top." Was White bothered by the joke? "The way I feel is this," he said. "Some jokes should not be taken too far. Once, maybe twice, but after a while it gets to be too much." Whenever anyone would joke with him on the set about the nickname, he would always respond by saying his hair was prematurely gray, so in the long run, he still was able to joke about the joke.

If anything, White felt that when the Serena character would come on to him, "it was a harmless bit of fluff . . . but in the beginning, Larry was quite a flirt himself. And if they hadn't toned down that aspect of his personality, he would have been presented as a totally rotten character."

Did White ever watch himself on the show during its initial run? "I did for two reasons," he said. "One, if I thought it was a very good script, and very well done on all accounts—acting, writing, directing—and two, on the rare occasion when it wasn't a good script, I just wanted to see how it turned out."

Some of David's favorite episodes included the third-season opener, No. 76, "The Moment of Truth," and No. 105, "Bewitched, Bothered and Infuriated," also from the third season.

"Truth" had to do with Samantha's finding the courage to tell Darrin that Tabitha is a witch, and keeping the Tates from seeing Tabitha's hocus-pocus one night while they're over for dinner. One reason this segment was a favorite of White's is that "Larry and Louise really get a chance to interact with each other . . . and to show some honest affection for each other."

At one point during "Truth," Samantha tries to induce Larry supernaturally to believe he's drunk, so that he and Louise may leave before they see any of Tabitha's magic-making. Both Sam and Darrin go as far as to request that Larry take a sobriety test of sorts in their living room. Larry agrees, and when he begins to walk a straight line, Sam twitches him to fall into Louise's arms, where the now-ruffled Larry asks his wife, "Louise . . . is that you?" The Tates then decide to go home.

Yet it's in No. 109, "Toys in Babeland," that White recalled one of his most favorite scenes from the series. In this outing, Tabitha brings her toys to life, and Larry ends up having a drink with a toy soldier at a bar. On trying to convince Larry that he's mixing with the wrong company, Darrin hysterically blurts out to his obstinate boss about the soldier, "Larry, he's a doll!" To which an oblivious Mr. Tate replies, "Well, make up your mind, Darrin. Do you like him or not?"

"Now, that's funny," said White, "and like every scene in the show, we played it for real . . . which added to the humor."

Besides "Truth" and "Toys," the segments that first came to David's mind were the show's seventh season visits to Salem, Massachusetts, which White enjoyed. "I had a lot of fun," he said. "I had never been to Boston or to Salem or the House of the Seven Gables [which was featured in No. 203 and No. 208], and it was different for me."

What did he recall specifically about the House of the Seven Gables? Only that "people must have been smaller when that place was built because I remember almost hitting my nose on the doorways," he said with a laugh. "I had to bend over [going] from one room to the next."

David White was a flexible actor who brought great wit and style to Larry. "Larry Tate was a rude character," says E. W. Swackhamer, "but David's ability as an actor took the edge off the character and made him likable."

"I always loved watching him," adds Elizabeth. "He was so funny. But half the time, I really don't think he knew how funny he was. Fortunately, everyone else did."

Of White's comedic timing and double takes, Bill Asher delivers great praise: "David's performance was like quicksilver."

T*V's most beloved supernatural family. (Columbia Pictures Television.)*

M*arion Lorne as Aunt Clara. (Columbia Pictures Television/Wide World Photo/Fredric Tucker.)*

THIS AND OTHER WORLDLIES

Very rarely, if ever, did we settle for anything less than we initially desired for any role or character on Bewitched. *The size of the role or the actor's work history was not a concern. We were always after the quality of talent.*

—Elizabeth Montgomery

Throughout the eight years of *Bewitched,* the cast was constantly evolving. Many characters left and many new characters were created. These transitions enhanced the mortal/supernatural conflict of *Bewitched.* The world of Samantha and Darrin opened up to include funny and zany relatives and friends; witches and warlocks faced off against neighbors, clients, and random historical figures. This team of supporting actors was essential to keep the audience captivated season after season.

Witches and Warlocks

Of the performers who portrayed the nonearthly roles on *Bewitched,* Richard Michaels states: "They were a talented group of actors who had a bundle of laughs playing these fantasy characters, and they instilled laughter in the audience." No argument there, but let's delve a little deeper into what—and who—made these characters tick.

Aunt Clara

Aunt Clara was an odd egg. Though high-spirited and experienced, she was a totally inefficient and most unskilled witch. But pick on her? Certainly not when Samantha was around. Clara was her favorite aunt and she often acted as Tabitha's babysitter.

No matter how many times Clara's powers failed, Samantha always came to her defense, as in No. 95, "The Trial and Error of Aunt Clara," when Endora and the Witches' Council set out to have Clara stripped of her powers.

Here, Samantha pleaded emotionally that Clara's kind of love was a rare find. This, of course, did not sit well with Judge Bean (Arthur Malet), and just as he was about to despell Clara, a surprising turn of events took place.

First, Darrin came home early, and right before he had a chance to get a close view of his living room (which had been transformed into a witchy court), Clara waved her arms and, as she said, "everybody disappeared," thus saving Darrin's nerves and Samantha's marriage.

These occurrences resulted in two very important developments, as Clara proved to the Witches' Council that when push came to shove, she was ready and powerfully prepared. And it also expressed just how much she loved Samantha. As Sam loved Clara, Elizabeth too loved Marion. "She was a blast to be around," says Liz. "When Aunt Clara would hit those walls [as she'd try to go through them], it was hysterical because we all would hear this shriek on the set, which was Marion's hearing aid conflicting with the microphones on stage."

Elizabeth recalls an even more humorous mechanical interference the night Marion contacted her from the famed Beverly Hills Hotel. "She called me from her room," says Liz, "and insisted I come to see her. When I finally got to her room, she was awfully nervous, and she kept on saying, 'I did it! I did it!' And she told me that I was the only one who would understand."

It seems Marion thought she had truly attained some kind of magical powers. She was unaware that her bracelets had created a form of electrical current that was on the same frequency as her room's television set. "Every time her arm would move," recalls Elizabeth, "the bracelets would clink and the channels would change. But I wasn't about to tell her what was really going on, because she was walking on air."

However, Elizabeth stresses that this story is misleading. "Marion was a very smart lady," she says, "and a brilliant performer who knew exactly what she was doing as Aunt Clara."

Lorne chose to have Clara stammer, and it became her trademark. "I remember once, early on in the series," says producer Davis, "when Marion was stumbling over her lines and taking a lot of time. I finally said to her, 'Honey, don't worry about it, you're going to screw it up anyway when you read it.' And she said, 'You don't understand. I have to know exactly how to say it before I screw it up.' And I'll never forget that because I loved so much that she said it. She was just naturally funny."

Of working with Lorne, *Bewitched* costar Kasey Rogers says: "On and off the screen, Marion Lorne was Marion Lorne—and she was a dear."

Uncle Arthur

Paul Lynde's Uncle Arthur was one of *Bewitched*'s most memorable characters. The outrageous and somewhat obnoxious warlock specialized in dousing people with water and playing other practical jokes that raised Darrin's temperature and caused nothing but trouble for Sam. Yet he was family.

Though Samantha's lineage was mostly unclear (one of the series' few faults), one thing was clear: Uncle Arthur was Endora's younger brother.

Arthur's zany capers accounted for only a small part of his appeal, as most of the credit must go to Lynde for adding so much dimension to Arthur in so few appearances. He made only ten in the role, and one as Harold Harold in No. 26.

Episode No. 26, "Driving Is the Only Way to Fly," was Lynde's debut episode. Here he played a nervous driving instructor who teaches Samantha how to drive the mortal way. "After we used him in that first show," says Bill Asher of Lynde, "we had to have him back in some regular capacity. Liz loved him . . . they were crazy about each other."

"Driving" is one of Elizabeth's "all-time favorite" episodes, and it's solely because of Lynde. "I truly enjoyed every minute of it," she says, "and when you're working with someone who is as totally off-the-wall as Paul was, it gives you a lot of freedom creatively.

"His instincts were fascinating, and Bill [Asher] had known him for a long time, and they really trusted each other's instincts, as well. We all had a great social relationship, which kind of just bled into Samantha's relationship with Uncle Arthur. Paul and I really appreciated each other. . . . We got along very well."

Almost too well at times. She recalls: "One morning, we got so hysterical over some little joke that Bill threw his hands up in the air and called lunch at ten thirty [A.M.]. Paul looked at me and said to Bill, 'It's her fault.' Bill laughed a little bit, but we both were so obnoxious to the point of being totally useless on the set."

Lynde was a comedic treasure.

"He was unique," says writer Bernie Kahn, "flat-out wonderful. And he just seemed to glory in his own uniqueness." Kahn refers to Lynde's classic line delivery and comedic timing. For example, on *Bewitched*, he would tip his head, shake it with cynicism, and utter the short phrase "Hiya, Sammi" to Elizabeth, and the results were hysterical.

Publicity shot of Paul Lynde. (ABC-Television.)

Adds Ed Jurist, who had written for *The Paul Lynde Show* and *Temperatures Rising* (both produced by Bill Asher): "I think if we did *The Paul Lynde Show* today, it would be a shoo-in. But Paul's outrageousness was not acceptable then [in the early 1970s] in a main character. He was just too much to take on a weekly basis because all he would have to do was moan [a line like] 'Oh, my knees' and he'd get a roar."

Through all his performances, Lynde was applauded for this novel line delivery: that sarcastic, smiling twang. How did he come to develop this working trait? According to his older sister, Helen Lynde [there were six children in Lynde's family, and he was the middle of four boys], "It was a natural ability. He always talked that way."

She admits, however, that "when we were growing up, I didn't think he was that funny, and neither did our mother. She would always tell him, 'Oh, stop being so silly.' She loved him dearly, but she just didn't get his humor."

Helen continues by explaining that when her brother did *Bewitched*, he had a great affection for the show, and he loved playing exaggerated roles like Uncle Arthur. He knew the appeal the show had for children, and he was always amazed at the reaction he received from them, because of *Bewitched*, and also because of his appearances on *Hollywood Squares* (the popular game show, where he was situated as center square).

Helen also confirms Paul's fondness for the *Bewitched* cast, particularly Elizabeth. "He *loved* her," she says, "and he was also very fond of Agnes Moorehead."

Behind the laughter, Paul Lynde was a very private person, and he also had a very serious and poignant side that he rarely revealed. David White remembered catching a glimpse of Paul's almost invisible reserved nature once during rehearsal. "He brought his dog down to the set one day—it was a very exotic-looking animal, I forget exactly what kind—but he used to talk to it all the time, just like many people do who care deeply for their pets. Anyway, he turned to the dog and said, 'Now, listen . . . you behave yourself or I will never bring you down here again. Do you understand?' And the dog just kept looking at him . . . and looking at him . . . and it was just a very touching moment."

It can be said that Paul Lynde touched everyone with his ability to make others laugh. He was a natural, and as Bill Asher says, "a favorite."

Esmeralda

When Marion Lorne passed away, "we needed someone else to mess up the magic as Aunt Clara did," says *Bewitched* story editor Ed Jurist. Consequently, Alice Ghostley's shy, inept witch-maid of Samantha's, Esmeralda, faded into the picture. Though "fading" was actually an integral part of Esmeralda's makeup (when she felt incompetent or saw Darrin, she would literally fade away), Ghostley herself gradually came into the *Bewitched* picture.

Like Paul Lynde, she first appeared in an early episode of the show and was asked back as a regular because of her most positive first impression. This first outing, entitled "Maid to Order" [No. 53], seemed to foreshadow Ghostley's future role on *Bewitched*, as she played Larry and Louise's temporary maid Naomi who is hired to replace their regular housekeeper who, ironically, was named Esmeralda.

Samantha's maid Esmeralda was not the first regular role Ghostley was approached about playing on *Bewitched*. When Alice Pearce passed away, Ghostley was offered the role of the new Mrs. Kravitz, but she declined. "Alice was a friend of mine," says Ghostley, "whom I had known from New York. We had worked together in many of the same clubs [including the popular Blue

Angel]. So when they called me in to do Gladys, I said no. I guess I was superstitious about replacing her."

And even though Ghostley had also worked with Marion Lorne (in the 1967 theatrical film *The Graduate*), she did not know Lorne socially and agreed to play an Aunt Clara-like character. So she said yes to playing Esmeralda. "And I couldn't have been happier," says Bill Asher. "I always wanted her on the show."

Referring to the dysfunctional magic of Esmeralda (she'd sneeze or hiccup and some kind of catastrophe would arise), Ghostley explains: "Esmeralda would sometimes take the long way around a situation, but she still had powers that would cause excitement one way or the other. But there were certain aspects of her personality—her shyness, for one—that I think could make her very lonely. She was really very amiable and wanted to be part of everything, but I believe her bashful nature may have stopped her. But at the same time, I think this made her more a human-witch than a witch-witch."

Does Ghostley ever catch any of Esmeralda's antics on *Bewitched* in reruns? "It's funny," she says, "I seldom watch myself, and I don't know why. I guess I watch the screen and say, 'Is that really what I look like? Oh, dear, I wouldn't watch this if I were someone else.'" Then she adds, "It's always difficult for me to critique myself."

Even so, Ghostley has two favorite *Bewitched* episodes: No. 226, "Samantha's Magic Mirror," and No. 232, "Samantha's Not-So-Leaning Tower of Pisa."

"Mirror" concerned Esmeralda's rendezous with an old warlock boyfriend, and her more than usual nervousness. To boost her maid's ego in other areas, Samantha zaps the hall mirror into presenting a beautiful likeness of Esmeralda each time she gazes into it.

"I loved that one in particular," Alice says of "Mirror," "because Esmeralda had the chance to express some varied emotions, and it gave the audience a chance to get to know other sides of her as well. To maybe understand why she was so shy . . . or to at least explore that aspect of her personality a little further."

"Mirror" also is a favorite because of guest star Tom Bosley, who is best known for his role as Ron Howard's father, Howard Cunningham, on TV's *Happy Days*, and whom she had known since the early days of television. "We had been friends for a long time," she says, "and it was nice working with him again."

Alice remembers the "Pisa" segment for more comedic reasons. In this episode, it's made known that Esmeralda is the reason why the famous Leaning Tower of Pisa (in Italy) leans. It seems that centuries ago, during its construction, Esmeralda was working for Bonano Pisano, and on ordering his lunch, she accidentally incanted a sandwich to be made "lean." Instead, the tower obliged.

"I went to Italy years later," says Alice, "and just looked at that thing and thought, 'Wow! It's so *large* and *powerful*, not even I could move it.' The reality of the situation set in."

Several years later, when Alice played orphan housemother Miss Hannigan in the musical based on the comic strip *Little Orphan Annie*, she was almost unrecognizable. Yet as she recalls, "That didn't matter to the children in the audience. All they wanted to see was Esmeralda . . . and I was in that show for over two years. After every matinee, they'd be standing outside the theater waiting to see me and screaming, 'Esmeralda! Esmeralda!' "

Today Ghostley is back on television as the dippy Bernice Clifton on the CBS hit *Designing Women*. And even with the popularity of this show and her varied theatrical experiences, does it matter to her that she is still best known for her days as Sam's magic maid?

"Not in the least," she says. "I loved playing Esmeralda, and I am ever amazed at the strength of the show's popularity." And just in case her loyalty to *Bewitched* is ever truly doubted, she leaves a constant reminder on the set of *Designing Women*. When the studio audience rallies around her for autographs at the close of the show's taping, she signs, "Best witches, Alice Ghostley."

Dr. Bombay

"Calling Dr. Bombay! Calling Dr. Bombay! Emergency! Emergency! Come right away!" This was Samantha's plea to the metaphysical continuum whenever there wasn't exactly domestic bliss on the Stephenses' home front. In such a case, the indispensable witch Dr. Bombay would appear, played by the English actor Bernard Fox.

The witches, not being humans, did not have ordinary prescriptions or cures. To relieve a given witch experiencing a dry spell or to right some witchery gone wrong, he would always try to diagnose the magic ills with the proper incantation; at times this required the additional assistance of one of his many attractive witch-nurses or supernaturally medicinal contraptions.

In fact, in the *Tabitha* TV series starring Lisa Hartman (Episode No. 11, "Tabitha's Party," directed by William Asher), it is learned that Dr. Bombay has married one of his nurses, who also happens to be a mortal. By this time, it seems the Witches' Council has not only reversed its position on mixed marriages but has decreed that one must marry a mortal every year.

If all else failed, he would try to cover his mistakes with poor attempts at humor that were singularly unappreciated by others. He would comfort himself with a "Ha-ha! Ha-ha!"—followed by dead silence as no one shared in his humor.

Where does an actor find inspiration to portray such a gregarious character as Dr. Bombay? One who was labeled a quack on many an occasion?

"I never wanted him to be a run-of-the-mill character," says Bernard Fox of the role he's most associated with. Consequently Fox based Bombay "on a commanding officer I encountered while serving in a naval transit camp in what was then Ceylon.

"This elderly gentleman had, in civilian life, been a veterinary surgeon of the old school and was hard of hearing. And he assumed everyone else was also, so he constantly yelled at everybody.

"Some twenty years later, when I came to play Dr. Bombay, I was searching for something more colorful than the everyday doctor, and that officer came to mind." As Paul Lynde said of Bombay in No. 190, "Super Arthur," he had "the bedside manner of an orangutan."

Says Elizabeth of the Bombay character: "Bill and the writers always had a good time with him because he was so outrageously odd. And we were ever on the lookout for unique characters on the show." Of Fox's contributions to the role, Liz says, "One of the great things about Bernie is that he would always come up with all these really weird kinds of aspects to Dr. Bombay."

Was Fox's energy what made Bombay a unique character? "All the characters on the show were unique," the actor, who is reserved in real life, modestly states. "The success of *Bewitched* is largely due to all the talented people on the screen and behind the scene." Of the actors, Fox singles out Agnes Moorehead and Maurice Evans as "two highly trained performers of the theater. You rarely find such talent in the business."

Next to Dr. Bombay, Bernard Fox is probably best known to television audiences for his role as Colonel Crittenden on *Hogan's Heroes*. Of his characters, Fox states, "I tried to play them all energetically." Like Paul Lynde and Alice Ghostley, Fox appeared in an early episode of *Bewitched* before establishing a regular role on the series. In No. 65, "Disappearing Samantha," he played Osgood Rightmire, a mortal debunker of witches.

Fox claims that the hardest part of playing Dr. Bombay was the character's long, breathless constructions and incantations. "They were a difficult study," he says, "and I usually have a good head for names and titles and lines when I'm working, but *his* dialogue was most complicated."

Fox has many fond memories of working on *Bewitched*, one involving a favorite piece of dialogue from No. 200, "Make Love, Not Hate," that took place between Bombay and Samantha. It went something like this:

> Bombay: Where's the clam dip?
> Sam: In the kitchen sink.
> Bombay: I may join him. I could do with a swim.

During the filming of "Make Love," numerous puns on *dip* and *swim* abounded on the set, and at one point Fox was required to squeeze a lemon into the clam dip, which led to another humorous incident between him and Elizabeth. He explains:

"Having found the dip, I proceeded to squeeze the lemon, and a tiny squirt shot out from one side, straight into Elizabeth's eye. She reacted instantly, and we both thought it funny, but something was technically wrong so we had to have another take. Elizabeth said, 'Bet you can't do it again,' but it did happen again, and even on the third take, and so there it is on film for posterity."

Fox's fondest memory of *Bewitched* is of a Christmas party on the set for cast and crew. "My wife and I were invited, of course, and as my eighty-year-old mother was visiting from England, we took her along. Mother (an actress herself) wasn't too thrilled with the idea, as she evidently envisioned herself sitting off to one side like a bump on a log and being totally ignored.

"The first one to sit down to chat with her was Elizabeth, then Bill Asher wandered over, and soon she was the center of a chatty, happy group. Mabel Albertson, a terrific talent, was playing the piano like the expert night club performer she had been. The group then moved over to her, and in no time at all, my mother was singing songs from the old musicals (*Desert Song*, *Rose Marie*, etc.) and having a ball.

"My mother left for England a few days later, and because of doctor's orders was never able to visit us again. But she took with her a warm and wonderful memory of that night, for which I never cease to thank Elizabeth, Bill, the cast, the crew, and all the delightful people that I met and worked with on *Bewitched*."

Sandra Gould's first season as Gladys Kravitz, 1966. (Columbia Pictures Television.)

Tabitha

In May 1966 the twins Erin and Diane Murphy auditioned for the role of Tabitha and started in the series a day before their second birthday. At first they shared the role. After the fourth season Erin played the part and Diane acted as her double.

On the set, the sisters had a private tutor for three hours every day. "That was the law then," says Erin. (It still is.) The law was another reason twins were chosen to play Samantha's twitchy daughter. Child actors are allowed only a certain amount of air time on television and film, and having twin actors means the workload for each child will be cut in half.

This is still being done today on such TV shows as *Full House*, where Mary Kate and Ashley Olsen play little daughter Michelle to Bob Saget's Danny.

But on *Bewitched*, why did Erin take over the role of Tabitha? "We were fraternal twins," she says, "and in the beginning we were very interchangeable, but as we got older, I started to look more like Elizabeth."

Working on the show, she says, "was a lot of fun . . . and a lot of work." She jokes that she should have received hazard pay for riding ponies and for the physical humor that was required. She refers to Episode No. 189, "Tabitha's Very Own Samantha," where Tabitha conjures up her "very own" mother, one she doesn't have to share with anyone, specifically her brother Adam (played by another set of twins, David and Greg Lawrence).

In "Very Own," Tabitha is wearing a Band-Aid on her chin because she tried flying at too young an age. Actually, Erin had hurt herself on a pony ride that takes place in this segment. The writers just wrote in the reference to flying later.

Erin says she "always remember[s] being a little afraid of the special effects and the animals on the show. I remember seeing hooked wires all over the place and not really understanding why they were there."

What about the adults on the show? How did the Murphy twins get along with them? "Everyone was really great," says Diane. "I enjoyed [the show] while I was doing it, but I realized later that acting was not something I would be interested in pursuing as a career."

"We both called our TV parents 'Darrin Daddy' and 'Mantha Mommy,'" she says, "to distinguish them from our real parents. In the beginning, we couldn't pronounce 'Samantha,' so that's why we just kind of shortened it."

Of Elizabeth, Diane recalls, "I remember she used to like to eat coffee ice cream with honey on it, which Erin and I called the 'Mantha Mommy Special.' Her dressing room door was covered with autographs, and I was real excited when she let me sign it. I wrote a big *D*, but my mother said I shouldn't take up too much room, so I wrote the rest of my name inside the *D*."

What were some of Erin's favorite episodes from the show? "I enjoyed all the ones with other kids in them," she says, "and the times Tabitha was seen attending school [No. 248, "Tabitha's First Day at School" and No. 171, "Samantha and the Beanstalk"]. It was on the latter segment that Erin met child star Johnny Whitaker, who guested as Jack from the Beanstalk.

"He was my first date," Erin says. "And it was really funny, because we recently appeared on *Good Morning America*, in a show about former child actors [Whitaker was one of the young leads in TV's *Family Affair*], and we mentioned how we first met on *Bewitched*."

Little Tabitha and Jack from the Beanstalk? Could work.

Adam

Like Erin and Diane Murphy, David and Greg Lawrence were brought into the *Bewitched* fold to offer a double play as Adam,

Tabitha's younger brother. And it's all because of actress Barbara Feldon . . . yes, Barbara Feldon.

Feldon, who played Agent 99 on the spy sitcom *Get Smart*, was pregnant, and future scripts called for her to give birth to twins. A enterprising talent agent who had no six-month-old twins as clients began calling pediatricians in an effort to locate potential candidates. When she reached Dr. David Rottapel, a pediatrician in Sherman Oaks, California, he said, "I don't have six-month-old twins, but I have absolutely gorgeous, small for their age, nine-month-old twins. Let me call their mother for permission to give you their names."

As fate would have it, *Get Smart* was canceled. But having seen pictures of David and Gregory Lawrence, the agent knew she had a winning combination to work with.

The twins were soon in demand for commercials; David and Gregory achieved a 100% batting average, landing every role for which they auditioned. *Bewitched* was no exception.

After an exhaustive search and a look at sets of twins throughout the state of California, the producers decided to go with the Lawrence twins—not only because of their dark hair, blue eyes, rosy cheeks, cleft chins, and great smiles, but because they had the same quizzical quirk of their right eyebrows that Elizabeth had.

The boys enjoyed working on the show and even fought over whose turn it was to be in a scene. Although they found Agnes Moorehead's Endora a bit intimidating, their favorite was Grandpapa, Maurice Evans, who, according to the boys' mother, "was a truly warm and loving gentleman." And though Elizabeth was generally very busy on the set, she still found time to play with the boys. One day she suddenly grabbed David, threw herself on the floor, and began bouncing him on her knees, much to the chagrin of wardrobe mistress Vi Alford, since Liz was in a shimmering white pleated skirt for the next scene and the floor was filthy. Though viewers would be hard pressed to detect it, both boys had ear infections and raging fevers during the filming of their biggest show, No. 242, "Adam, Warlock or Washout." They were real troupers, however, and refused to quit until shooting was completed, probably because they found it such fun to be wired to fly (this feeling was not totally shared by their mother).

When the final season of *Bewitched* ended, the Lawrence

David and Greg Lawrence. (Mark Gilman.)

twins' parents made the decision to retire them from show business, preferring to see them grow up as just regular kids. "If an acting career is meant to be, let it be their own decision when they're old enough to make one," said their mother, "but for now I'd rather they not be exposed to the somewhat distorted values I've seen with stage children and the pressures imposed by the hectic schedule and distorted life-style."

Today neither David, Greg, nor their mother expresses any regrets for this decision. Strangely enough, the young men, who are adopted, discovered at age fourteen that their natural father is an actor of extraordinary fame and celebrity. It's anyone's guess as to how things might have turned out had they been raised by him.

Mr. Majestic

There is no better way to close a section on the central supporting "supernaturals" of *Bewitched* than with a profile of the classically trained and very charismatic actor Maurice Evans, and his portrayal of Samantha's father, also named Maurice.

Though Evans and his television counterpart shared their first names, Evans preferred the proper British pronunciation, Morris, while his TV self demanded that his name be pronounced

Mor-eece. All of this led to some behind-the-scenes humor during the filming of No. 168, "Samantha's Good News."

In that episode, after Maurice makes Endora jealous by hiring a beautiful witch-secretary, she seeks emotional revenge by enlisting the assistance of warlock John Van Millwood, played by Murray Matheson. When Van Millwood refers to Evans's character as Morris, Maurice cringes, emphasizing the pronunciation of his name. None of this, however, matters to Samantha, who knows her father only as Daddy.

Maurice Evans and his warlock persona shared the spelling of their first name as well as a penchant for all things Shakespearean, but this is where the similarities between the two end. Evans himself was nowhere near as threatening as Samantha's father, who proved to be an even stronger adversary for Darrin than Endora.

On the other hand, Elizabeth confirms that Evans was "charming and gallant," and that she "truly adored him. He was the best!" She also goes on to explain that Evans (who died in 1989) had a "marvelous sense of humor. . . . One night," she says, "Maurice, some friends, and I went out to dinner. When the waiter came over to take our order, Maurice gestured toward me and said, 'My daughter will have a glass of champagne' . . . and everyone just roared."

With specific regards to Evans's casting as Samantha's father, Liz states: "The one aspect of Evans's personality that made him perfect for Maurice was that he didn't look flamboyant. . . . He wasn't six feet four. But whatever he lacked physically, he made up for with his huge talents as an actor."

Elizabeth mentions that actors Vincent Price and Cesar Romero were also considered for the role. "Either one of them would have been bliss," says Liz, "and I even wanted my father to do it [he said no], but I thought it was tremendously beneficial that Evans could play Maurice with so much demonstrative strength."

Therefore, Maurice Evans balanced a sophisticated sense of style with Maurice in much the same manner as Agnes Moorehead performed Endora. An impression his life and career almost demanded.

Of his tenure on *Bewitched*, Evans wrote in his autobiography:

> I have special reason to be grateful to have been cast as Samantha's father in *Bewitched,* since, apart from the enjoyment of working with Elizabeth Montgomery and her merry gang of witches and warlocks, it put me for the first time on more than a nodding acquaintance with my grandnephews and -nieces. Up until then their uncle Maurice's career in America was to them a topic of yawning dimensions, but as I began to appear regularly on the show they became eager to get to know me, insisting that I enlighten them on the magic tricks that made *Bewitched* so much more than just another domestic comedy.
>
> I was voted "in" as a regular member of Samantha's household, and, although it involved commuting constantly between New York and Hollywood in the 1960s, it was a thoroughly enjoyable experience.

Bewitched director E. W. Swackhamer states it was just as pleasurable to work with Evans. "He was a remarkable actor who never turned any part down. And it didn't have to be Hamlet or Macbeth. But that's the way most English actors are," continues Swackhamer. "If you go to direct a project over in England, you get the most incredible people that walk into a casting office.

"You end up pinching yourself, as if to say, 'You mean I can really get these guys to work with me?' And the answer is 'yes.' Even if they're starring on the stage in some major production, they'll come in and do small parts for you. Acting is acting to them.

"America doesn't have that attitude . . . unhappily. But Maurice did. He was like that totally. He would come up with the most incredible ideas, and give himself over completely to a role."

Adds *Bewitched* producer/writer/director Jerry Davis: "I had done a film called *Kind Lady* (1951) with Maurice, who played the villain, and when he came on *Bewitched,* it was a nice reunion for us. I never had anything but a pleasant relationship with the man."

Marveled Mortals

"Comedy is all about reaction," says *Bewitched* story editor Ed Jurist, "and the human characters on *Bewitched*—whether they knew it or not—were reacting to the very unnatural phenomena that were presented to them."

The Kravitzes

Gladys and Abner lived across the street from the Stephenses at 1168 Morning Glory Circle. Mrs. Kravitz was convinced from the onset that Samantha was "different," though she could never prove it. And Abner didn't help matters, as he never listened to her.

Explains Richard Baer: "Mrs. Kravitz accepted what she had seen, however strange, and would run back to the house and tell Abner, who just wanted to read the newspaper or watch the ball game. And he would always tell his wife when she would complain about what she had seen: 'Again with across the street?' He'd then tell her to take a pill and relax, and she would try, but then she would see an elephant on the roof or something."

This type of evidence would unfortunately disappear when Gladys ran to her husband to spread the news. "Abner," she would scream, "you're not gonna believe this," and assuredly, he would not, and would only advise his wife to at least take a nap.

From a different perspective, Gladys, though thought of as an airhead by her husband or any public or government official whom she would bring in to confront Samantha's secret, may be viewed as probably one of the smartest and most aware mortal individual characters on the show.

Think about it: Did Larry, in all the years he knew Darrin and Samantha, ever really suspect that Samantha or his employee's household could ever be anything other than normal? Granted, Samantha made this very difficult, as she was a most beautiful witch, and she tended to derail the average mortal male with her nonwitchy charms. But other than a chosen few dream sequences or spellbinding situations, Larry remained pretty much in the dark about what was really going on with the Stephenses. Yet their perceptive neighbor, housewife Gladys Kravitz, thought by many to be weird herself, proved otherwise.

Because she lived right across the street from the Stephenses, she was more accessible to what was really going on in the neighborhood, but then again, so was Abner, and he never once suspected a thing.

How interesting then, for someone who was thought to be so "crazy" to have really been onto the Stephenses' secret. Gladys was constantly being made a fool of by—and often in front of—her husband. But who was fooling whom?

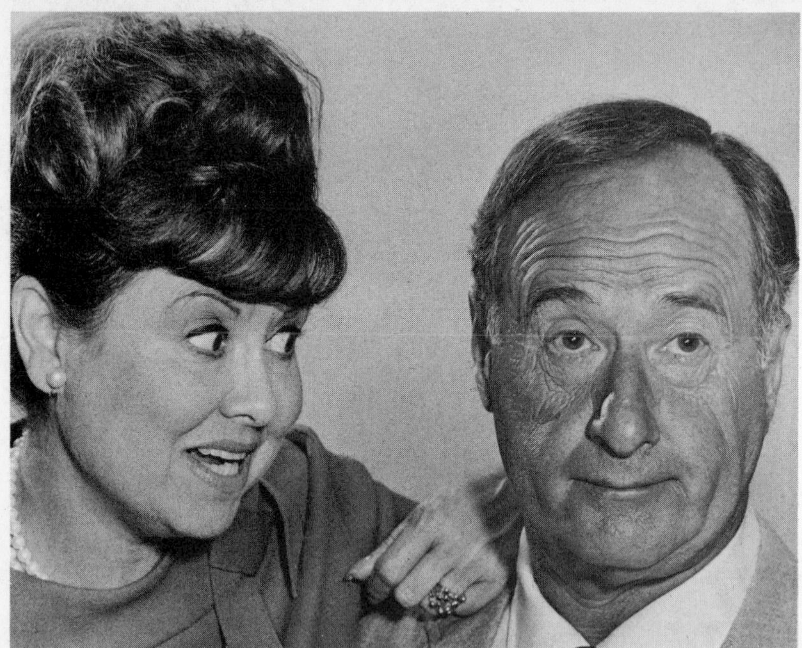

Sandra Gould and George Tobias as Gladys and Abner Kravitz. (Columbia Pictures Television.)

A publicity shot of Dick York and Elizabeth Montgomery. (Columbia Pictures Television.)

Just as Dick York and Dick Sargent offered varied Darrin interpretations, Alice Pearce and Sandra Gould presented two different Gladyses.

"Alice had that scream of hers that made her almost more maniacal," says Marvin Miller, "and I think that made you feel more sorry for her. And I think Sandra played it down more than Alice, but [was] almost more defiantly opposed to Samantha's witchcraft. When Alice would get scared, you really believed that Mrs. Kravitz was going to pieces, whereas I think Sandy offered a more shocked reaction."

Pearce, who died of cancer while still working on the show, told the *TV-Radio Mirror* in 1965: "When I first heard that I was going to play a character called Gladys Kravitz, I couldn't understand how they could invent such a nutty name. Well, the day before I was to report on the set of *Bewitched* for the first time, I came down with one of those minor upsets and I needed a doctor real fast. A friend recommended someone. His name? Dr. Kravitz." It was quite a coincidence that boded well for *Bewitched*.

On playing Gladys, Alice told the *Mirror*, "I'm playing someone who's going over big with kids. They stop me and want to know if I can wiggle my nose like Liz Montgomery. And they like my snooping and poking around. The more frenzied my reactions are and the louder my 'eeks' get, the better."

According to Harry Ackerman, "Alice was offered the part of Gladys without auditioning since her talents were well known to Danny [Arnold], Bill [Asher], and myself, and she got along splendidly with the other members of the cast. She never admitted the onslaught of cancer, although it was painfully obvious to all of us that she was losing weight rapidly. Actually, she worked almost literally up until the day she died."

Prior to *Bewitched*, however, Alice did audition for the part of Grandmama Addams on *The Addams Family*, but she was too young, and the part was given to Blossum Rock. And only a few years before this audition took place, Pearce told an interviewer, "Playing strange, sweet oddballs is exactly my cup of tea."

She also commented on her unique appearance, which was partly caused by slipping from a swing during a visit to Brussels as a child. "Look at me," she said, "I'm a chinless wonder. If I'd sustained no accident as a kid, if I had developed an ordinary chin, today I'd probably be just another starving, middle-aged character actress."

When Sandra Gould replaced Pearce, did she feel obligated to imitate Pearce's interpretation as Gladys? "I couldn't," she says. "That would have been unfair to myself and to Alice's memory. I knew I couldn't change the character. That was left up to the writers and the producers. All I knew was that I had a part to play, and that it was my job as an actress to act out that part."

Was George Tobias supportive of Gould? "George and I had been friends years before *Bewitched*," she recalls. "I was what they called a 'stage child.' I started in the theater when I was nine years old, and that's when I met George."

Tobias, Orson Welles, and actor Eddie O'Brien were friends. "They took care of the kid," says Gould, "which was I. And it was the funniest thing in the world when I grew up to play George's wife, because he was something like twenty years older than I."

Since there was quite an age difference between Gould and Tobias, was she asked to age or to look older on *Bewitched*? "No, they didn't do anything about it. Though, now I think I would be better for the part than I was then," she says with a laugh. "And they didn't do anything to George either. If anything, if you really do watch the show, I really do think George looks a lot older than I do."

How did Tobias come to *Bewitched* in the first place?

"I had met him when he was a star at Warner Brothers Studio," recalls Harry Ackerman. "He made quite a few pictures for them [including *Air Force* in 1943 and *Yankee Doodle Dandy* in 1942], and I think maybe doing a semiregular role on a TV show was a bit of a comedown for him, but I believe he was just very grateful to have the part.

"He was in his mid-sixties when I approached him, and work was few and far between for him at the time. And Abner was also such a different role for him to play. He was always used to much tougher and more physical-type roles. And by the time he came to *Bewitched*, he was more suited to character roles, which is exactly what Abner was."

Twin Louises

Louise Tate, wife of the self-devoted Larry Tate, was played by Irene Vernon from 1964 to 1966, and after Vernon left to

Irene Vernon publicity shot. (Columbia Pictures Television.)

pursue a career in real estate, Kasey Rogers took over for the show's last six years.

Were their interpretations of Louise as varied as Dick York's and Dick Sargent's were of Darrin? Or as different as Alice Pearce's and Sandra Gould's were of Gladys?

"You had to look at Larry," said David White, "and see whom he would marry. He would marry someone who would further his career . . . who would schedule his dinner parties, and who was—more or less—in control. And to that extent, I think Irene Vernon's Louise was more along those lines. She was colder in the role than Kasey, which worked better for the character, but Kasey was more animated in the role, which worked better for the show's comedy."

How did Vernon see the character? "I really never had a clear picture of who she was. She always seemed to be groping, so that's how I played her. In the very first show I did [No. 3, "It Shouldn't Happen to a Dog"], she was just one of the guests invited to

Darrin and Samantha's dinner party. She maybe had one or two lines, but that was it."

Vernon does say, "I think Louise was the antithesis of how Larry saw her, and what he thought she was. I remember Danny [Arnold] saying that he didn't want Louise to be the bossy, nagging wife; he wanted her to be attractively sweet and an understanding partner for Larry. And that's the person I tried to present on screen."

From Vernon's viewpoint, "there really wasn't that much comedy to draw from." She felt that Elizabeth was the show's center comedian, and "since many of my scenes were with her, she should get the laughs because it was her show.

"When two actors are doing a scene together," she continues, "they should be able to play off each other well, and not try to outact one another" (but, rather, contribute to each other's performance). Tying in with David White's philosophy on comedic acting, Vernon states, "If two actors are trying to be funnier than each other, or trying to be funny, period, then the scene they're working on won't fall into place.

"Though I've always been a little afraid of comedy," she admits.

Did Kasey Rogers feel she brought anything to the role that may have differentiated her interpretation of Louise from Vernon's? "I just played it as they wrote it," she says. But, she admits with a laugh, "it took me a couple of shows before I shouted my first 'Larry!' properly." She was referring to the verbal exclamation that became a trademark of the Louise character.

"I don't even think I knew I was doing it," she says, "but people still come to me and ask if I would please do the 'Larry yell.'"

When Rogers first auditioned for Louise, her hair was red and of medium length. "So they asked me if I would mind wearing a black wig," she says, "so as not to create a jolt to the viewer's eyes [since Irene Vernon's hair was black]."

However, by the end of the fifth season (Rogers's third year with the show), she asked Bill Asher if she could stop using the black wig. Much to her surprise, he replied, "Sure. But why did you start wearing it in the first place?"

Irene Vernon "loved playing on *Bewitched*," though she doesn't regret leaving the show for a successful career in real estate. "I'm saner. But the show was a wonderful experience for me. It taught me a lot about life and myself. And in that sense, it really was magical."

"Louise, I love you," says Kasey Rogers, "and thank you for allowing me to be party to *Bewitched.*"

The Other Mr. and Mrs. Stephens

As noted in Chapter 2, not much of Darrin's family was seen on *Bewitched*, as it was thought best if he was the principal mortal on the show. Sol Saks had written a sister for him in the pilot episode, but she never came to be in the show.

Other than Uncle Albert in No. 68, and Cousin Helen in No. 129, the only relatives of Darrin's that were regulars were his parents, Frank and Phyllis Stevens. Phyllis was played by veteran stage, film, and television performer Mabel Albertson (sister of actor Jack *Chico and the Man* Albertson), and the role of Frank was shared by Robert F. Simon and Rob Roberts.

Just as Samantha had two Darrins, Darrin had two fathers. It seems to have run in the family. Dick York, of course, was replaced because of his poor health, but what was the story with Simon and Roberts?

"We were operating on the theory of actor availability and character necessity," says Bill Asher. "There were times when we couldn't get either Robert or Roy, so we had to switch from time to time. And we were allowed to do that because neither was under contract with the show."

Roberts has passed on now, but Simon is alive and well in Reseda, California, and as he recalls playing Darrin's dad: "I never gave too much thought as to how to interpret the role. The show was so well written that the characters literally spoke for themselves."

Adds Robert Simon of Albertson: "Both Mabel and Aggie [Moorehead] were hard to know, I thought. They were both very strong women. I mean, they were kind enough, but they both seemed to want to have power over everyone in their life. I always try to stay clear of women like that, if not anyone like that. But they certainly were both very clever performers."

One of Mabel's more prominent episodes, No. 182, "Samantha's Double Mother Trouble," was directed by David White.

"She was always ready and willing to try anything," said White. "And when I gave her an instruction, she understood exactly what I was talking about. Just to have the chance to work with Mabel made it all worthwhile."

Bill Asher praised both Simon's and Roberts's work on the show, but states: "As long as we had Mabel Albertson, we'd be fine. She was the key to the conflict that we needed where Darrin's parents were concerned. She was the one who was overreactive, who was more apt to jump to conclusions and make assumptions of her own. Whereas Mr. Stephens was thought of as a very easygoing kind of guy.

"Phyllis was the typical mother-in-law, always looking to find a dirty house, and one who would offer the humorous opposition to Endora. We could have done a show [as they did] without Darrin's father, but we couldn't have done one without his mother.

"There are certain aspects of a show that you can't mess around with," Asher firmly states, "and replacing Mabel was one of them."

"That woman was hysterical," says Elizabeth Montgomery of Albertson. "She was a superb actress, and she really gave it her all when she played Phyllis. And one of the great things about her was that she was one of the people [like Paul Lynde] who was not afraid to pull out all the stops when it came to her performance. Whoever was directing her would say, 'Now, Mabel, relax a little bit, come down in your performance a couple notches.' She was great that way. She was never afraid to go too far with her acting. And she was just as strong-willed as Aggie [Moorehead].

"When I'd see the two of them together, I would just sit back and say, 'Okay, well, let's just see how this turns out.'"

Special Guests

Bewitched was painstakingly cast, from its lead characters to its walk-on roles. Besides those already mentioned, people like Nancy Kovack, Dick Wilson (Mr. Whipple from the Charmin commercials), Charles Lane, Bernie Kopell (*The Love Boat*), Steve Franken (*Dobie Gillis*), Parley Baer, Sara Seegar (*Dennis the Menace*), David Huddleston, Henry Gibson (*Laugh In*), Jay Robinson, and Julie Newmar (Catwoman on *Batman*, guesting as a catwitch on *Bewitched*)—among many others—each offered theatrical expertise to various guest-starring roles.

Moreover, several screen legends appeared on the show, including Mercedes McCambridge, Cesar Romero, Peter Lawford, and Estelle Winwood, while Adam West (*Batman*), Raquel Welch, Peggy Lipton (*The Mod Squad* and *Twin Peaks*), Star Trekkers James Doohan and Grace Lee Whitney, Bill Daily (*I Dream of Jeannie* and *The Bob Newhart Show*), and Richard Dreyfuss—all made their television debuts on *Bewitched*.

Then there were the show's stalwarts, like Ruth McDevitt, Reta Shaw, Madge Blake, Jane Connell, and a host of child actors, such as Johnny Whitaker (*Family Affair*), Billy Mumy (*Lost in Space*), Maureen McCormick (*The Brady Bunch*), and Danny Bonaduce (*The Partridge Family*)—the latter three making two episodes each—among several other actors who kept the magical cast alive.

Was there ever any question of whether anyone felt the audience would grow tired of seeing the same actors on the show in various roles? "If I like an actor's style," says Bill Asher, "or know of his talents, I never have any qualms about using him or her again and again. Some producers do . . . I don't."

Elizabeth adds, "You see some shows and you say, 'Now, why didn't they take a little more time with the recurring roles or guest players?' And then you realize that the persons were cast because they were from some corporate office and considered the better choice because they had a 'name.' I don't agree with that philosophy, and we never used it on *Bewitched*. We always went with the best possible people, conceding to their abilities as actors and capabilities with the roles being cast."

She concludes: "I thought everyone on the show was extraordinary."

ASSORTED ARTS AND WITCH CRAFTS

One of the most amazing things I learned while filming Bewitched *is that at any given moment, the crew is infinitely more important than any actress or actor working on a television show.*

—Elizabeth Montgomery

Special effects were vital to the success of *Bewitched*.

"Technically," says Bill Asher, "*Bewitched* was a tough show to direct. In the early years I made sure I directed all the episodes that were more magic-oriented because I knew how to move things along more readily. And there were also times when we were enough ahead of schedule and air date that I was allowed to shuffle directing random scenes for different episodes out of sequence."

In the event that Asher could not finish shows, he would arrange time at the end of the third day (the series shot in four days) to complete scenes that took place in the Stephens house with the regular cast members, and would hand the rest over to the assistant director. And after the last frame was filmed, he would edit all the scenes together and fit them in.

"Today you can't do that," he says. "At times, we would have one of those thirteen-page days when the sides [dialogue between actors] would just fly by. But we more or less maintained a balance."

The optical illusions on *Bewitched* took a long time to devise and film—and time is money. Circa 1970, while comedies like *The*

Odd Couple had a budget reaching $90,000, each half hour of *Bewitched* cost approximately $115,000. This may not seem expensive by today's standards (*Star Trek: The Next Generation* is fortunate if it stays under $1,000,000 an episode), but during Samantha's original run, it was a high figure.

"It was more expensive to shoot than a regular show because of the effects," says Asher, "but after a while, we had it down to a science."

"At first," adds Bernard Slade, "we really didn't use any exuberant special effects. It wasn't as if we were doing *Star Wars*. We kept things simple because we felt the magic was not all-powerful. And we wanted to keep it within the boundaries of believability."

"In the later years," says Asher, "the budget grew as the show grew, but that just meant we worked harder. We did the same amount of dialogue as *The Donna Reed Show* or *Father Knows Best*, but we had to correlate the magic, which took some doing."

There were several individuals who brought these special effects to life. After veteran Willis Cook oversaw the *Bewitched* pilot (and went on to other projects), Screen Gems brought in Richard Albain, who had worked on features for Columbia, including *Bell, Book and Candle*.

When Albain left to work with Sidney Sheldon on *I Dream of Jeannie*, Marlowe Newkirk, Hal Bigger, Terry Saunders, John Bendowski, and Roy Maples lent their assistance through the years.

"We'd receive a script two or three days in advance of rehearsal, and then go over it in a production meeting with the rest of the cast and crew, noting any changes to be made. Then an hour or two before we went to shoot the gag, Bill, or whoever was directing, would come over and give his okay, or say something like, 'I'd like this [prop] to do this' or 'I'd like to see this [prop] float over here.'"

If it was a rather involved special effects sequence, Albain says, "it would have to be rigged [positioned] in advance. And we all just worked around it until it came time to shoot."

There were several camera tricks that were employed on the show, but the most frequently used sight gag was the appearance or disappearance of various witches and warlocks on the show. For this effect, the graphic camera was used. Albain explains:

"We'd get an angle on whoever was about to pop in or out and then mark the lens where the character would swing his arms or whatever, and then someone would mark the other camera in the same way. Then we'd stop tape [filming] at the proper time on one camera and keep another one on to give the illusion of someone disappearing."

When objects appeared or disappeared from Samantha's or anyone else's hand, that person would freeze and hold the mark. Albain would then come on the set and take the object away. When the episode was viewed, the object would appear to vanish.

To make it look as if there were particular people or objects levitating in midair, Albain used an old diving board and crane that Columbia had discarded. He situated the board between the catwalks in the ceiling on the set, where there was a six-foot clearance. "And I would secure the special wires and strings from up there."

Albain then explained the puff-smoke effect: "At first they wanted Samantha to pop in and out in a puff of smoke, called a screen explosion. So I developed the idea. When they did the pilot, they used black powder, and they put three or four feet of it in front of the camera, which would black out the whole screen after somebody blew on it.

"So then I thought of building a trough to put at Samantha's feet at such an angle that it would deflect the heat. This way, the smoke and the heat would blow far from the camera and Elizabeth, keeping her cool and the camera from exploding. And then when she would pretend to disappear, we would just 'puff' her out. The director would cut, and then Elizabeth would change her clothes or whatever, and be ready for the next shot."

Other effects included the dry-ice or mist effect used in many of the "Salem" segments during the Witch Convention scenes in the seventh season. This technique was employed to create a cloudlike look in No. 252, "A Good Turn Never Goes Unpunished," in which the Stephenses argue, and Samantha is forced to retreat with Tabitha and Endora, literally, to Cloud Nine.

This effect was also used in No. 144, "Darrin Gone and Forgotten," in which Sam flies to the abode of witch Carlotta up yonder to plead for the release of Darrin, whom the not so nice witch has replaced with her son (Steve Franken).

To produce the heavenly effect, carbon dioxide was solidified into a white, icelike substance. This, in block form, is called dry ice, and was extensively employed as a coolant. Permitted to warm, the dry ice gradually dehumidified and gave off clouds of white vapors as it returned to its original gaslike form.

Dry ice was not costly, and it was kept on hand so it could be easily manipulated—as in "Gone" and other episodes. The only essential precaution was to avoid prolonged skin contact. During the filming of No. 171, "Samantha and the Beanstalk," Elizabeth found the dry ice made it difficult to breath. "I was pregnant during that time," she says, "and I was more apt to become queasy around that stuff, but I didn't realize how strong those vapors could be. It was real scary."

To a less harmful extent, small pieces of dry ice were used in many of the *Bewitched* episodes involving Dr. Bombay's potions. Minute cantlets would be dropped into a test tube or a glass of water, and the result was a bubbling or swirling white steam.

Some other special effects:

To showcase Samantha's and Endora's flying (as in No. 127, "If They Never Met," where the two travel back in time), a technique adopting multiple wind implements was employed, localizing the bewitching breezes as much as possible.

Yet when mass confusion had to be created in Samantha's house (as when High Priestess Hepzibah arrived in No. 201), apparatus capable of various speeds and larger wind machines were utilized so that props could fly all about.

When Bernie Kopell's apothecary character from the witch world was seen in his laboratory, it was covered with cobwebs. A novel instrument empowering a rubber solution to trickle onto a revolving fan blade helped to produce this webbed look. The pitched substance was usually spun over extended black cotton threads. To add more to this effect, the crew would dust the webs with a substance called Fuller's Earth, which made the webs more visible.

When ghosts and specters would partially appear or disappear on the show (as in No. 130, "McTavish," or No. 235, "The Ghost Who Made a Spectre of Himself"), the spirit actor would be placed in front of either a black or a blue background, and the chroma-key effect would be put to use.

As a result, any body part or clothing that was supposed to disappear would be cloaked in the same black or blue material, so that headless torsos and various bodiless arms and legs appeared. This technique was used extensively with Alice Ghostley's character, Esmeralda, who (as already explained in Chapter 8) would continually fade in or out on a nervous whim.

Every once in a while, when Samantha or Endora wove a magic spell or spoke an incantation, a gleaming light effect would be added to the projected scene. Here glitter, stardust, and other glimmering agents, patterned with sequins or something similar, would be employed. Occasionally metallic dust was used for sparkling coiffures, as on Elizabeth's hair just before Samantha was crowned Queen of the Witches.

When dream sequences were needed on the series (as in No. 135, "I Confess"), the ripple reflection effect was applied. This commonly used technique involved having a machine hold a receptacle of water. It was held in a crisply centralized light stream, as its image was projected on a nearby surface that the camera then filmed.

Another effect used on the show when the Stephenses' home was being rocked by the angry supernatural force of the moment was simply called tilting the picture. This technique was created by having various mirrored lens attachments handy to enable the special effects people to rotate the picture. By superimposing a regular scene on a tilted one, the illusion of a slanted frame is easily created.

This process was extensively employed on the *Batman* TV series. It was also used on the classic *Star Trek* series whenever the *Enterprise* was under attack by an alien vessel, and the crew would be seen swaying from side to side.

Certain props used on *Bewitched* shows almost had a life of their own. One such prop was the mobile chair with collapsible legs used in No. 86, "Sam's Spooky Chair." Says Elizabeth: "We had an absolutely wonderful propman named Fairchild who used to doze off on the set quite often . . . and he had this habit of going off to a corner and resting. Well, when we had that chair built, we had to be very careful about where we placed it when we weren't using it because everyone had this vision of him walking over to the chair and sitting down and having him collapse in it."

Kasey Rogers (Louise Tate) recalls two wonderful props that she was allowed to keep after they were used in the show. In No. 198, "Mona Sammy," the Tates see a portrait they assume to be of Samantha. It is really her grandaunt Cornelia. The Stephenses convince them that Darrin is the artist. Consequently, Louise asks Darrin to paint a portrait of her. Sam zaps Darrin, turning him into a true artist. Just as he is finishing a most flattering portrait of Louise, Endora rezaps him so that the picture is a hideous likeness.

Rogers got to keep both portraits, and as she says, "I still have this fantasy of having the pretty picture hanging on my den wall at the beginning of a party, only to turn it around and have the ugly one on the other side by the end of the party."

In No. 114, "Birdies, Bogeys and Baxter," Samantha and Endora cast a spell on Darrin and make him a superior golfer one day when he and Larry are playing with a client. A golf pro was brought in to substitute for Dick York during the sequences showing Darrin's newfound abilities, and according to York, this professional "couldn't get one of those balls to hit the green . . . it was the funniest thing in the world. So we had to keep on fixing the shoot.

"Then I gave it a shot myself. I damn near hit some of the golfers on the other side of the green. And everyone joked that if they'd known I could do that, they would never have hired the other guy."

One of the most bizarre props ever used on the show, according to York, was the wings off a dead fly in No. 113, "No Zip in My Zap." In this segment Darrin thinks Samantha has transformed herself into a fly to spy on his meeting with a client, who also just happens to be an old girl friend. "I remember that as one of the grossest days on the show. The prop guys took the wings off this poor little fly and placed them right on my nose."

Dick York's recollection of working with that fly is just one of the many live special effects experiences on *Bewitched*. Marvin Miller relates a few other instances where much larger creatures were used: "I remember one time when we were working with an ostrich, which can be very mean—and Bill [Asher] asked me to go and stand between the ostrich and Marion Lorne [Aunt Clara]. I said, 'What do you mean?' He said, 'Well . . . Marion's afraid to be too close to the ostrich.' And I said, 'Well . . . I'm not too happy about it either.'

"But in order to get the ostrich to move, we had to flag it down . . . and this particular bird was temperamental. You had to be careful—it usually takes two people to ride them out."

Miller describes another animal problem early in the series: on the set of No. 3, "It Shouldn't Happen to a Dog," Samantha turned a client (Jack Warden) of Darrin's into a dog. "We were out at the Columbia ranch and I asked the trainer about a certain scene with the dog we were using. We were ready to start filming and I said to him, 'Now, we're all set . . . is the dog ready?' and he said, 'Oh, yeah . . . no problem.' Well, the dog was supposed to be level with the ground and then run up to this car and put his paws on the hood. Later we found out that the hood was hot and the dog was smarter than the trainer. He wouldn't put his paws up there. And it delayed shooting for quite some time that day. And that's when I learned that whenever I heard an animal trainer say, 'No problem,' I'd get nervous because I knew there would be a problem."

Miller also remembers a few other animal scenes gone awry, including "a penguin that couldn't control himself" and left "droppings all over the place" and the pink elephant from No. 89, "A Gazebo Never Forgets." Of the latter, he says: "We had to get that elephant to go up the stairway [in the Stephenses' house]. But he was just too big and too wide, and the steps couldn't hold him."

Dick Sargent also remembers some of the animals on the show being difficult to work with: "Liz and I were very nervous about having those monkeys [in No. 218, "The House that Uncle Arthur Built"] on the set. There were ten or twelve of them running around the living room and we weren't exactly sure of what they were going to do next. But they had real big mouths and teeth, and rumor had it that they got vicious after seven years of age. And these monkeys were way past that stage."

One of the main audiovisual techniques employed on *Bewitched* was the split-screen effect, showcasing Samantha and Serena side by side, with the assistance of Elizabeth's stand-in, Melody Thomas. Director Richard Michaels explains how this effect was achieved.

"The first thing we would do was to secure two cameras in identical positions, with angles situated on Elizabeth and Melody. We then would shoot the over-the-shoulder shots with Elizabeth as Samantha and Melody as Serena before we did the master shots of Elizabeth as Serena and Melody as Samantha, only because Elizabeth used heavy makeup and a wig as Serena, while Melody used only the black wig.

"Next, we'd do the sound track with Elizabeth as Samantha and Melody as Serena, and then vice versa. But how it sounded really didn't matter as much as how long it took to record it, as we could perfect the sound quality and character distinction later on when editing."

Melody's voice-over of both Samantha and Serena (which was used just for timing purposes during filming) was edited out, and only Elizabeth's voice performances were edited in during an additional dubbing session.

Overall, the special effects were probably the most difficult part of filming *Bewitched*. "There were times," recalls Dick York, "when I would get a line perfect, and the magic was off. And I remember once having to wait almost twelve hours for the crew to shift the furniture in the living room as it was zapped in and out, in and out." [No. 2, "Be It Ever So Mortgaged"]

"But," he concludes, "we were all masters of making the magic work."

IN WITCH CONCLUSION

Bewitched is one of the pantheon of classical American TV shows that were created before the medium itself lost its innocence. We seemed to have lost the formula. And now all we have is a medium that is only bothering and bewildering.

—Professor Arthur Asa Berger, San Francisco State University; author, *The TV Guided American*

Many elements contributed to the success of *Bewitched*, and the show was created week after week with care and dedication. This may explain why most contemporary shows pale in comparison to this series, and why it's still shown in syndication.

When the show first appeared in the 1960s, it had compassion. It wasn't severely conservative or reactionary or broadly comedic. Instead it displayed a great deal of humanity.

When Samantha first began to twitch, the majority of television characters were lovable and flawless people. Rarely would a three-dimensional person show up in a situation comedy. To address an audience, television types had to be likable and never really cry or display any extreme emotion. There were good guys and bad guys, but hardly any in between.

On *Bewitched*, the producers, directors, writers, and actors were able to make the witches and warlocks more dimensional because they weren't human.

In the quintessential episode discussed in Chapter 4, No. 17, "A Is for Aardvark," Samantha cries real tears when Darrin presents her with a watch inscribed I LOVE YOU EVERY SECOND. And in No. 251, "School Days, School Daze," Samantha grows increasingly angry with her daughter's mortal teacher, who invades the Stephens household one time too many, seeking an explanation for Tabitha's genius, which Endora has given the child.

Uncle Arthur was outlandish and irresponsible, Serena was a little wild and loose, and Endora was ungenerous and grudging. Each was permitted to stray from the norm and do the outrageous because they were all part of an outside world . . . the supernatural world.

Endora displayed emotional distaste for Darrin every week and flaunted traits that are most unappealing to a human being. Though her conduct was considered inappropriate by Samantha and Darrin, it was given the stamp of approval by the audience. In keeping with the programming philosophy of the times, Endora was a "bad" good witch.

"I think fantasy shows like *Bewitched*," said Harry Ackerman, "filled a great gap in television in the 1960s. And I also think that the networks were much too quick to wipe out the *Bewitched* type of programming . . . and to replace it almost immediately with *All in the Family* and comparatively realistic shows."

To the viewer's satisfaction, Samantha controlled her witchcraft and twitched only on occasion and in an emergency. She remained a witch without succumbing to what Bernard Fox's Dr. Bombay might have termed primary mortalitis, and, as a result, she continues to enjoy her immortal success in television. Had she become human, the show would have obviously no longer been about a witch, and Samantha's reign as Queen of the Witches would have been curtailed.

During the show's original run, *All in the Family* was programmed against it in 1972. Samantha held her own against Archie Bunker, and a ninth season was planned, but *Family* prevailed as the time-period lord, and *Bewitched* was cancelled . . . but not forgotten.

The mark of Samantha has been ingrained in the minds of the general television-viewing, music-listening, and moviegoing public.

Bewitched entered national syndication in September 1973 via Screen Gems, and was renewed in 1988 via barter with Dancer, Fitzgerald & Sample of New York. The show is televised in approximately 122 markets worldwide, 83 percent of which are in the United States.

In the fall of 1989, cable's Nickelodeon channel, Nick at Nite, began showing the first two black-and-white seasons, which had not been seen in over a decade. Other cable networks like TBS televise the show weekdays, as do independent stations and network affiliates across the country. As a result, *Bewitched* can be seen as many as four times a day in places like New York City, Chicago, Los Angeles, and Phoenix.

There are thousands of female mortals around the world who were named after little Tabitha, who was "born" on January 13, 1966.

Several comedians perform monologues about *Bewitched*. *Saturday Night Live*, *Newhart*, *Cheers*, *The Golden Girls*, and *The New Leave It to Beaver* have each included dialogue pertaining to two Darrins, and ABC's Sunday night drama, *Life Goes On*, features Ray Butenica as a Larry Tate-inspired advertising man named Jerry Berkson.

On a more direct television line, ABC tried to duplicate its *Bewitched* success in 1977 with the *Tabitha* series. And ABC tried again in 1989 with *Free Spirit*, featuring a witch who was the housekeeper for a divorced father and his three children. Alas, the last spell was cast after only three months on the air.

Syndicated supernatural sitcoms reminiscent of *Bewitched* have enjoyed better luck . . . at least for two seasons or so. *Small Wonder*, *Out of This World*, and *Down To Earth* (which starred Dick Sargent) have been aired. And NBC's once highly rated sardonic success, *Alf*, now popular in reruns, features Mrs. Ochmonek, a nosy neighbor in the vein of Mrs. Kravitz.

Even more spooky is the relationship between *Bewitched* and the ABC series *Who's the Boss*, starring Tony Danza as housekeeper Tony Micelli to Judith Light's Angela. Angela owns her own advertising agency; she refers to her mother, Mona, played by Katherine Helmond, in much the same manner as Samantha referred to Endora. Helmond's hair color is as red as Agnes Moorehead's was. And Mona is just as interfering as Endora was, though Mona mostly sides against Angela. What's more, Danza's TV daughter, played by Alyssa Milano, is named—of all things—Samantha, and the front door to Angela's house is a replica of the Stephenses' door in *Bewitched*. *Who's the Boss* is filmed on the very same lot in Hollywood as *Bewitched* (then ABC Studios, now Sunset-Gower Studios), owned by the same company (Columbia),

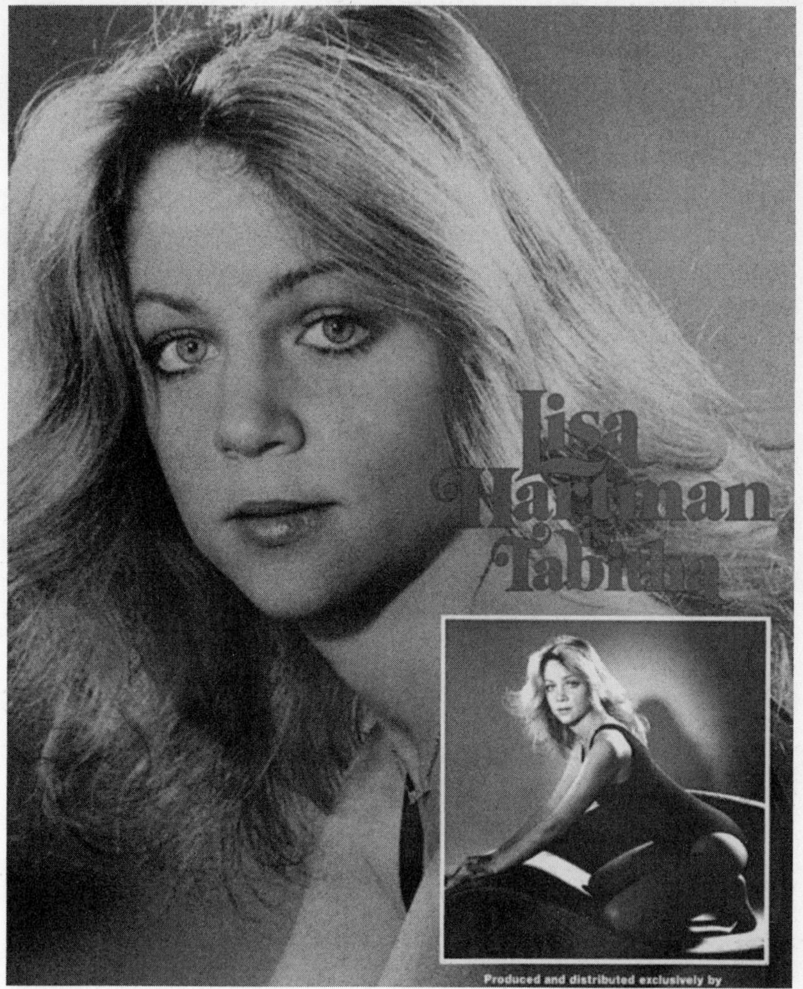

Lisa Hartman as Tabitha in the TV show Tabitha. *(Columbia Pictures Television.)*

and aired on the same network. Somebody put a spell on somebody.

On the big screen, the theatrical films *Big* (1988), in which a young boy suddenly becomes a man (played by Tom Hanks), and *Bill and Ted's Excellent Adventure* (1989), which involves historical figures visiting the present, both employed devices that were first used on *Bewitched.* And *The Witches of Eastwick* (1987) and *Warlock* (1991) made forthright references to *Bewitched.*

Of musical note, the rock band Redd Kross recorded their own version of the Boyce and Hart composition, "Blow You a Kiss in the Wind," which was sung by Elizabeth as Serena in No. 192,

"Serena Stops the Show." There is also a Los Angeles rock band who named themselves The Larry Tate Experience.

Even Edie Brickell, of the New Bohemians band, recently stated in *Rolling Stone* that all she ever "really wanted was to have a job like Darrin Stephens on *Bewitched* . . . [one] where you could be creative all the time."

Advertising man Craig Winner of Los Angles, California, took his *Bewitched* inspiration one step further and opened McMann, Tate and Stevens, Advertising, Inc., adding and slighting altering Darrin's last name.

"I always wanted to be an advertising man like Darrin," says Winner. "So I made my dream come true and I'm successful due to a lot of hard work . . . and the inspiration I received from *Bewitched*."

Does the actual ad business differ from the way it's portrayed on *Bewitched?* "The pace is just as hectic," he says, "and there's just as much on-the-spot decision making and slogan creating" at his company as there was on the show. He admits to one major distinction between Darrin and himself, however: "I'm not married to a witch."

The Liberated Point of View

In September of 1990, an article written by Irene Lachner entitled "She Worship" appeared in the *Los Angeles Times* with some interesting things to say about how real witches are viewed today. Lachner wrote:

> For some, goddess worship is emerging as the latest wave in the evolution of women's rights. If feminism first took on economic issues in the 1960s and 1970s, and then moved on to questions about family life in the eighties, then the nineties are seeing women grappling with a more elusive target.

With regard to *Bewitched,* similar comments are made by two of the shows associates: guest star Bernie Kopell and writer Barbara Avedon.

"Women loved to be liberated," says Kopell. "And they love to have great powers . . . and whether Darrin realized this or not, Samantha motivated his life, something he possibly felt impotent to do."

"I think people in the 1960s watched *Bewitched*," notes Avedon, "and said, 'Yes, it's right, Samantha shouldn't use her powers.' They might have felt that if she did, they would have had to relinquish their strengths as well . . . and give in to society and just go along with the norm.

"Every woman does for the man in her life, and I think—in a sense—Darrin was the voice of society. The one who would say, 'Sam, what have you been up to?' I mean, it wasn't the outside world that was telling her not to fly her child to school, it was absolutely within her relationship with Darrin that she held herself back. Not because she simply wanted to live the mortal life as a challenge in and of itself, but because she chose to live the mortal life because she loved Darrin.

"The Stephenses' marriage," she continues, "may have even been the basic metaphor for the male-female relationship of the 1960s—when women really kept their own strengths hidden within the prescribed boundaries of marriage."

Does this mean there is truly a message behind the magic of *Bewitched*?

"If I can't write a message into the script I'm working on," Avedon replies, "then I don't go up to the plate. If a story doesn't teach some kind of lesson, then it's not worth writing. But if it's written totally as a message, then it should be sent as a telegram. Then again, if it's delivered with some drama or comedy—or hopefully both—and it says something, then that's art . . . because without the message, it's not art."

Conversely, *Bewitched* director E. W. Swackhamer says: "Television is supposed to take your mind off what happens during the day, not necessarily to sit there and teach you something. If that's what viewers want, they certainly have that opportunity with public television and A&E [the Arts and Entertainment network on cable TV], but I think that basically situation comedy should be fun and escapist and make you feel good."

"I think television comedy is a great medium to get things across," adds Marvin Miller. "But I don't think that many of the episodes we did on *Bewitched* had any hidden messages. Elizabeth was pretty clear and up front about what she said and did as Samantha.

"When you're a star and you have a hit show, then of course you'll have a forum where it's easier to discuss matters that are

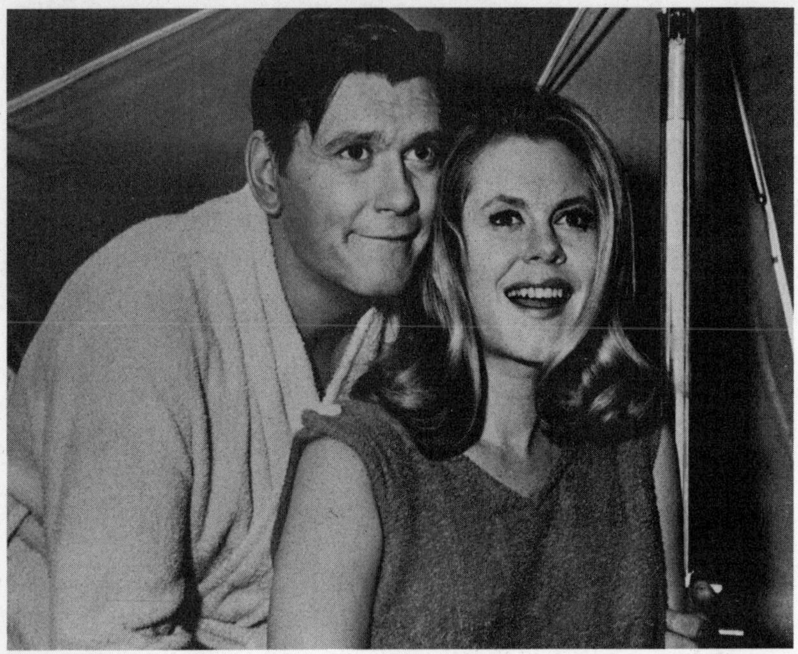

H*appily married Darrin and Sam. (Columbia Pictures Television/Milton T. Moore, Jr.)*

important to you and to have people listen to your perspective. Or maybe the audience might not even like the politics of the subject matter, but they're going to listen to whatever is said because they like and respect the actor who's saying it. And because the actor has made himself or herself accessible to the viewer. Whereas if I (a person behind the scenes) got up and spoke on a topic on the air, no one would know who I was and they wouldn't listen."

However, there were times when Elizabeth would have preferred to be even more political on *Bewitched,* but as it was a comedy, she thought "there were certain parameters we could not have passed."

In all, Miller concludes: "Television is a very strange medium. For people to welcome shows into their homes, they have to feel comfortable with the performers on the screen. That's why some actors make it on TV, and some don't. They may succeed in the theater and in motion pictures (as it is more of a physical choice and effort to see a play or a film), but if the audience isn't comfortable with them on their living room television, the actors or actresses can forget it."

Of course, the ongoing success of *Bewitched* subliminally rests with its star power.

Elizabeth's Samantha was quite attractive, and as *Bewitched* writer John L. Greene (creator of *My Favorite Martian*) says, "you can just see the intelligence in her eyes." Furthermore, Samantha was—for the most part—an independent lady, as it was *her* decision to surrender her sorcery for the mortal life. (For this behavior to be accepted by the 1960s viewer, the female lead in a series probably would have had to be a supernatural woman.)

Elizabeth was the first female sex symbol of the TV generation, and she arrived on the tube long before *Charlie's Angels* and Suzanne Somers combed the hairwaves. The latter's popularity stemmed strictly from her frosted locks, loose apparel, the right amount of jiggle, and constant displays and mentions of her unmentionables.

The trouping of Dick York and Dick Sargent on *Bewitched* also proved most advantageous to viewers. Their idiosyncratic interpretations of Darrin almost allow the series to be screened as two different shows. This contributed to the show's longevity.

Expanding on other actors who shared the same role on *Bewitched*, Richard Michaels states: "We couldn't get another actor to play Aunt Clara [Marion Lorne] the way we replaced Dick York with Dick Sargent as Darrin. Darrin was a critical character, and we really didn't want to tinker with the basis of the show.

"But with Aunt Clara and Esmeralda [Alice Ghostley], the disappearance of a bumbling aunt and the appearance of a bumbling maid were acceptable because both were not as central to the show's basic premise as Darrin was."

Regarding Alice Pearce and Sandra Gould as Gladys Kravitz, Michaels explains: "We were either going to hire someone new to play Gladys after Alice passed away or move in new neighbors to replace the Kravitzes altogether. Obviously, we opted for the former due to the fact that Gladys's interplay with Abner was too funny, and, yes, too essential to the show's format."

On Irene Vernon and Kasey Rogers as Louise Tate, Michaels says: "We couldn't have Larry just marry someone else, because the character of Louise softened his persona. So for him to get a divorce or even become a widower would have made him less appealing and too bitter. It was just cleaner to hire Kasey after Irene left."

In each of these replacement cases, it should be noted that it was never a question of recasting a character because of an actor's unacceptable performance. The decision to replace an actor was made because the performer died (Marion Lorne and Alice Pearce), became ill (Dick York), left on his own accord (Irene Vernon), or had filming conflicts with other projects (Robert F. Simon and Roy Roberts).

Agnes Moorehead and her performance as Endora cannot go without final mention in analyzing the everlasting appeal of *Bewitched*. It was Moorehead's Shakespearean delivery of Endora's spells and incantations that continues to enchant viewers.

Of Moorehead's lasting reputation, writer Bernie Kahn says: "She was brilliant . . . a forerunner who added a great deal of class to Endora. Agnes was just way ahead of her time."

Bewitched . . . Again?

In view of the enormous popularity of *Bewitched*, would Elizabeth ever agree to do a reunion movie, updating the adventures of Samantha and Darrin?

"I don't see any reason to do that," she says. "I think once you have completed a project, you should go on." And she adds, "I am very proud of *Bewitched*, and I seriously doubt that whatever type of reunion could be made would ever top what we did on the series, or even come close."

Which may lead one to wonder what Elizabeth's involvement with the *Tabitha* series in 1977 was.

"I had absolutely 'zero' to do with the show," she says. "But I still received mail from people who were outraged that Erin and Diane Murphy were not involved with it. The letters would say, 'What in the world is going on here?! Tabitha is in her twenties! This doesn't make any sense!' And I responded to each and every person who was looking for an answer. I felt an obligation to them. They were annoyed and felt betrayed."

There were two pilots produced for Tabitha. The first starred Liberty Williams in the lead, Bruce Kimmell as Adam, and Archie Kahn as the love interest Cliff, in *Tabatha* (with an *a* instead of an *i*, as it was originally spelled early on in *Bewitched*).

The Williams-Kimmell-Kahn version was not purchased by ABC. Thus a second pilot starring Lisa Hartman was made and sold to the network. And somewhere during or in between these consecutive pilots, actress Susan Dey was approached about playing the lead.

Bewitched writer Ed Jurist thought Dey's casting "would have been perfect," as "she is an exact double for Elizabeth." Yet Dey declined. Three years before *Tabitha*'s premier, she had completed four seasons as Laurie Partridge on *The Partridge Family*, and she set out to break the sweet-daughter mold, something she finally accomplished with her role as Grace Van Owen on NBC's highly acclaimed prime-time hit, *LA Law.*

Lisa Hartman also resembled Elizabeth Montgomery and even possessed similar body language, but *Tabitha* still did not succeed.

Of winning the *Tabitha* lead in 1977, Hartman told the *Los Angeles Times* on May 12, 1987: "It was a real shock to get that. I came out here to make records and tour. I never really thought about [doing] a series." Hartman also told the *Times* that had it not been for continual bumping by Christmas specials, *Rudolph the Red-Nosed Reindeer* and *Frosty the Snowman*, the show might have had a better chance.

"After all," she said, "it was a hit in its time slot during [the] summer reruns." She conceded that perhaps *Tabitha*'s success was not meant to be. "I believe things happen the way they do for a reason."

"I wish they had waited a couple of years so I could have done the show," says Erin Murphy. "I would have loved to do it. But I was only thirteen years old when it came on the air." This did not jibe with how *Tabitha* was being developed.

As Elizabeth has confirmed, there was genuine outrage on the part of fans when *Tabitha* debuted without Erin or Diane Murphy. Sol Saks comments: "Whereas *Bewitched* had the feel of success from the beginning—everyone liked it and enjoyed it while they were making it—*Tabitha* had problems from the onset."

From what Saks recalls, Bill Asher (who helped to develop *Tabitha* and also directed one of its episodes, No. 6, "The Arrival of Nancy") asked him to work on the show. "I had something totally different in mind from what they finally produced," says Saks. "With *Tabitha*, they set out to do *Bewitched* without Samantha and the original cast."

Bernie Kahn was story editor on *Tabitha*, and even he admits, "We were floundering, and we didn't understand the character. We really didn't have a fix on the show."

What really made *Bewitched* unique? The series is the definitive fantasy sitcom because its special premise never outshone its characters. Its stories never tampered with the internal logic of its own imaginative realm. The dialogue was masterfully structured to give life to the characters—there was no mistaking Darrin for Larry Tate or Samantha for Endora.

"This is why the show was so successful," says story editor Bernard Slade. "Everyone took it so seriously." While writing for *Bewitched,* Slade also wrote for the sitcom *My Living Doll*, starring Julie Newmar as a mechanical woman. "So there I was," Slade says, "a grown man writing about a witch and a robot, sitting in rooms with other grown men debating things like, 'Would a witch really say that?' "

Ed Jurist was also amused by how seriously he and his colleagues took the series. "I remember working in Palm Springs one season with Bill Asher," he says, "and we were discussing the life of a frog [for Episode No. 106]. And I recall thinking, 'if someone overheard this conversation, they would think we were crazy.' "

Richard Baer remembers wondering, "Who's crazy here?" in considering the *Bewitched do*'s and *don't*s. "Uncle Arthur couldn't pop out of the kitchen cabinet, it would have to be a book, and this book could never have been an encyclopedia, it had to be *The Swiss Family Robinson.*"

Baer remembers fondly writing Samantha and Endora's lyrical spells. "I used to love writing those incantations," he says. "I would steal from Kipling all the time."

Of the show's continued popularity, Dick York may have said it best: "*Bewitched* remains successful because it's a show about faith and trust. It was first shown at the proper time . . . when we needed to return to innocence and sanity. It was the way things should have been after World War Two and the announcement of democracy. . . . If there's ever something to fear in life, and if you can't believe in miracles, then *Bewitched* makes you believe in magic."

Nothing sums up the vision held for the show by its cast and creative team better than Richard Baer's comment: "It was really our job to take something natural . . . and make it supernatural."

Cosmic Codex

VITAL STATISTICS

254 Episodes (74 in black and white, 180 in color)

Broadcast History:

ABC September 17, 1964, to July 1, 1972
ABC (Daytime) January 1, 1968, to September 1973
ABC Saturday Morning 1971 to 1973

Original ABC Schedule:

Thursday 9:00 P.M. September 17, 1964, to January 5, 1967
Thursday 8:30 P.M. January 12, 1967, to September 9, 1971
Wednesday 8:00 P.M. September 15, 1971, to January 5, 1972
Saturday 8:00 P.M. January 15, 1972, to July 1, 1972

Original ABC Nielson Ratings:

SEASON	RANK	AUDIENCE SHARE
1964–65	#2	31.0
1965–66	#7	25.9
1966–67	#8	23.4
1967–68	#11	23.5
1968–69	#12	23.3
1969–70	#25	20.6
1970–71	—	15.4
1971–72	—	10.4

CREDIT LISTINGS

Samantha/Serena	Elizabeth Montgomery (254 episodes as Samantha/24 as Serena)
Darrin (1964–69)	Dick York (116 episodes)
Darrin (1969–72)	Dick Sargent (84)
Endora	Agnes Moorehead (144)
Larry Tate	David White (166)
Gladys Kravitz (1964–66)	Alice Pearce (28)
Gladys Kravitz (1966–72)	Sandra Gould (29)
Abner Kravitz	George Tobias (53)
Louise Tate (1964–66)	Irene Vernon (13)
Louise Tate (1966–72)	Kasey Rogers (33)
Maurice	Maurice Evans (12)
Aunt Clara (1964–68)	Marion Lorne (28)
Uncle Arthur (1965–72)	Paul Lynde (10) (1 as Harold Harold in No. 26)
Dr. Bombay (1967–72)	Bernard Fox (18) (1 as Osgood Rightmire in No. 65)
Esmeralda (1969–72)	Alice Ghostley (15) (1 as Naomi in No. 53)
Phyllis Stephens	Mabel Albertson (19)
Frank Stephens (alternate)	Robert F. Simon (6)
Frank Stephens (alternate)	Roy Roberts (7)
Tabitha (1966–72)	Erin Murphy/Diane Murphy (100 varied episodes/scenes)

Adam (1970–72)	David Lawrence/Greg Lawrence (17 varied episodes/scenes)
Executive Producer/Creative Consultant (1964–72)	Harry Ackerman
Producer/Director (1964–72)	William Asher (directed 133 episodes)
Producer/Story Editor (1964–65)	Danny Arnold (wrote 3 episodes)
Producer/Director/Writer (alternate/1966–67)	Jerry Davis (directed 4 episodes/wrote 2)
Producer (1967–68)	William Froug
Pilot Creator	Sol Saks
Associate Producers (alternate)	Jerry Brisken, Ernest Losso, and Richard Michaels (who also directed 54 episodes)
Directors (alternate)	R. Robert Rosenbaum (22 episodes), Richard Kinon (8 episodes), and E. W. Swackhamer (8)
Assistant Director (alternate)	Marvin Miller, Maxwell Henry, Mark Sandrich, Hal Polaire, Gil Mandolik, Jerome Siegal, Jack Orbison, Michael Dmytryk, Jack R. Berne, and Anthony M. Ray
Story Editor/Writer (1964–66)	Bernard Slade (wrote 17 episodes)
Story Editor/Writer (alternate)	Ruth Brooks Flippen (wrote 2 episodes)
Story Editor/Writer (alternate)	Ed Jurist (wrote 52 episodes plus 2 as cowriter = 54)
Story Editor/Writer (alternate)	Michael Morris (wrote 22 episodes)
Writers	James Henerson (10 episodes plus 2 as cowriter), Lila Garrett and Bernie Kahn (10), John L. Greene (8 episodes with Paul David, 5 with David V. Robison, and 5 solo), and Barbara Avedon (4 solo, 1 with William Asher)
Special Effects (alternate)	Willis Cook (pilot), Richard Albain, Marlowe Newkirk, Terry Saunders, and Hal Bigger
Wardrobe (1964–72)	Byron Munson (Department Head) and Vi Alford
Makeup	Ben Lane (Department Head), Rolf Miller (1969–72)
Hairstyles (alternate)	Peanuts and Cosmo

Production Supervisor	Seymour Friedman
Music	Warren Barker, Van Alexander, Pete Carpenter, and Jimmie Haskell
Title Song	Howard Greenfield and Jack Keller
Music Consultant	Don Kirshner
Music Supervisor	Ed Forsyth
Directors of Photography	Robert Tobey, Robert Wyckoff, Frederick Gately, and Lloyd Ahern
Postproduction Supervisor	Lawrence Werner
Art Direction	Ross Bellah, Robert Purcell, Malcolm C. Bart, and Robert Peterson
Set Decoration	Sidney Clifford, Louis Diage, Jack Ahern, Milton Stumph, and James M. Crowe
Film Editors	Aaron Nibley, Jack Ruggiero, Hugh Chaloupka, Jack Peluso, Asa Clark, Michael Luciano, and Gerald J. Wilson
Casting Directors	Burt Metcalfe, Ernest Losso, Al Ornorato, and Sally Powers
Opticals	Photo Effex
Sound Effects	Fred J. Brown, Sid Lubow, Sunset Editorial
Music Effects	Sunset Editorial
Elizabeth Montgomery's Wardrobe	PFC Inc., York Town Juniors, Tony Lynn Maternities
Dick York's Wardrobe	Phoenix Clothes, Michaels-Stern
Dick Sargent's Wardrobe	Botany 500, Michaels-Stern
Tabitha's (infant) Wardrobe & Furnishings	Babycrest
Props	George Ballerino
Camera Operator	Val O'Malley
Gaffer	Arthur D. Kaufman
Head Grip	Charles Gibbs
Assistant to the Producer/Production Secretary	Bobbi Shane
Color by	Pathé, Perfect Pathé, Berkey Path

EPISODES

THE FIRST SEASON: 1964 to 1965

No. 1

"I, Darrin, Take This Witch, Samantha" (9-17-64)

Written by Sol Saks. Directed by William Asher. Guest cast: Nancy Kovack, Gene Blakely.

Samantha and Darrin get married before he discovers she's a witch. When Endora disapproves, Sam begs her not to meddle. After Darrin learns the truth, he makes Sam promise never to use witchcraft. Later, his old girl friend, Sheila Sommers, invites the Stephenses to a dinner party, making every effort to embarrass Samantha, who eventually "lets Sheila have it."

Note: This pilot was filmed in November 1963.

No. 2

"Be It Ever So Mortgaged" (9-24-64)

Written by Barbara Avedon. Directed by William Asher.

Endora is dismayed when Samantha chooses to live the mortal life. Yet Sam does resort to her witchy ways when faced with having to bake a cake. Her powers also come in handy when she and Endora inspect the house Darrin plans to purchase. Much to Gladys's dismay, the two witches have a good time rearranging the new place.

Note: The Stephenses' address is 1164 Morning Glory Circle.

No. 3

"It Shouldn't Happen to a Dog" (10-1-64)

Written by Jerry Davis. Directed by William Asher. Guest cast: Jack Warden, Grace Lee Whitney.

Samantha holds a dinner party to impress Darrin's client Rex Barker, who flirts with her after he has a couple of drinks. When

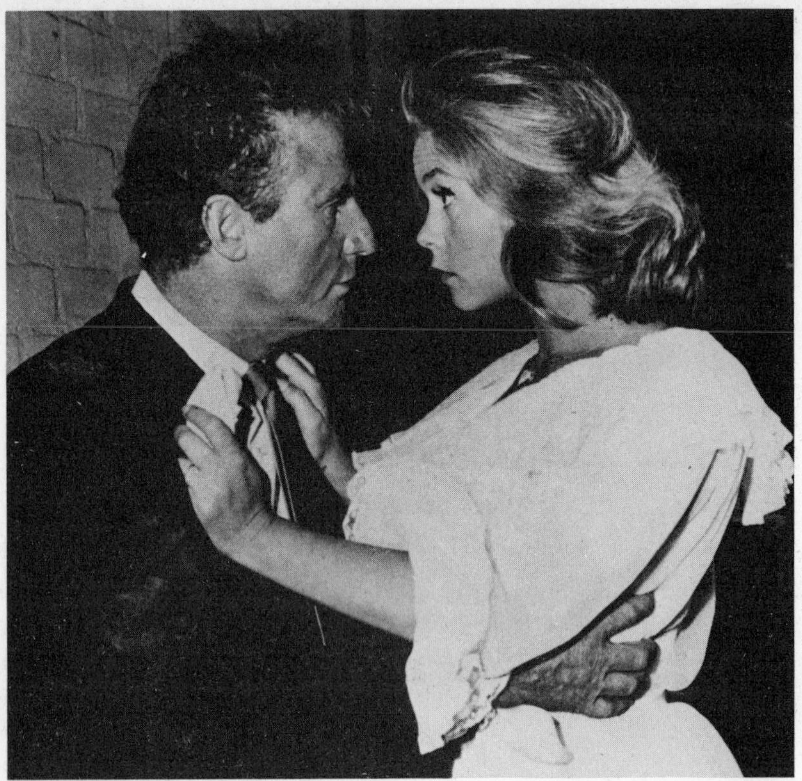

Jack Warden as Rex Barker with Elizabeth in "It Shouldn't Happen to a Dog." (Columbia Pictures Television.)

Barker becomes too aggressive, Sam changes him into a dog and becomes angry with Darrin, who thinks only of losing the account. When she eventually changes Barker back, he continues to make passes at her. And this time, Darrin knocks him out.
Note: First Larry and Louise/first client show. Remade as Nos. 196 and 245.

No. 4

"Mother Meets What's-His-Name" (10-8-64)

Written by Danny Arnold. Directed by William Asher. Guest cast: Hollis Irving, Alice Backes.

Gladys tries to convince her neighbors of the weird goings-on at the Stephenses' and Endora adds to the mayhem by roping up three neighborhood boys. As Gladys struggles to convince the boys' mothers of how impossible it was for them to tie themselves up, Darrin becomes furious with Endora, who threatens to turn him into an artichoke.
This is the first Darrin/Endora episode.

Endora modeled four different costumes when she prepared to meet Darrin for the first time. (Columbia Pictures Television/Dan Weaver Collection.)

No. 5

"Help, Help, Don't Save Me" (10-15-64)

Written by Danny Arnold. Directed by William Asher. Guest cast: Charlie Ruggles.

Darrin grapples to produce a campaign for Caldwell Soup. When Sam offers her suggestions, he suspects witchery, and presents his own ideas to Philip Caldwell, who rejects them. Endora is then in her glory when Sam and Darrin fight, as he accuses her of influencing Caldwell's decision. After they make up, Darrin realizes Caldwell truly disliked his slogans, and Sam makes sure Darrin still gets the account.
Note: Remade as No. 252.

No. 6

"Little Pitchers Have Big Fears" (10-22-64)

Written by Barbara Avedon. Directed by William Asher. Guest cast: June Lockhart, Jimmy Mathers, Joe Brooks.

Sam caters to ten-year-old Marshall Burns, whose overprotective widowed mother leaves her son with an inferiority complex. Sam tries to restore his confidence by convincing him to play Little League baseball. At first, she makes Marshall a star player, later allowing him to succeed on his own account—much to his mother's delight.
Note: Partially remade as No. 90.

No. 7

"The Witches Are Out" (10-29-64)

Written by Bernard Slade. Directed by William Asher. Guest cast: Shelley Berman, Reta Shaw, Madge Blake.

When Darrin is assigned to create a trademark for a new Halloween candy, Sam, Aunt Clara, and witch friends Bertha and Mary grasp the chance to change the popular conception of witches into a more flattering image. Yet the candy's promoter, Mr. Brinkman, wants things to remain status quo and Sam and her friends haunt him until he changes his mind.
Note: First Halloween show.

No. 8

"The Girl Reporter" (11-5-64)

Written by Paul David and John L. Greene. Directed by William Asher. Guest cast: Cheryl Holdridge.

Teenager Liza Randell interviews Darrin about his advertis-

Elizabeth with Alice Pearce as Gladys Kravitz in "Little Pitchers Have Big Fears." (Columbia Pictures Television.)

Elizabeth Montgomery, Dick York, June Lockhart, Jimmy Mathers, and Joe Brooks from "Little Pitchers Have Big Fears." (Columbia Pictures Television.)

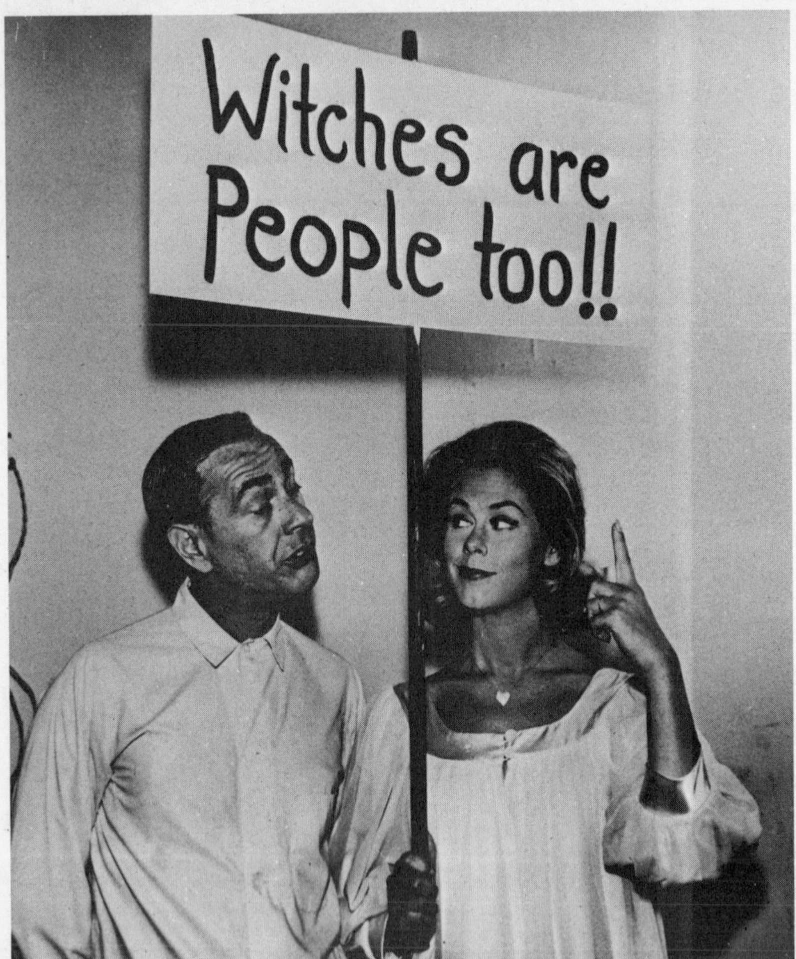

Samantha celebrates her heritage in "The Witches Are Out." (Columbia Pictures Television.)

ing career for a school paper. After he takes her to McMann and Tate, her jealous boyfriend—a football star—sets out to beat up Darrin. Samantha explains that Darrin and Liza's relationship is innocent, but things take a turn for the worse when Liza's beau develops a mad crush on Sam.
Note: Partially remade as No. 194.

No. 9

"Witch or Wife" (11-12-64)

Written by Bernard Slade. Directed by William Asher. Guest cast: Raquel Welch.

Darrin's work load adds up after Larry and Louise fly to Paris to see a fashion show for a client. Simultaneously—and unknowingly—Samantha accepts an invitation from her mother to fly to Paris for lunch. When they run into the Tates, Larry phones Darrin. When Sam pops home, Darrin tells her he thinks their marriage has been a mistake, even though she tries to persuade him he's wrong. She then returns to Paris, only to be followed by Darrin, who apologizes.
Note: Larry and Louise meet Endora.

No. 10

"Just One Happy Family" (11-19-64)

Written by Fred Freeman and Lawrence J. Cohen. Directed by William Asher. Guest cast: Thomas Anthony, Charlie Dugdale.

Endora warns Sam that Maurice is coming for a visit, and that he'll be upset once he finds out about Darrin. When Maurice arrives, the conversation proceeds nicely until Sam reveals the truth about her marriage. Maurice then dematerializes Darrin until Samantha begs for his return.
Note: First Maurice episode.

No. 11

"It Takes One to Know One" (11-26-64)

Written by Jack Sher. Directed by William Asher. Guest cast: Lisa Seagram, Robert Cleaves.

Darrin needs a "Miss Jasmine" for a perfume account, and Endora sets out to create doubt in Samantha's mind regarding Darrin's fidelity. When Larry and Darrin agree that a beautiful model, Janine Fleur, is their "Miss Jasmine," Sam learns that Janine is a witch hired by Endora to separate her and Darrin.
Note: Remade as No. 240.

No. 12

". . . And Something Makes Three" (12-3-64)

Written by Danny Arnold. Directed by William Asher. Guest cast: Maureen McCormick

Larry coincidentally visits his dentist in the same building where Sam has gone to the obstetrician with Louise. Thinking Sam is expecting, Larry tells Darrin, who imagines his children as little witches and warlocks. That night, the Tates have dinner with the Stephenses and the misunderstanding is cleared up when Louise announces she's pregnant.

No. 13

"Love Is Blind" (12-10-64)

Written by Roland Wolpert. Directed by William Asher. Guest cast: Adam West, Kit Smythe.

Sam's average-looking friend, Gertrude, expresses envy for Sam's happy marriage. Against Darrin's wishes, Sam sets Gertrude up with Darrin's artist buddy, Kermit. Darrin suspects Gertrude is a witch and arranges a match between Kermit and Susan, a former girl friend of his. Since Gertrude isn't a witch, all ends well when Kermit proposes to her.

Note: Samantha goes to church.

Adam West and Kit Smythe guest in "Love Is Blind." (Columbia Pictures Television/Milton T. Moore, Jr.)

No. 14

"Samantha Meets the Folks" (12-17-64)

Written by Bernard Slade. Directed by William Asher.

When Darrin's parents visit Samantha for the first time, Phyllis hopes to find her daughter-in-law lacking in domestic skills. The tension builds when Aunt Clara makes a surprise visit, causing Darrin to worry about a confrontation with his parents. Clara, intent on helping her niece look good in front of the elder Stephenses, conjures up an exotic feast for dinner. This upsets Phyllis, and Darrin becomes angry with Clara, who leaves in a fury. Darrin attempts to mend Samantha's and Clara's feelings by asking Clara to return.

Note: Recut as No. 56.

No. 15

"A Vision of Sugar Plums" (12-24-64)

Written by Herman Groves. Directed by Alan Rafkin. Guest cast: Sara Seegar, Bill Daily, Billy Mumy.

While a seven-year-old orphan named Tommy spends Christmas with the Kravitzes, six-year-old Michael, also an orphan, stays with the Stephenses. Tommy believes in Santa Claus; Michael doesn't. To help change Michael's mind, Samantha whisks both him and Darrin to the North Pole to meet St. Nicholas himself.

Note: First Christmas show. No. 51 is a recut version.

No. 16

"It's Magic" (1-7-65)

Written by Tom Waldman and Frank Waldman. Directed by Sidney Miller. Guest cast: Cliff Norton, Walter Burke.

When Samantha is named entertainment chairperson of the Hospital Fund Auxiliary, she is limited to a $50 budget. Consequently, she hires Zeno, a broken-down magician who drinks. However, she uses witchcraft to make Zeno a hit of the show, which leads him to a TV appearance, and this prompts a client of Darrin's to hire him.

No. 17

"A Is for Aardvark" (1-14-65)

Written by Earl Barrett. Directed by Ida Lupino.

Darrin sprains his ankle and is confined to bed. After Samantha gets tired of running up and down the stairs at his beck and call, she grants him use of her supernatural powers. Darrin misuses his newfound magic and realizes the special qualities of being mortal.

No. 18

"The Cat's Meow" (1-21-65)

Written by Richard and Mary Sale. Directed by David McDearmon. Guest cast: Martha Hyer, Harry Holcombe, George Ives.

Client Margaret Marshall insists Darrin fly to Chicago to help her campaign for her cosmetic company. To do so, Darrin sidesteps a six-month anniversary celebration with Samantha to meet Margaret on her yacht. On board, Darrin sees a cat and feels it may be Sam, prompted by Endora to check up on him. After Margaret tries to seduce him, Darrin takes the cat home, only to be greeted by Sam.

No. 19

"A Nice Little Dinner Party" (1-28-65)

Written by Bernard Slade. Directed by Sherman Marks. Guest cast: Lindsay Workman, David Garner.

Sam arranges a dinner party for Darrin's parents to meet Endora, who promises not to make any trouble. When Mr. and Mrs. Stephens arrive, Endora is most courteous to Phyllis, but flirts with Frank, which causes a marital rift between the two. Upset, Phyllis boards a train to Arizona, while Frank takes a plane beginning a world tour. Using their combined powers, Sam and Endora reunite Phyllis and Frank at Angel Falls, where he proposed to her.

Note: Salem is revealed as Endora's birthplace.

No. 20

"Your Witch Is Showing" (2-4-65)

Written by Joanna Lee. Directed by Joseph Pevney. Guest cast: Jonathan Daly, Peggy Lipton.

Endora's upset when Darrin forbids Samantha to fly to Egypt for a cousin's wedding. Instantly, Darrin starts having trouble at work, and Larry enlists an assistant, who Darrin thinks is a warlock hired by Endora to steal his job. Once Samantha intervenes, Darrin realizes the new man is mortal and deals with him on a human level by punching him out.

No. 21

"Ling Ling" (2-11-65)

Written by Jerry Davis. Directed by David McDearmon. Guest cast: Jeremy Slate, Greta Chi.

Darrin hopes to find a model for the Jewel of the East campaign so that it may boost the confidence of Wally Ames, a temporary photographer with McMann and Tate. On cue, Sam changes a cat into a beautiful oriental woman named Ling Ling, who everyone feels is the perfect Jewel model. The Stephenses give a dinner party to celebrate, and Ling Ling and Wally begin to date. When this transpires, Sam is forced to tell Darrin the truth.

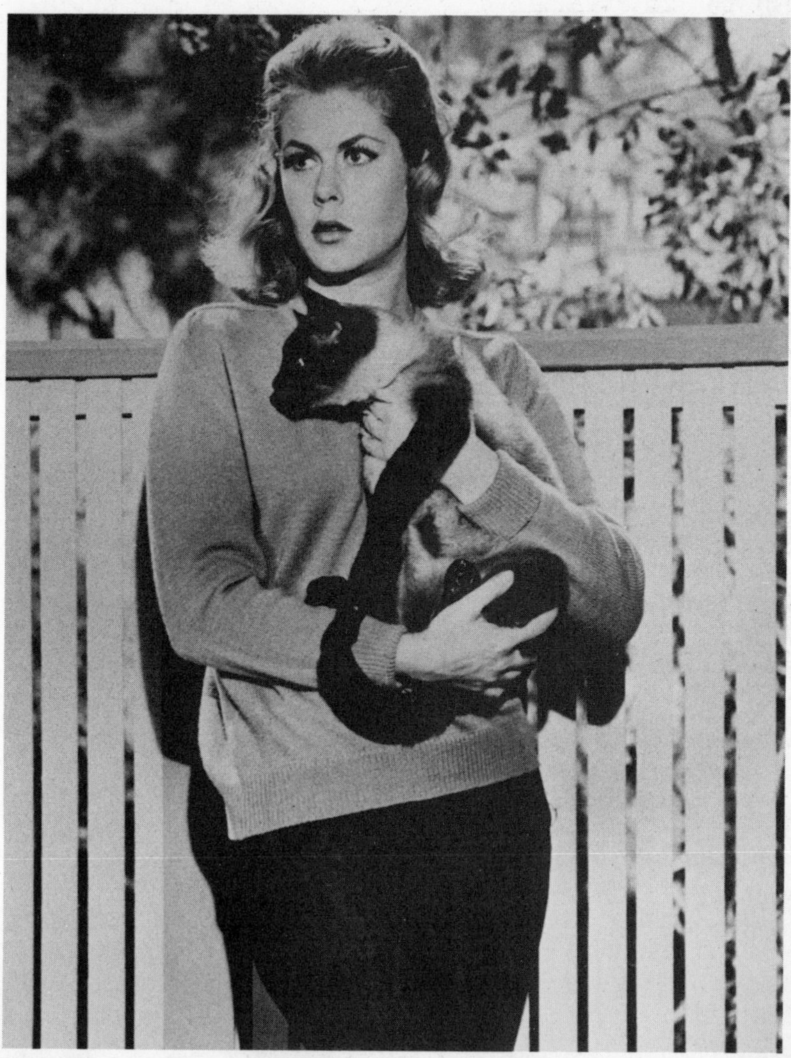

Samantha and a very sly cat in "Ling Ling." (Columbia Pictures Television/Milton T. Moore, Jr.)

No. 22

"Eye of the Beholder" (2-25-65)

Written by Herman Groves. Directed by William Asher. Guest cast: Gene Blakely, Peter Brocco.

When Endora superimposes Samantha's face on an ancient print entitled MAID OF SALEM, Darrin is compelled to buy the painting. However, he then envisions himself as a senile old man paired with an ever-youthful Samantha. After Endora tells Samantha that she may age along with Darrin, if she prefers, Darrin realizes his mother-in-law is to blame for his doubts.

Note: Samantha's birthday, June 6, is mentioned in this segment.

No. 23

"Red Light, Green Light" (3-4-65)

Written by Roland Wolpert. Directed by David McDearmon. Guest cast: Dan Tobin, Vic Tayback.

The Stephenses become politically involved with constructing a traffic light on their street. Darrin creates an ad for a rally, but the mayor says the light is unnecessary. After Samantha magically ties the mayor up in traffic, he changes his mind.

No. 24

"Which Witch Is Which" (3-11-65)

Written by Earl Barrett. Directed by William D. Russell. Guest cast: Ron Randell, Monty Margetta.

When Samantha doesn't have time for a dress fitting, Endora helps out by turning herself into Sam's double. While being fitted, Endora-Samantha captures the heart of author Bob Fraser, who also happens to be Darrin's friend. And when Gladys sees the twosome, she thinks Sam is having an affair. Meanwhile, Darrin tells Samantha to expect a visit from Bob, only to have Endora save the evening by claiming to be Samantha's exact double.

No. 25

"Pleasure O'Riley" (3-18-65)

Written by Ken Englund. Directed by William D. Russell. Guest cast: Ken Scott, Kipp Hamilton, Norman Burton.

New neighbor and beautiful model Priscilla "Pleasure" O'Riley is hiding from her jealous boyfriend, an offensive fullback. When Darrin helps Pleasure hide, the boyfriend visits Sam, who inadvertently gives the impression that Darrin is Pleasure's new beau. To save Darrin's hide, Sam turns him into his grandmother,

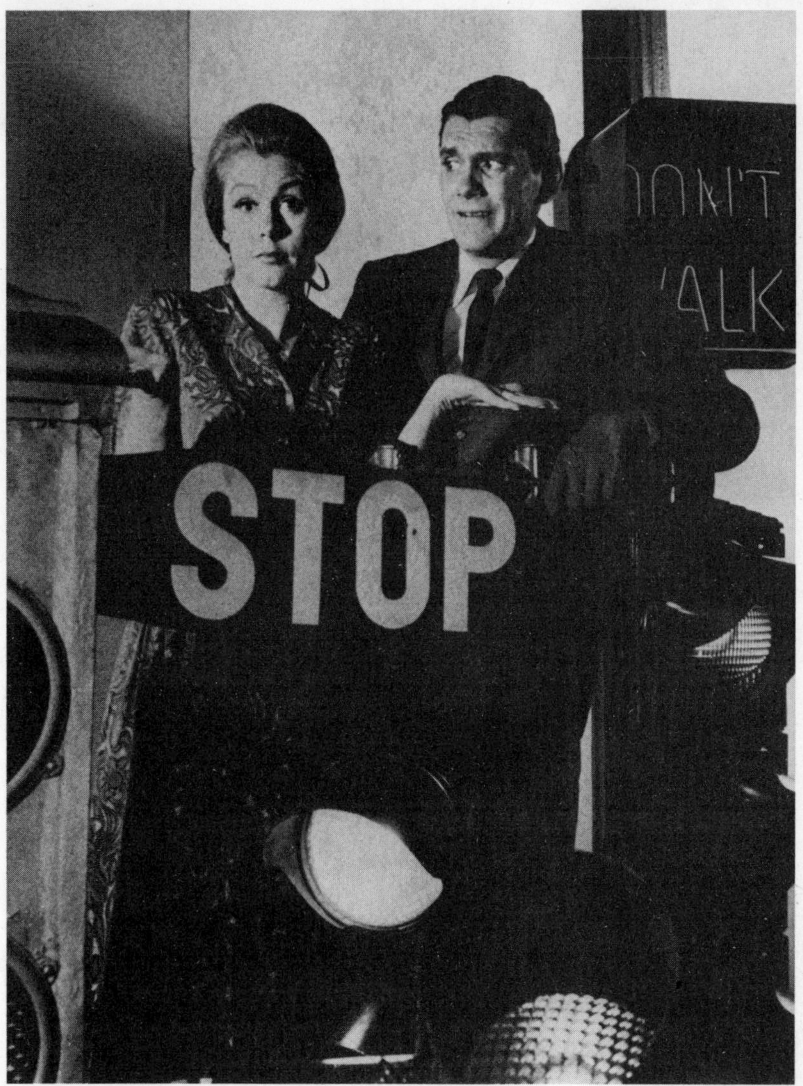

Samantha and Darrin in "Red Light, Green Light." (Columbia Pictures Television.)

leaving Pleasure's friend to mistake Abner Kravitz as the "other man."

Note: Pleasure's sister appears in No. 30.

No. 26

"Driving Is the Only Way to Fly" (3-25-65)

Written by Richard Baer. Directed by William Asher. Guest cast: Paul Lynde (in non-Uncle Arthur role), Paul Bryar.

When Samantha enrolls in driving school, her driving instructor is the very nervous Harold Harold. During their test drive, Samantha uses witchcraft to avoid accidents, which makes Harold doubly uneasy. Endora makes matters worse by speaking from the backseat, while invisible. When Harold is fired, Sam threatens to switch schools unless he's rehired.

No. 27

"There's No Witch Like an Old Witch" (4-1-65)

Written by Ted Sherdeman and Jane Klove. Directed by William Asher. Guest cast: Reta Shaw, Karen Norris.

While suffering from a power failure, Aunt Clara stays at the Stephenses. To cheer her up, Sam and Darrin take her out with the Caldwells, whose baby-sitter doesn't show up. Clara tries to help by offering her services as a baby-sitter.
Note: Remade as No. 243.

No. 28

"Open the Door Witchcraft" (4-8-65)

Written by Ruth Brooks Flippen. Directed by William Asher. Guest cast: Hal Boker, Baynes Barron.

Fascinated by electric garage-door openers, Samantha creates her own. Unhappy about Samantha's witchcraft, Darrin sacrifices new fishing gear to buy a real remote control. After radio signals from various aircraft conflict with the doors, Sam and Darrin argue over her use of witchcraft. Sam stands by her vow not to use her powers, and she and Darrin are locked in the garage when a plane flies overhead.

No. 29

"Abner Kadabra" (4-15-65)

Written by Lawrence J. Cohen and Fred Freeman. Directed by William Asher.

After Gladys sees "moving pictures" at the Stephenses, Samantha convinces her that she has ESP powers. Although Samantha cautions her, Gladys begins using her alleged powers to attempt supernatural feats. When she tries to stop the rain from falling and tells Abner to dry up, Sam changes him into a pile of dust, causing Gladys to retire her ESP powers forever.

No. 30

"George the Warlock" (4-22-65)

Written by Ken Englund. Directed by William Asher. Guest cast: Christopher George, Beverly Adams.

Darrin offers to help D. D. "Danger" O'Riley, Pleasure's beautiful younger sister while she's on vacation for a couple of weeks. Endora seizes another opportunity to break up her daughter's marriage by persuading a Casanova-type warlock named George to romance Samantha.

Note: A raven whistles the series' theme.

No. 31

"That Was My Wife" (4-29-65)

Written by Bernard Slade. Directed by William Asher. Guest cast: Warrene Ott.

The Stephenses decide to take a short vacation, and reserve a room at the President Hotel. Unaware that Larry's in the lobby, Samantha, on a whim, arrives wearing a black wig. When she goes to hug Darrin, Larry thinks Darrin is having an affair. When Sam pops home to get a book, Larry comes to comfort her.

No. 32

"Illegal Separation" (5-6-65)

Written by Richard Baer. Directed by William Asher. Guest cast: Dick Balduzzi.

When the Kravitzes have a fight, Abner stays with the Stephenses and becomes much too comfortable as a guest. A frustrated Darrin tells Sam to deal with the problem and talk Gladys out of a divorce. To bring her mortal neighbors back together, Sam uses a dream spell, projecting Abner and Gladys back to the day Abner proposed.

Note: Remade as No. 140.

No. 33

"A Change of Face" (5-13-65)

Written by Bernard Slade. Directed by William Asher. Guest cast: Gene Blakely, Paul Barselow, Marilyn Hanold, Dick Wilson.

While Darrin's asleep, Endora rearranges his face. At first Sam objects, later adding some cosmetic changes of her own. When Darrin awakes, he demands an explanation, which Sam can't offer. He then begins to worry about his looks, and his

confidence suffers. To boost his ego, Sam transforms herself into a beautiful Frenchwoman who tells Darrin he is handsome.
Note: First Dick Wilson show.

No. 34

"Remember the Main" (5-20-65)

Written by Mort. R. Lewis. Directed by William D. Russell. Guest cast: Edward Mallory, Byron Morrow.

The Stephenses get involved with Ed Wright's campaign for city council. At Darrin's suggestion, Ed debates his challenger, John C. Cavenaugh, on TV, focusing on the illegal fund allocations for a new drainage system. When a water main bursts, Wright looks like the easy winner until Darrin suspects Samantha caused the flood. Endora, however, admits to it in the end.

No. 35

"Eat at Mario's" (5-27-65)

Written by Richard Baer. Directed by William Asher. Guest cast: Vito Scotti, Alan Hewitt.

Mario's, a favorite dining spot of Samantha's and Endora's, is going out of business because Mario refuses to sell pizza. Unaware that Darrin's new client, Mr. Baldwin, owns a successful pizza franchise, Samantha conjures up a full-page newspaper ad for Mario. Endora plugs him on a TV show, which happens to be sponsored by Mr. Baldwin. Once Sam realizes Darrin's job is at stake, she enlists her mother's help to save the Baldwin account.

No. 36

"Cousin Edgar" (6-3-65)

Written by Paul Wayne. Directed by E. W. Swackhamer. Guest cast: Arte Johnson.

While McMann and Tate tries to hold onto the Shelley Shoes account, Endora summons Sam's cousin Edgar, an elf, in another attempt to separate Sam and Darrin. After Edgar makes trouble for Darrin at the office, Sam convinces Edgar that she's happily married. This causes Edgar to annoy Darrin's competitors. Consequently, Darrin succeeds with the Shelley campaign and features an elf most similar to Edgar in the ad.

THE SECOND SEASON: 1965 to 1966

No. 37

"Alias Darrin Stephens" (9-16-65)

Written by Richard Baer. Directed by William Asher.

Aunt Clara celebrates the Stephenses' first anniversary by bringing gifts. She accidentally changes Darrin into a chimpanzee. Unable to change him back, she returns home for an antidote. When Sam steps out of the house, Endora stays with Darrin (the chimp). Darrin leaps out the window and runs into Gladys, who takes him to the zoo. After Sam retrieves him, Clara returns and changes him back, and Darrin learns that Sam is pregnant.

No. 38

"A Very Special Delivery" (9-23-65)

Written by Howard Leeds. Directed by William Asher. Guest cast: Gene Blakely, Dort Clark.

As Darrin contemplates his imminent fatherhood, Larry convinces him that all women would make a career of motherhood if they could. He gives Darrin a book on the topic that asserts that if an expectant mother is active, she and her child will be happier and healthier. Darrin starts ordering Sam around, which angers Endora, who makes Darrin believe *he's* pregnant.

No. 39

"We're in for a Bad Spell" (9-30-65)

Written by Bernard Slade. Directed by Howard Morris. Guest cast: William Redfield, Richard X. Slattery.

Aunt Clara informs the Stephenses that Darrin's friend Adam Newlarkin has inherited an ancient witch-curse that was placed on his ancestor, a judge in Salem, centuries earlier. To counteract the curse, Adam has to kiss a dog, be dunked in water, etc., or else he'll be accused of a crime. After Sam, Darrin, and Clara carry out the spell-steps to Adam's recovery, a colleague of Adam's at the bank where he works is arrested for robbery—a crime of which Adam would have been accused.

Note: Remade as No. 179.

No. 40

"My Grandson, the Warlock" (10-7-65)

Written by Ted Sherdeman and Jane Klove. Directed by E. W. Swackhamer. Guest cast: Kendrick Huxham, Minnie Coffin.

When Darrin and Samantha baby-sit for little Jonathan Tate,

Gladys assumes the Stephenses are now proud parents. When Maurice arrives, Gladys congratulates him on the birth of his grandson. This leads to much confusion, especially for Maurice, who is upset that his "grandson" is not being guided in the ways of a warlock babe.

No. 41

"The Joker Is a Card" (10-14-65)

Written by Ron Friedman. Directed by E. W. Swackhamer. Guest cast: Douglas Evans.

After a failed meeting between Endora and Darrin to settle their differences, Uncle Arthur tricks his nephew-in-law into believing he can use magic against Endora. When Darrin realizes he's been had, he joins Samantha and Endora to teach Arthur a lesson about practical jokes—one that leads him to believe that Darrin has transformed Endora into a parrot . . . permanently. Note: First Uncle Arthur episode.

No. 42

"Take Two Aspirin and Half a Pint of Porpoise Milk" (10-21-65)

Written by Bernard Slade. Directed by William Asher. Guest cast: Philip Coolidge, Maudie Prickett.

Paul Lynde in his first Uncle Arthur appearance, "The Joker Is a Card." (Columbia Pictures Television.)

Samantha falls ill and loses her powers after contact with a black Peruvian rose. A doctor decides her health is perfect, and when Gladys sees the physician's car, she brings over some chicken broth. Later Aunt Clara arrives with a witch-antidote from a supernatural apothecary and cures Samantha.
Note: First witch-illness show. Remade as No. 253.

No. 43

"Trick or Treat" (10-28-65)

Written by Lawrence J. Cohen and Fred Freeman. Directed by E. W. Swackhamer. Guest cast: Jack Collins, Maureen McCormick.

Ignoring Endora's request that her daughter accompany her to a Halloween party, Darrin demands that Samantha remain at home to entertain Larry, Louise, and a client and his wife. To seek revenge, Endora impersonates a child in a gypsy costume and turns Darrin into a werewolf. After Darrin persuades Sam to lock him in the closet because he fears what might happen, Sam confronts Endora and accuses her of being the stereotypical witch she claims to disdain. Endora then apologizes to both Darrin and Samantha, and changes Darrin back.
Note: Second Halloween show.

No. 44

"The Very Informal Dress" (11-4-65)

Written by Paul David and John L. Greene. Directed by William Asher. Guest cast: Max Showalter.

When Larry invites the Stephenses to a dinner for a prospective client, they find they have nothing to wear. Aunt Clara conjures up a new dress for Samantha and a new suit for Darrin. To show his appreciation, Darrin invites Clara along for the evening. He regrets his decision when he goes to park the car and Clara removes a fire hydrant. Later in the evening it reappears and Darrin gets a parking ticket. Then Sam's and Darrin's new clothes begin to vanish, causing more embarrassment.

No. 45

"And Then I Wrote" (11-11-65)

Written by Paul Wayne. Directed by E. W. Swackhamer. Guest cast: Tom Nardini, Eileen O'Neil.

A psychiatrist at a rest home tells Samantha his patients would like to celebrate the centenary of the end of the Civil War. When Samantha tells the doctor that Darrin will publicize the function, Darrin appoints Samantha to write the script. He then tells her that she has created wooden characters, and on Endora's advice, Sam literally brings them to life.

No. 46

"Junior Executive" (11-18-65)

Written by Bernard Slade. Directed by Howard Morris. Guest cast: Oliver McGowan, Billy Mumy.

While Darrin is contemplating a model ship for the Harding Toys account, Samantha wonders whether their child will look like Darrin. To help answer her question, Endora turns her son-in-law into an eight-year-old boy. Mr. Harding sees the young Darrin at McMann and Tate and urges Larry to hire the child to create a slogan for his company. Darrin completes the slogan for the Harding account while acting out his childhood in the park.

Note: Remade as No. 224.

No. 47

"Aunt Clara's Old Flame" (11-25-65)

Written by Bernard Slade. Directed by E. W. Swackhamer. Guest cast: Charlie Ruggles.

Hiding from her warlock boyfriend, Hedley Partridge, Aunt Clara pays a visit, fearing Hedley will discover her magic is out of synch. Endora feels Hedley is the perfect mate for Clara, and invites him to meet her at the Stephenses. On the sly, Samantha assists Clara with her witchcraft and so she is able to match Hedley trick for trick. Clara's fears are allayed when Hedley admits his witchcraft isn't what it used to be either.

Note: Remade as No. 226.

No. 48

"A Strange Little Visitor" (12-2-65)

Written by Paul David and John L. Greene. Directed by E. W. Swackhamer. Guest cast: James Doohan, Craig Hunely.

While Samantha's witch friends attend a convention, she baby-sits for their ten-year-old warlock son, Merle, who promises not to do any witchcraft in front of Darrin. His commitment is tested when a burglar breaks in and overpowers Darrin. Yet Merle sticks to his promise, only to give in finally and help capture the crook.

No. 49

"My Boss the Teddy Bear" (12-9-65)

Written by Bernard Slade. Directed by William Asher. Guest cast: Jack Collins, Henry Hunter.

After Larry allows Darrin time to take Sam to a witch wedding, Endora brings Larry a much-sought-after teddy bear for his son. Darrin, who is working on the Harper's Honey account, is sure Endora has changed Larry into the bear. There is much confusion because Louise, too, has bought a teddy bear toy and must return one to the store. Thinking Larry might be the one she brought back, Darrin buys all the bears at the store, brings them home, and tries to find which one is Larry.

No. 50

"Speak the Truth" (12-16-65)

Written by Paul David and John L. Greene. Directed by William Asher. Guest cast: Elizabeth Fraser, Diana Chesney, Charles Lane.

Endora delivers to Darrin's office a statue that makes people tell the truth. Some bad experiences result from too much truthfulness, but Darrin finally establishes a good rapport with a new client. Larry gives him a raise—a consequence of the truth spell. This surprises Endora, who thought that only chaos would come from her truth-telling device.
Note: Remade as No. 254. First show with Charles Lane.

No. 51

"A Vision of Sugar Plums" (12-23-65)

Note: This is a recut version of No. 15, with a new opening.

No. 52

"The Magic Cabin" (12-30-65)

Written by Paul Wayne. Directed by William Asher. Guest cast: Peter Duryea, Beryl Hammond.

Larry persuades a fatigued Darrin and Samantha to stay at his log cabin, which he hasn't seen in years—and which he's also put up for sale. On arrival, Darrin forbids Sam to use magic to clean up the cabin, which is a shambles. He quickly changes his mind when a storm breaks out. When Larry apprehensively sends prospective buyers to inspect the cabin, he's shocked when—because of Sam's magic cleaning—they want to buy it.

No. 53

"Maid to Order" (1-6-66)

Written by Richard Baer. Directed by William Asher. Guest cast: Alice Ghostley (not as Esmeralda), Elvia Allman.

Bumbling maid Naomi, looking for work so she can send her son through medical school, is hired by the Stephenses temporarily until the baby is born. When Larry and Louise come to dinner, Sam tries to make a good impression by helping Naomi with her duties. Then Louise hires Naomi, but without Sam's help Naomi is incompetent. But when she displays her ability at calculation (by adding the number of dishes she breaks), Sam persuades Darrin to give her a job in the accounting department at McMann and Tate.

No. 54

"And Then There Were Three" (1-13-66)

Written by Bernard Slade. Directed by William Asher. Guest star: Eve Arden.

Samantha gives birth to a daughter and Endora names her Tabitha. Darrin doubts the baby will grow up to look like Samantha, so Endora proposes to turn the baby into an adult, so he can see. Meanwhile, Serena, Sam's cousin, visits her in the hospital. On seeing Serena for the first time, Darrin thinks Endora's magical threat has been put into action.

Note: Tabitha is born; first Serena show.

No. 55

"My Baby the Tycoon" (1-20-66)

Written by Richard Baer. Directed by William Asher. Guest cast: Jack Fletcher.

After Gladys and Abner give Tabitha a share of their stock, it appreciates exponentially. Tabitha's random pointing at the newspaper stocks causes Darrin to think her witchcraft has developed early and is in full gear. Later, the Kravtizes lose their life savings and the stock returns to normal. Darrin realizes there was a logical explanation for the stock's behavior.

No. 56

"Samantha Meets the Folks" (1-27-66)

Note: This is a recut version of No. 14.

No. 57

"Fastest Gun on Madison Avenue" (2-3-66)

Written by Lee Erwin. Directed by William Asher. Guest cast: Herbie Faye, Herb Vigran, Roger Torray.

While dining, Darrin tries to protect Samantha from heavyweight champion Joe Kovak, who's making passes at her. When Darrin tries to defend himself, Sam twitches her nose and Kovak is knocked out. Consequently, the newspapers proclaim Darrin the future champ. Later, after Darrin ends up knocking out Joe a second time (again with the assistance of Sam), he runs into Tommy Carter, another champ, who accidentally knocks himself out, this time indirectly due to Sam.

No. 58

"The Dancing Bear" (2-10-66)

Written by James Henerson. Directed by William Asher. Guest cast: Arthur Julian.

Robert F. Simon and Mabel Albertson as Darrin's parents in "The Dancing Bear." (Elizabeth Montgomery/William Asher collection.)

Darrin's parents come to visit Tabitha, and as usual, Endora and Phyllis don't get along. Adding fuel to the fire, Phyllis brings a toy bear identical to Endora's, except that Endora's bear dances—magically. This leads to Frank's misconception that there is a fortune to be made from dancing bears.

No. 59

"Double Tate" (2-17-66)

Written by Paul Wayne. Directed by William Asher. Guest cast: Irwin Charone, Kathee Francis.

Unaware that Endora has given him three wishes for his birthday, Darrin suddenly receives instant elevator service at McMann and Tate and sees a beautiful girl in a bikini. Later, when a prominent client demands to see Larry, who's in Chicago, Darrin unknowingly wishes he was the boss for "just one day." This leads to a double crossing between him, Samantha, and the Tates.

No. 60

"Samantha, the Dressmaker" (2-24-66)

Written by Lee Erwin. Directed by William Asher. Guest cast: Dick Gautier, Barbara Morrison, Harry Holcombe.

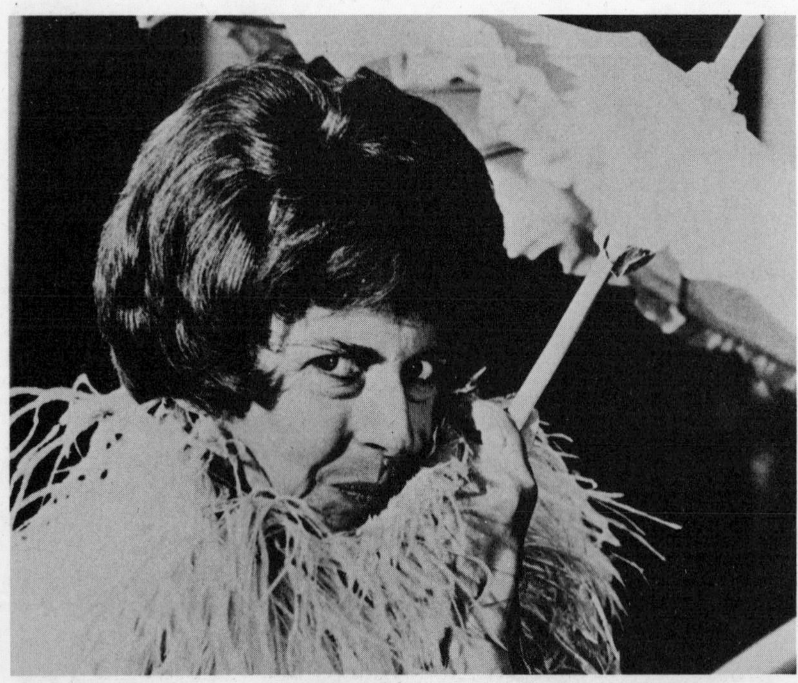

Alice Pearce as Gladys Kravitz in "Samantha, the Dressmaker." (Columbia Pictures Television/ Fredric Tucker.)

When Sam fails to make her own dress for client J. T. Glendon's party, Endora flies her to the Paris showroom of Aubert, a designer who has not succeeded in the American market. Back home, Samantha magically reproduces an Aubert original, and suddenly finds herself a dressmaker for Mrs. Glendon, Mrs. Kravitz, and others. Yet Sam is unaware that Aubert is a client of McMann and Tate's, and he threatens to sue the company when he sees the women wearing his designs.

No. 61

"The Horse's Mouth" (3-3-66)

Written by Paul David and John L. Greene. Directed by William Asher. Guest cast: Sidney Clute, Patty Regan.

Samantha transforms an escaped racehorse into a woman named Dolly, who claims she's been coerced into throwing races so her sister horse can be the victor. In the meantime, Dolly tips Darrin's inventor friend, Gus, on how to win races and make money on marketing a new idea. After Sam turns Dolly back into a horse, the Stephenses persuade Gus to bet on her. Dolly's a winner, and Gus makes money.

No. 62

"Baby's First Paragraph" (3-10-66)

Written by James Henerson. Directed by William Asher. Guest cast: Clete Roberts.

While Samantha and Darrin meet an important client, Endora baby-sits with Tabitha and promises not to use any magic. Yet when Mrs. Kravitz visits with her nephew Edgar and starts boasting about his intelligence, Endora supernaturally induces Tabitha to talk. As a result, Tabitha becomes a world sensation. Things get cleared up when Endora admits to being a ventriloquist.

No. 63

"The Leprechaun" (3-17-66)

Written by Paul David and John L. Green. Directed by William Asher. Guest cast: Parley Baer, Henry Jones.

Sam tells Darrin that visiting leprechaun Brian O'Brian is not one of her relatives, but one of his. Brian wishes to reclaim his pot of gold, which is hidden in a fireplace in the States. The gold was brought here by James Dennis Robinson, whose company would be a very desirable account for McMann and Tate. After a failed

Elizabeth and Henry Jones in "The Leprechaun." (Columbia Pictures Television/Milton T. Moore, Jr.)

solo attempt, Brian is assisted by Sam in recovering his golden treasure, and his powers are restored.
Note: First Parley Baer show. A St. Patrick's Day show.

No. 64

"Double Split" (3-24-66)

Written by Howard Leeds. Directed by Jerry Davis. Guest cast: Julie Gregg, Martin Ashe.

At Darrin's request, Sam tries to be nice to a snobbish daughter of a major client. Frustrated by the girl's demeanor, Samantha twitches a canapé in her face, which angers Darrin. When Larry criticizes Sam's behavior, Darrin quits McMann and Tate. Samantha and Louise then have to restore their husbands' friendship.

No. 65

"Disappearing Samantha" (4-7-66)

Written by Paul David and John L. Greene. Directed by William Asher. Guest cast: Bernard Fox (not as Dr. Bombay), Foster Brooks, Nina Wayne.

Darrin publicizes Osgood Rightmire, who makes a name for himself by exposing fraudulent witches. When the Stephenses and the Tates attend a lecture given by Rightmire, he melodramatically presents himself as a witches' scapegoat, which angers Sam. Rightmire then recites an incantation causing Samantha to disappear and reappear against her will. Later, when Osgood is at the Stephenses, Endora and Sam discover his powers come from an ancient ring he wears, which Sam destroys and replaces with a replica.

No. 66

"Follow That Witch" (Part 1, 4-14-66)

Written by Bernard Slade. Directed by William Asher. Guest cast: Steve Franken, Robert Strauss, Virginia Martin.

Elizabeth with Robert Strauss and Virginia Martin in "Follow That Witch." (Columbia Pictures Television.)

While Darrin is closing a deal with Robbins Baby Food, Mr. Robbins and his assistant, George Barkley, agree that their company must maintain a wholesome image. This leads to an investigation of Darrin's home life, and the discovery of Samantha's secret.
Note: First two-part episode.

No. 67

"Follow That Witch" (Part 2, 4-21-66)

(Same credits as in Part 1 with additional guests Renie Riano, Jack Collins.)

Private detective Charlie Leach threatens to reveal Sam's witchery unless she makes him rich. Realizing that Darrin's account is at stake, she conjures up a new car and a newly remodeled apartment for Leach. Later, Sam forces Barkley to admit he wants to take over his boss's job; Robbins fires Barkley and hires Darrin. Darrin then gives Sam permission to get back at Leach.

No. 68

"A Bum Raps" (4-28-66)

Written by Herman Groves. Directed by Jerry Davis. Guest cast: Herbie Faye, Cliff Hall, Ann Prentice.

With Darrin's Uncle Albert about to arrive, two ex-vaudeville performers who are also con artists prowl the neighborhood. One impersonates Uncle Albert and robs the Stephens home. When Sam realizes what's happened, she magically makes the crooks return with the stolen goods.

No. 69

"Divided He Falls" (5-5-66)

Written by Paul Wayne. Directed by R. Robert Rosenbaum. Guest cast: Joy Harmon, Susan Barrett, Frank Maxwell.

Sam and Darrin's much-delayed vacation is postponed when Larry begs Darrin to work on the Stern Chemical Company account. Thinking she has the perfect remedy for the situation, Endora splits Darrin in two: (1) a hard worker and (2) a fun-loving guy. After Endora persuades Samantha to vacation with the second Darrin, she reluctantly brings them back together.
Note: Remade as No. 185.

No. 70

"Man's Best Friend" (5-12-66)

Written by Bernard Slade. Directed by Jerry Davis. Guest cast: Richard Dreyfuss.

Just as Darrin's about to celebrate Sam's 30-day nonuse of witchcraft, a pesty warlock named Rodney appears and insists that Samantha run away with him. When she refuses, Rodney turns himself into a shaggy dog, and Darrin takes a liking to him. Sam convinces her husband that the canine is Rodney in disguise. When Rodney turns himself back into a human, Darrin punches him.

Note: Partially remade as No. 209.

No. 71

"The Catnapper" (5-19-66)

Written by Howard Leeds. Directed by R. Robert Rosenbaum. Guest cast: Marion Thompson, Virginia Martin, Robert Strauss.

Detective Charlie Leach pays another visit, and this time he discovers that both Samantha and Endora are witches. Meanwhile, Sam and her mother see Darrin with Toni Devlin, an attractive client. This prompts Endora to turn Toni into a cat, and Charlie steals the cat for evidence. Yet when he arrives home, Sam turns Charlie into a mouse. Eventually Sam and her mother undo their spells.

No. 72

"What Every Young Man Should Know" (5-26-66)

Written by Paul David and John L. Greene. Directed by Jerry Davis.

With Samantha's permission, Endora sends the Stephenses back to the past to see if Darrin would have married Sam if he had known she was a witch. A first look then shows Darrin running when he finds out her secret. Then, Darrin asks Sam to have Endora continue the test, since he believes his mother-in-law is creating the problems in their relationship. A second look shows Darrin insisting that Sam give up witchcraft when they get married. The third look, however, shows that no matter what Endora does to him, Darrin still convinces Sam that he loves her in spite of her heritage.

Note: The word "bewitched" appears in script.

No. 73

"The Girl with the Golden Nose" (6-2-66)

Written by Syd Zelinka and Paul Wayne. Directed by R. Robert Rosenbaum. Guest cast: Oliver McGowan, Owen McGiveney, Alice Backes.

Because Larry has refused him an assignment with a substantial account, Darrin feels his career is at a dead end. After he tells this to Samantha, Larry gives him the account. This leads Darrin to believe that his wife used witchcraft to help his career. Furious, Samantha transforms their house into a beautiful mansion with several housekeepers. Darrin protests by saying he wants to succeed the mortal way. Sam convinces him that he's been doing that all along. The house is restored to its former condition and their relationship is secured.

No. 74

"Prodigy" (6-9-66)

Written by Fred Freeman and Lawrence J. Cohen. Directed by Howard Morris. Guest cast: Jack Weston.

As a child, Gladys's brother, Louis Gruber, made an embarrassing violin debut at Carnegie Hall—his knickers fell down. Abner feels that Louis is still a loser. To boost Louis's confidence, Samantha arranges for him to play a hospital benefit, and uses all her magic to help him utilize his musical ability to the fullest. Louis is unaware of all this, and he performs wonderfully at the function. This leads to a TV appearance where he loses his pants . . . again.

Note: This is the last black-and-white episode.

THE THIRD SEASON: 1966 to 1967

No. 75

"Nobody's Perfect" (9-15-66)

Written by Douglas Tibbles. Directed by William Asher. Guest cast: Robert Q. Lewis, Lindsay Workman, David Lewis.

Though Endora is ecstatic at the news that Tabitha is a witch, Samantha stays up all night worrying about how she is to break it to Darrin. Because of her lack of sleep, Sam dozes off while Darrin takes Tabitha to top baby photographer Diego Fenman, a man Tabitha magically drives to his wits' ends. But Sam still hasn't told Darrin about Tabitha's powers.

No. 76

"The Moment of Truth" (9-22-66)

Written by David V. Robinson and John L. Greene. Directed by William Asher.

While Aunt Clara is paying a visit, Samantha searches for a way to tell Darrin about Tabitha, who magically makes a mess of the living room. When Larry and Louise come over to celebrate the Stephenses' anniversary, Samantha warns that Tabitha may add a glitch to the evening. Darrin discovers Tabitha is a witch and he and Sam convince the Tates that Larry is drunk, and should be taken home.

Note: First Kasey Rogers episode.

No. 77

"Witches and Warlocks Are My Favorite Things" (9-29-66)

Written by David V. Robinson and John L. Greene. Directed by William Asher. Guest cast: Estelle Winwood, Reta Shaw.

Tabitha's powers are tested by Aunt Hagatha, Aunt Enchantra, Aunt Clara, and Endora. Endora argues with Maurice, who pays a visit during the proceedings. Later, just as Darrin arrives, Tabitha impresses the coven so much, they decide she is a superior talent and opt to enroll her in Hagatha's school for little witches. Outraged, Sam, Darrin, and Aunt Clara side together against the rest, and Samantha calls upon her father for help.

No. 78

"Accidental Twins" (10-6-66)

Written by Howard Leeds. Directed by William Asher.

Sam and Darrin frantically try to keep Larry and Louise from learning that Aunt Clara has mistakenly transformed their little Jonathan into twins. The Stephenses persuade the Tates to

Samantha and Maurice Evans as her father in "Witches and Warlocks Are My Favorite Things." (Columbia Pictures Television/Milton T. Moore, Jr.)

leave their son overnight so that the next day they can throw two separate birthday parties for the two Jonathans. Meanwhile, since Aunt Clara can't remember how to reverse the spell, Sam makes her ten years younger, so the Tates again have just one son.

No. 79

"A Most Unusual Wood Nymph" (10-13-66)

Written by Ed Jurist. Directed by William Asher. Guest cast: Kathleen Nolan, Michael Ansara.

Claiming to be a friend of Darrin's aunt, beautiful Gerry O'Toole pays a visit to the Stephenses. When Endora suspects Gerry is a wood-nymph—a mortal arch enemy of witches—Sam confronts her, putting Darrin in a deep freeze. Endora's suspicions are confirmed when Sam learns that Gerry is out to perpetuate a curse on Darrin's family. To reverse the curse, Endora sends Samantha back to meet up with Darrin the Bold, a fifteenth-century ancestor of Darrin's.

No. 80

"Endora Moves in for a Spell" (10-20-66)

Written by Robert Riley Crutcher. Directed by William Asher. Guest cast: Sid Clute, Paul Smith.

Uncle Arthur visits and he and Endora clash over how Tabitha's witchcraft should be guided. Endora vows never to return. Later, Darrin complains about Arthur's influence over Tabitha and tells Sam he'd rather deal with Endora, who instantly appears. Arthur and Endora then keep making a house across the street appear and disappear while they debate which of them will move into the neighborhood. They continue to quarrel until Samantha insists they make up.

Note: First episode with Sandra Gould.

No. 81

"Twitch or Treat" (10-27-66)

Written by Robert Riley Crutcher and James Henerson. Directed by William Asher. Guest cast: Willie Mays, Barry Atwater, Joan Huntington.

Endora decides to hold her Halloween party at Samantha and Darrin's, and extravagantly remodels the living room. Among the guests: a warlock named Boris, his feline companion, Eva (a catwoman), and Willie Mays, who Sam assures Darrin is a warlock. In the meantime, Uncle Arthur and Endora are still battling over the house and continuing to confuse Mrs. Kravtiz, not to mention Councilman Green.

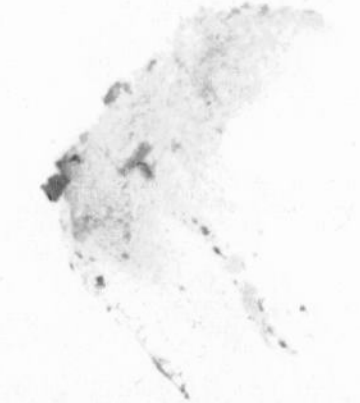

No. 82

"Dangerous Diaper Dan" (11-3-66)

Written by David Braverman and Bob Marcus. Directed by William Asher. Guest cast: Marty Ingels.

Diaper Dan, secretly working for A. J. Kimberly Advertising Agency, plants a microphone in a baby rattle he gives to Tabitha. Later, Samantha is angry when Darrin tells her she might be

Darrin caught between Endora and Samantha at a cocktail party. (Columbia Pictures Television/Milton T. Moore, Jr.)

responsible for a leak of ideas from McMann and Tate. When Endora protests such an accusation, Sam finds out about Dan's plan, as she and her mother drive the diaper man up a tree, by popping the wheels and doors off his van.

No. 83

"The Short Happy Circuit of Aunt Clara" (11-10-66)

Written by Lee Erwin. Directed by William Asher. Guest cast: Arthur Julian, Reginald Owen.

Darrin consents to Aunt Clara's baby-sitting when he and Sam are invited to the Tates' to meet Mr. MacElroy, a shoe client. However, the picture darkens when Aunt Clara accidentally knocks the lights out on the entire Eastern Seaboard. Desperate for help, she summons Ocky, her old warlock boyfriend, who can keep the lights on only at the Stephenses' by raising his arms. Larry then insists the dinner meeting be continued at Darrin and Samantha's. Once back at home, Darrin opens the closet door and a pair of shoes walk out—it's Ocky in disguise. But MacElroy thinks it's part of Darrin's ad campaign and loves it.

No. 84

"I'd Rather Twitch than Fight" (11-17-66)

Written by James Henerson. Directed by R. Robert Rosenbaum. Guest cast: Norman Fell, Parley Baer, Bridget Hanely, Burt Mustin.

Darrin is enraged when Sam gives his favorite sport jacket to Goodwill. As a result, they both seek marital advice from the Tates—Darrin from Larry, Sam from Louise. Shocked by such amateur counsel, Endora summons Dr. Sigmund Freud, who settles Sam's problems, then gets into a free-for-all with the Tates' analyst. Sam and Endora dematerialize each analyst to his proper environment.

No. 85

"Oedipus Hex" (11-24-66)

Written by David V. Robinson and John L. Greene. Directed by William Asher. Guest cast: Paul Dooley, Ned Glass, Irwin Charone.

While Samantha serves on a fund-raising committee, Endora casts a spell on a bowl of popcorn. This spell alters Darrin's work habits, making him lazy. The milkman and the TV repairman are also afflicted. When Sam returns home, she finds the house a shambles and Darrin and the others loafing the day away. Recognizing her mother's handiwork, Sam removes the spell on the happy-peppy-popcorn, and gets the loafers to contribute heavily to her committee.

No. 86

"Sam's Spooky Chair" (12-1-66)

Written by Coslough Johnson. Directed R. Robert Rosenbaum. Guest cast: J. Pat O'Malley, Anne Seymour.

Samantha buys a chair that, unknown to her, is bewitched. That night she prepares dinner for the Tates and client Max Cosgrove and his domineering wife. Mrs. Cosgrove wants to buy the chair. In the Cosgroves' possession, the chair immediately begins making life miserable for them. Endora explains to Samantha that the haunted chair is really Clyde Farnsworth, a warlock who transformed himself years ago after Samantha rejected him.

Samantha with Fred Wayne as Benjamin Franklin. (Columbia Pictures Television.)

No. 87

"My Friend Ben" (12-8-66)

Written by James Henerson. Directed by William Asher. Guest cast: Fredd Wayne, Harry Holcombe.

Aunt Clara mistakenly conjures up Benjamin Franklin to fix a lamp, and Darrin can't convince Larry that Franklin is not part of an ad campaign. Later, Ben gets lost and Sam, Darrin, and Clara search for him. Inadvertently, Ben has started an old fire engine and slams into a curb. He is later taken to court.

Note: Part 1 of 2. Remade as No. 249.

No. 88

"Samantha for the Defense" (12-15-66)

Written by James Henerson. Directed by William Asher. Guest cast: Fredd Wayne, Mike Road, Paul Sand, the Real Don Steele.

Assistant D.A. Chuck Hawkins feels Ben Franklin's appearance is publicity for McMann and Tate and tells Darrin that

Franklin ("or whoever he is") will be prosecuted to the full extent of the law. Later, while in court, Samantha disappears and returns with a plaque from the fire engine Ben was accused of stealing. The plaque bears his name. Winningly, she states that a person can't be convicted of stealing what he already owns.
Note: Part 2 of 2. Remade as No. 250.

No. 89

"A Gazebo Never Forgets" (12-22-66)

Written by Jerry Devine and Izzy Elinson. Directed by R. Robert Rosenbaum. Guest cast: Steve Franken, Paul Reed, Dodo Denny.

While Aunt Clara baby-sits for Tabitha, Samantha applies for a bank loan to transform her gazebo into a rumpus room. When a bank inspector is sent to review the construction site, he sees a large pink elephant that Aunt Clara has created from a toy Tabitha desired. After a close call with Larry and the bank president, whose brother holds a profitable account with McMann and Tate, Clara returns the elephant to its normal state.
Note: First show Dick York missed.

No. 90

"Soap Box Derby" (12-29-66)

Written by James Henerson. Directed by Alan Jay Factor. Guest cast: Michael Shea, William Bramley.

Sam helps prepare twelve-year-old Johnny Mills for the Soap Box Derby. Gladys brags that her nephew will win the local race and go on to victory in Akron. Later, at the track, both Darrin and Gladys keep an eye on Sam, making sure she doesn't assist Johnny with magic. Yet, when Johnny does triumph on his skill alone, Gladys calls for a hearing, where the young boy proves he knows his go-cart. Furthermore, his father, who earlier was reluctant to support his son, now shows up in Johnny's defense.
Note: Partial remake of No. 6.

No. 91

"Sam in the Moon" (1-5-67)

Written by James Henerson. Directed by R. Robert Rosenbaum. Guest cast: Dort Clark, Tim Herbert.

Sam baffles Darrin by choosing not to watch a TV newscast about the moon, flippantly stating that she's been there. Later she flies to Tokyo with Endora and buys some unique tea from a Japanese warlock. Darrin then takes the tea to have it analyzed, thinking because of Sam's earlier remark that it may be moon dust. After slight confusion involving the pharmacist's brother-in-law (who is from Nassau County, not NASA), Darrin is almost certain that the tea is genuine.

No. 92

"Ho Ho the Clown" (1-12-67)

Written by Richard Baer. Directed by William Asher. Guest cast: Joey Forman, Dick Wilson.

Samantha and Endora take Tabitha to a live taping of the *Ho Ho the Clown* show on TV, which is sponsored by Darrin's client, the Solow Toy Company. Endora is enraged when Tabitha is excluded from the show's contest because she's related to Darrin, so she magically makes sure her granddaughter wins anyway—while on the air. Darrin then feels his career is over when Solow finds out he's Tabitha's father. Ever to the rescue, Sam conjures up a "Tabitha" doll, and claims that her daughter's TV appearance was a publicity stunt for the new toy.

Note: First show with Dick Wilson as a client.

No. 93

"Super Car" (1-19-67)

Written by Ed Jurist. Directed by William Asher. Guest cast: Irwin Charone, Dave Madden, Herb Ellis.

Thinking she's doing Darrin a favor, Endora gives him the prototype of a new car that she steals from its creators in Detroit. Unaware of the trick at first, Darrin loves the car, and he and Samantha take a test drive. However, when client Mr. Sheldrake shows interest in the auto, Darrin learns its true origin and insists Endora return it. She does so, only with Sheldrake in the driver's seat.

No. 94

"The Corn Is as High as a Guernsey's Eye" (1-26-67)

Written by Ruth Brooks Flippen. Directed by William Asher. Guest cast: Don Penny, William Thegoe, Howard Smith.

Larry tells Darrin to forget the Morton Milk account, since another agency plans to promote Morton's famous guernsey cow in McMann and Tate's office building lobby. Meanwhile, Aunt Clara is despondent and Sam tries to cheer her up by taking her to lunch with Darrin. At McMann and Tate, Sam leaves Clara for a moment and returns to find Clara nowhere in sight. Thinking the frazzled witch has turned herself into the Morton cow, Sam twitches the beast home with her. After a ruckus is raised over the missing cow, Darrin finds Clara and phones Sam to return the cow.

No. 95

"The Trial and Error of Aunt Clara" (2-2-67)

Written by Ed Jurist. Directed by William Asher. Guest cast: Nancy Andrews, Arthur Malet, Ottola Nesmith.

Because her magic is failing, Aunt Clara is put on trial by the Witches' Council (presided over by Judge Bean, with Endora). The Council plans to sentence her to be earthbound. As court begins session in the Stephenses' living room, Samantha acts as her aunt's defense counsel and secretly helps Clara during a series of witch tests. When Sam momentarily steps away, Clara gets very confused. Then when Darrin arrives, she magically and magnificently makes the judge and all in the court disappear, thus proving her powers are still intact.

No. 96

"Three Wishes" (2-9-67)

Written by Robert Riley Crutcher. Directed by William Asher. Guest cast: Linda Gaye Scott, Robert Stiles.

Endora once again grants Darrin three wishes to prove his love for Samantha. First Darrin wishes that Larry go on a Hawaiian business trip instead of him because Sam can't go. When Darrin tells Sam that he has to go to a business meeting with a beautiful model named Buffy, Endora can't wait to hear what she thinks his next wish will be. Later he and Buffy fly to Boston on a business trip. Sam phones Darrin's hotel room, and Buffy answers because Darrin let her stay there as there was only one room available. When Sam angrily suspects that Darrin has used up his last two wishes on Buffy, he wishes Endora to appear . . . which she does.

No. 97

"I Remember You . . . Sometimes" (2-16-67)

Written by David V. Robison and John L. Greene. Directed by William Asher. Guest cast: Dan Tobin, Grace Albertson.

When Darrin tries to improve his memory for better business success, Endora puts a spell on his wristwatch, which gives him total recall whenever he has it on. Later the Tates and the very boastful client Mr. Pennybaker and his wife are invited to the Stephenses' for dinner. Darrin monopolizes the conversation with his overactive memory and knowledge (something Mr. Pennybaker prides himself on). Sam soon realizes that the watch is bewitched and zaps it off Darrin and onto Mrs. Pennybaker's wrist. The client's wife recites verbatim her husband's "party" stories. Mr. Pennybaker realizes that at times he, too, is a bore.

No. 98

"Art for Sam's Sake" (2-23-67)

Written by Jack Sher. Directed by William Asher. Guest cast: Arthur Julian, Paul Sorenson.

Endora becomes disgusted with Samantha's amateurish attempt at painting and replaces Sam's picture of a fruit bowl with a masterpiece. Unaware of what her mother's done, Samantha wins first prize at a charity exhibit. Consequently Darrin, the Tates, and perfume client Mr. Cunningham accompany her to the art show. But when she recognizes Endora's hand in her affairs, and when Mr. Cunningham actually purchases what he thinks is her masterpiece, trouble brews. A bargain is made when Samantha persuades Mr. Cunningham to use her named-on-the-spot perfume, "I Know You," for his company.

No. 99

"Charlie Harper, Winner" (3-2-67)

Written by Earl Barrett. Directed by R. Robert Rosenbaum. Guest cast: Angus Duncan, Joanna Moore.

Samantha and Darrin entertain Charlie Harper and his wife, Daphne. Charlie, an old college chum, has surpassed Darrin in every category since school. He's handsome, rich, and the father of triplets. So Samantha conjures up a fur coat to impress the Harpers, but ends up hurting and angering Darrin. When Sam realizes how upset her husband really is, she also strengthens and confirms her love by giving the coat to Daphne, who initially wanted to buy it.

No. 100

"Aunt Clara's Victoria Victory" (3-9-67)

Written by Robert Riley Crutcher. Directed by William Asher. Guest cast: Jane Connell, Robert H. Harris.

Aunt Clara fondly remembers her days as lady-in-waiting to Queen Victoria and tries to return to the Victorian Age. Instead, the Queen herself (with throne) appears in the Stephenses' living room. Later, client Mr. Morgan and the Queen first hit it off, then clash. After Sam bewitches Morgan with a dream-spell to make him believe he's Queen Victoria, she reveals to Her Highness that she and Clara are witches. Victoria is furious; Clara becomes angry and tries to return the Queen to her own time. Unfortunately, Prince Albert appears instead.

Note: A non-Darrin episode.

No. 101

"The Crone of Cawdor" (3-16-67)

Written by Ed Jurist. Directed R. Robert Rosenbaum. Guest cast: Julie Gregg, Dorothy Neumann.

Samantha has to prevent Darrin from kissing beautiful young client Terry Warbell, who, Endora says, is really the Crone of Cawdor, an old hag who steals the youth from those mortals she kisses. On first hearing that Darrin will age 500 years if he touches the youthful-looking woman, he thinks it's ridiculous. And just as he is about to kiss her to spite Samantha, she transforms the Crone into her true aged self, which shocks Darrin.

No. 102

"No More Mr. Nice Guy" (3-23-67)

Written by Jack Sher. Directed by William Asher. Guest cast: Larry D. Mann, Paul Barselow, George Ives.

Endora casts a spell on Darrin that makes everyone hate him. Upset, Darrin seeks the counsel of a psychiatrist. After Sam finds out his job's in jeopardy because of Endora's shenanigans, she demands that her mother remove the spell.

No. 103

"It's Wishcraft" (3-30-67)

Written by James Henerson. Directed by Paul Davis (Alice Pearce's husband). Guest cast: Heather Woodruff.

When Darrin's parents visit, he and Samantha try to conceal Tabitha's powers. Sam even asks her mother to help, but Endora only ends up aggravating the situation by insulting Darrin in front of his mother. Consequently, Phyllis thinks Sam and Darrin are having marital difficulties. To soothe his mother's mind, Darrin remains happy and chipper as ever in front of his parents, even kissing Endora. The elder Stephenses never find out the truth about Tabitha, or about Samantha, for that matter.

No. 104

"How to Fail in Business with All Kinds of Help" (4-6-67)

Written by Ron Friedman. Directed by Richard Kinon. Guest cast: Henry Beckman, Lisa Kirk.

Darrin thinks Madame Maruska, a very domineering client, is Endora in disguise. As a result, he doesn't play what he thinks is Endora's game. Maruska, however, is upset with Darrin's arrogance and refuses to do business with McMann and Tate. Once he learns that Endora was with Samantha at the time in question, Darrin immediately runs to Maruska's office to apologize, only to meet Larry, who's already begging for the account. Samantha then takes Darrin's layout and boldly prints it in the newspaper, winning the Maruska account for McMann and Tate.

No. 105

"Bewitched, Bothered and Infuriated" (4-13-67)

Written by Howard Leeds. Directed by R. Robert Rosenbaum. Guest cast: Jack Fletcher.

Aunt Clara pops up a ten-year-old newspaper that states Larry Tate broke his leg on his honeymoon. Sam and Darrin think it's today's paper, and because Larry and Louise are going on a second honeymoon, the Stephenses make nuisances of themselves trying to prevent Larry from breaking his leg. Darrin even encourages Sam to use her powers—though she objects to his rude behavior. When they learn the paper is just another example of Clara's inept witchcraft, Sam and Darrin leave the Tates alone (and Larry doesn't break his leg).

No. 106

"Nobody but a Frog Knows How to Live" (4-27-67)

Written by Ruth Brooks Flippen. Directed by Richard Kinon. Guest cast: John Fiedler, Dan Tobin.

A frog has been turned into a man named Fergie by a witch. Samantha learns that a girl-frog is waiting for him back at the lily pond. Gladys wonders about this strange person. Samantha takes pity on him and changes him back into a frog.

No. 107

"There's Gold in Them There Pills" (5-4-67)

Written by Paul Wayne and Ed Jurist. Directed by R. Robert Rosenbaum. Guest cast: Milton Frome.

When Darrin catches a cold, Endora calls for Dr. Bombay, who prescribes a supernatural pill that cures Darrin's flu but also causes side effects: his voice gets higher. Before this happens, however, Darrin is delighted with a fast recovery, offering the pills to Larry and a client who both have colds. Their instant return to good health prompts Darrin and Larry to think about marketing Bombay's pills, until the side effects surface, and Sam discovers an antidote.

Note: The first Dr. Bombay episode.

THE FOURTH SEASON: 1967 to 1968

No. 108

"Long Live the Queen" (9-7-67)

Written by Ed Jurist. Directed by William Asher. Guest cast: J. Edward McKinley, Ruth McDevitt.

The Queen of the Witches retires and crowns Samantha the new queen, and at first Darrin doesn't mind. However, after the house is invaded by a blackbird, a walking chair, and an odd assortment of animals, objects, and supernatural beings, he heads for his favorite bar. There he converses with a pathetic drunk and a sympathetic bartender who help him decide to return home to Sam.

No. 109

"Toys in Babeland" (9-14-67)

Written by Ed Jurist. Directed by William Asher. Guest cast: Burt Mustin, Jim Brooks, Dick Wilson.

While baby-sitting for Tabitha, Endora learns that she is expected at a party at the Taj Mahal. She breathes life into Tabitha's toy soldier so that it can take her place as sitter. Later, Larry believes he's missed out on a masquerade party, when Tabitha copies her grandmother's incantation and brings all her toys to life. Larry goes out for a drink with the human toy soldier, thinking it works for another agency that's trying to hire Darrin.

No. 110

"Business, Italian Style" (9-21-67)

Written by Michael Morris. Directed by William Asher. Guest cast: Renzo Cezana, Fred Roberto.

To please an Italian client, Darrin tries to learn the Italian language. While he is struggling with instructive recordings, Endora zaps Darrin into a native Italian who doesn't understand English. When the client is impressed with Darrin's progress, he insists that he speak English. This is impossible until Samantha forces Endora to remove the spell, and the account is saved.

No. 111

"Double, Double Toil and Trouble" (9-28-67)

Written by Ed Jurist. Directed by William Asher. Guest cast: Stanley Beck.

After Queen Samantha holds witch proceedings in the wee hours, Darrin orders her to clear court, which infuriates Endora.

Then while Sam's at a church fund-raiser, Endora and Serena conspire to dispose of Darrin by having Serena take Sam's place. Later, after a free-for-all pie fest between Sam, Endora, Darrin, and Serena, everything gets cleared up.
Note: First Serena color episode.

No. 112

"Cheap, Cheap" (10-5-67)

Written by Ed Jurist. Directed by William Asher. Guest cast: Parley Baer, Mary Lansing, Jill Foster.

After Darrin makes Samantha return an expensive coat she thought was a bargain, Endora turns him into a real cheapskate. Later, during a disastrous dinner party with thrifty client Mr. Bigelow, Sam tries to reverse Endora's stingy spell, succeeding only in turning Bigelow into a big spender. Endora finally reverses the spell.

No. 113

"No Zip in My Zap" (10-12-67)

Written by Barbara Avedon. Directed by Richard Kinon. Guest cast: Mala Powers, Dick Wilson.

When Samantha loses her powers, Dr. Bombay tells her it's because her magic is all built up through its infrequent use. He tells her she must levitate in midair for a time. Later, when Darrin phones from a meeting with a client (who happens to be someone he used to date), Endora tells him Samantha can't talk because she's flying. This leads Darrin to believe that his wife has turned herself into a fly, and is out to check up on his business encounter with his former girl friend.

No. 114

"Birdies, Bogeys and Baxter" (10-19-67)

Written by David V. Robison and John L. Greene. Directed by William Asher. Guest cast: MacDonald Carey, Joan Banks.

Larry wants Darrin to impress client Joe Baxter, who prides himself on being an excellent golfer. After Darrin wears himself out practicing, Endora gives him a little magical boost to better his game. When Darrin starts making incredible shots, Larry warns him not to beat Baxter. But when Mrs. Baxter tells Samantha that she wishes her husband would lose just once, Sam obliges and adds her own contribution to her mother's witchcraft.

Samantha and Darrin on the green in "Birdies, Bogeys and Baxter." (Columbia Pictures Television.)

No. 115

"The Safe and Sane Halloween" (10-26-67)

Written by James Henerson. Directed by William Asher. Guest cast: Felix Silla, Jerry Maren, Billy Curtis.

On Halloween, Gladys's nephew trades places with one of the goblins Tabitha has brought to life from her storybook. The ghouls continue to cause havoc by playing tricks on Darrin and the Tates (they turn Gladys's nephew into a goat). As Tabitha returns the spirits to their proper place in the storybook, Samantha considers the situation and tries to offer a logical explanation.

No. 116

"Out of Synch, Out of Mind" (11-2-67)

Written by Ed Jurist. Directed by Richard Kinon.

When Darrin's parents have a fight, Phyllis comes to stay with the Stephenses. Samantha suggests that Darrin show home

movies of Tabitha to ease the tension. Unfortunately, the audio and the visual of the film are out of synch. Aunt Clara, who is also visiting, casts a spell to splice the movie, but instead hexes Sam's voice to follow her lip movement. A call to Dr. Bombay is made, Sam is cured, and Phyllis is delighted when Frank comes to pick her up.
Note: First Roy Roberts show.

No. 117

"That Was No Chick, That Was My Wife" (11-9-67)

Written by Rick Mittleman. Directed by William Asher. Guest cast: Herb Voland, Sara Seegar.

Larry asks Darrin to go to Chicago to renew the Springer Pet Food account. When Samantha accompanies Darrin, the Stephenses reluctantly have Aunt Clara baby-sit for Tabitha. Learning that Tabitha has zapped life into a toy monkey, Sam pops home and runs into Louise, who tells Larry she has seen Samantha. When everybody's back in Connecticut, Sam explains it was Serena who went with Darrin to Chicago, just as Louise is on her way to the psychiatrist.

No. 118

"Allergic to Macedonian Dodo Birds" (11-16-67)

Written by Richard Baer. Directed by Richard Kinon. Guest star: Janos Prohaska.

When Endora loses her powers, she stays with Samantha and Darrin and becomes an irritating presence in the Stephens household, especially to Darrin. Meanwhile, Aunt Clara's witchcraft has inexplicably improved tenfold. Dr. Bombay is summoned, and he suggests that Endora's and Clara's powers have somehow been switched. Tabitha had zapped up a Macedonian dodo bird—which Endora is allergic to. All is well again when the creature is found, and Endora's and Clara's powers are rightfully reversed.

No. 119

"Samantha's Thanksgiving to Remember" (11-23-67)

Written by Tom and Helen August. Directed by Richard Kinon. Guest cast: Jacques Aubuchon, Laurie Main, Peter Canon.

Aunt Clara ineptly zaps the Stephens family, Gladys, and herself back to seventeenth-century Salem for Thanksgiving. When Samantha asks Darrin to light a fire, he strikes a match and is immediately accused of witchcraft. At Darrin's trial, Sam conducts his defense and asks his accuser to light the alleged witch's match. When he hesitates, Sam twitches the match into a flame, proving Darrin's innocence. Aunt Clara then remembers how to get everyone back to the twentieth century.

No. 120

"Solid Gold Mother-in-Law" (11-30-67)

Written by Ed Jurist. Directed by Richard Michaels. Guest cast: Jack Collins.

Client Mr. Gregson, who has an old-fashioned vision of the American family, asks to meet Endora after she inadvertently pops a picture of herself on Darrin's desk. Darrin reluctantly invites the Tates and Mr. Gregson over to dinner to meet Endora (he makes peace with her for the night). The evening goes well until after Gregson leaves, when Larry accuses Darrin of making him look inferior, as Gregson has asked Darrin to open his own ad firm. To make them friends again, Sam submits Darrin's ideas to Mr. Gregson with Larry's signature.

Note: First episode Richard Michaels directed.

Darrin's oversize ears in "My, What Big Ears You Have." (Elizabeth Montgomery/William Asher collection.)

No. 121

"My, What Big Ears You Have" (12-7-67)

Written by Ed Jurist. Directed by Richard Kinon. Guest cast: Joan Hotchkis.

When Darrin tries to surprise Samantha with an antique rocking chair, Endora—because of a call from the antiques shop saleswoman—suspects he's fooling around with another woman. To prove her point, Endora causes Darrin's ears to grow each time he lies. The more he lies to keep Sam from finding out about the rocker, the larger his ears get. Finally Sam is surprised with the chair, which Darrin has been hiding in the Kravitzes' garage. In disgust, Endora returns Darrin's ears to normal.

No. 122

"I Get Your Nanny, You Get My Goat" (12-14-67)

Written by Ron Friedman. Directed by William Asher. Guest cast: Hermione Baddeley, Reginald Gardiner.

Darrin's unhappy with Tabitha's new baby-sitter, Elspeth, a witch-maid hired by Endora who also took care of Samantha when she was a little girl. Later, Lord Montdrako, Elspeth's former warlock-employer, arrives at the Stephenses', furious because Darrin has taken his housekeeper. Sam then convinces Montdrako that he doesn't need Elspeth, who leaves on her own accord.

No. 123

"Humbug Not to Be Spoken Here" (12-21-67)

Written by Lila Garrett and Bernie Kahn. Directed by William Asher. Guest cast: Charles Lane, Don Beddoe, Martin Ashe.

Samantha teaches cranky client Mr. Mortimer all about Christmas; she whisks him off to the North Pole to meet Santa, and then returns him to New York to visit his ex-butler's underprivileged family. When Sam brings Mortimer home, he's confused as to whether he's been dreaming or not. The next day is Christmas Day, and he arrives at the Stephenses' with gifts and accepts Samantha's invitation to dinner.

No. 124

"Samantha's Da Vinci Dilemma" (12-28-67)

Written by Jerry Mayer and Paul L. Friedman. Directed by Richard Kinon. Guest cast: John Abbott, Irwin Charone, William Thegoe, Vince Howard.

To help Samantha with painting the house, Aunt Clara mistakenly conjures up master artist Leonardo da Vinci, tries to send him back, but fails. Meanwhile, Da Vinci is angry when he learns his famous *Mona Lisa* will be used to sell toothpaste in Darrin's campaign. To keep this from happening, Sam persuades Da Vinci to create another campaign involving tooth paint, with Leonardo's likeness on the package. Afterward Aunt Clara sends the artist back to his place in history.

No. 125

"Once in a Vial" (1-4-68)

Written by James Henerson and Ed Jurist. Directed by Bruce Bilson. Guest cast: Ron Randell, Arch Johnson, Henry Beckman.

Endora summons Rollo, a handsome warlock who once dated Samantha, to break up her daughter's marriage. By accident Endora drinks a love potion Rollo had intended for Samantha, and decides to marry the less than average Bo Callahan, a client of Darrin's. As Endora is about to say, "I do," the potion wears off.

No. 126

"Snob in the Grass" (1-11-68)

Written by Ed Jurist. Directed by R. Robert Rosenbaum. Guest cast: Nancy Kovack, Frank Wilcox, Allan Emerson.

When Darrin's old girl friend Sheila Sommers visits, Larry seizes the opportunity to acquire her father's account. During a dinner party, Sheila upstages Samantha, monopolizes Darrin, and

Serena's hippie blonde look in "Hippie, Hippie Hooray." (Columbia Pictures Television.)

sounds off on wives who are boring. Determined to leave, Darrin is derailed by Larry, and Sam gives Sheila a deserved twitch. Larry is angry at losing the Sommers account, but is satisfied when Darrin wins the Webley account.

No. 127

"If They Never Met" (1-25-68)

Written by William Idelson and Samuel Bobrick. Directed by R. Robert Rosenbaum. Guest cast: Nancy Kovack, Frank Wilcox, Allan Emerson, Paul Barselow, Gene Blakely.

Though Sam maintains that Darrin really loves her, she accepts Endora's challenge to see what would have happened if they had never met. Back in time, Darrin confides to Al, the bartender, that his girl friend Sheila is wonderful and a millionaire's daughter, but he's not sure he loves her. When Darrin bumps into Samantha, he wonders if he's delaying marrying Sheila and waiting for someone else. Back to the future, Darrin admits for once that Endora was helpful.

No. 128

"Hippie, Hippie, Hooray" (2-1-68)

Written by Michael Morris. Directed by William Asher. Guest cast: Ralph Story, Walter Sands, Jean Blake.

Serena, now the hippest of the hip, sings rock and roll and shakes up the Stephens household by pretending to be Samantha. To convince Larry that Serena is Sam's cousin, Darrin invites the Tates to see the two look-alikes together. With the table set for five, Darrin admits defeat and is sorry about an earlier confrontation with Serena.

Note: There is no laugh track on this episode.

No. 129

"A Prince of a Guy" (2-8-68)

Written by Ed Jurist. Directed by R. Robert Rosenbaum. Guest cast: Louise Glen, Stuart Margolin, William Bassett.

When Tabitha brings Prince Charming to life out of her storybook, Darrin's cousin Helen falls in love with him, which upsets her fiancé Ralph. Larry wants to hire the prince for TV commercials. Then to help Tabitha return Mr. Charming to the book, Sam conjures up an alluring Sleeping Beauty, as Helen and Ralph reunite.

Note: A non-Darrin episode. Only episode with Darrin's relatives other than his parents.

No. 130

"McTavish" (2-15-68)

Written by James Henerson. Directed by Paul Davis. Guest cast: Ronald Long, Reginald Owen.

Aunt Clara learns her old warlock boyfriend Ocky has opened up an old castle in England. However, McTavish, an ancestral ghost, is ruining business by scaring guests. Reluctantly Samantha agrees to help Ocky, and suggests that McTavish find a more comfortable place to haunt. As a result, the ghost comes to the Stephenses'. Ocky then tells McTavish that the guests miss him, and to come back.

No. 131

"How Green Was My Grass" (2-29-68)

Written by Ed Jurist. Directed by R. Robert Rosenbaum. Guest cast: Richard X. Slattery, Barbara Perry, Joseph Perry.

Darrin thinks Samantha has conjured up a synthetic lawn in their front yard, and they have a fight. Meanwhile, neighbor Bill MacLane is wondering what happened to the artificial grass he ordered. Before everyone finds out that MacLane's plastic lawn was installed on the Stephens property by mistake, the angry neighbor accuses Darrin of stealing it and raises his fist, only to have Sam twitch MacLane to hit the fence. She then zaps the proper lawns into place.

No. 132

"To Twitch or Not to Twitch" (3-14-68)

Written by Lila Garrett and Bernie Kahn. Directed by William Asher. Guest cast: Margaret Muse, Arthur Julian, Donald Journeau.

On the way to a client's dinner party, Samantha and Darrin argue about her use of witchcraft. It begins to rain and the car has a flat tire, and Sam refuses to help fix it. Consequently, Darrin gets soaked and ends up having to wear the client's too-small clothes at the party. Later Sam and Darrin continue their argument, prompting Sam to leave with Tabitha and go to Cloud Eight, and then to return when Darrin apologizes.

No. 133

"Playmates" (3-21-68)

Written by Richard Baer. Directed by William Asher. Guest cast: Peggy Pope, Teddy Quinn.

Phyllis takes Samantha and Tabitha to visit the Millhowsers. Gretchen, the mother, loves to dabble in child psychology.

Darrin in "To Twitch or Not to Twitch." (Columbia Pictures Television/Gary Matheson.)

Michael, the son, wishes he were a dog. Later Tabitha zaps Michael into a dog, turning the Millhowser household upside down. Fortunately, Samantha persuades her daughter to transform Michael back to his original self.
Note: A non-Darrin episode.

No. 134

"Tabitha's Cranky Spell" (3-28-68)

Written by Robert Riley Crutcher. Directed by William Asher. Guest cast: Sara Seegar, J. Edward McKinley, Harry Harvey.

While Louise's Aunt Harriet baby-sits for Tabitha, Larry hopes Samantha can help persuade his client Mr. Baker to modernize his firm, which was established by Uncle Willie. Meanwhile, Tabitha has led Aunt Harriet to believe that she has contacted her dead fiancé, Mr. Henderson. Later Sam impersonates and then meets the real ghost of Uncle Willie, and persuades Mr. Baker to change his company's image. On arriving home, she then convinces Aunt Harriet that it was all a dream.
Note: A non-Darrin episode.

No. 135

"I Confess" (4-4-68)

Written by Richard Baer. Directed by Seymour Robbie. Guest cast: Woodrow Parfrey, Herb Ellis, Dick Wilson.

When Sam uses witchcraft to fend off a man in the street, Darrin, thinking her only defense in life is her magical powers, gets angry. In his frustration, he decides to end his opposition to her use of magic, and is now ready to tell everyone his wife is a witch. Knowing Darrin doesn't mean what he says, Sam uses a spell to show him what life would be like if the whole world knew her secret.

No. 136

"A Majority of Two" (4-11-68)

Written by Ed Jurist. Directed by R. Robert Rosenbaum. Guest cast: Richard Haydn, Helen Funai.

Aunt Clara sets a low table, Japanese-style, and pops herself and Samantha into geisha girl costumes to entertain client Kensu Mishimoto, whom she charms. Later she expects him to propose, which prompts Sam to contact Clara's boyfriend Ocky. However, Mr. Mishimoto feels humiliated and leaves abruptly. Sam heads him off by literally allowing herself to lose face, and then convinces him to stay in Connecticut to finish his business with McMann and Tate.
Note: A non-Darrin episode.

Darrin, Sam, and Larry in "I Confess." (Columbia Pictures Television.)

No. 137

"Samantha's Secret Saucer" (4-18-68)

Written by Jerry Mayer and Paul L. Friedman. Directed by Richard Michaels. Guest cast: Steve Franken, Hamilton Camp.

Aunt Clara accidentally zaps a toy space ship into the real thing, including live spacemen/dogs Alpha and Orvis. In the meantime, Gladys has spotted the spacecraft and has notified the Air Force. Aunt Clara zaps the aliens back just before the Air Force arrives to inspect the UFO.

Note: The last episode to feature Aunt Clara.

No. 138

"The No-Harm Charm" (4-25-68)

Written by Ed Jurist. Directed by Russell B. Mayberry. Guest cast: Vaughn Taylor, Susan Tolsky, Paul Smith.

When Darrin's brochure for the multimillion Omega Bank mistakenly lists the bank's assets as $100, Larry suggests he take some time off. However, Darrin thinks he has Uncle Arthur's magic charm for protection, and he sets out to salvage the Omega account. When Samantha learns that Arthur's charm is a fake, she ends up saving Darrin from several blunders. On his own, however, Darrin impresses Omega's Mr. Markham by disarming a robber, and saves the account for McMann and Tate.

No. 139

"Man of the Year (5-2-68)

Written by John L. Greene. Directed by R. Robert Rosenbaum. Guest cast: Bill Quinn, Roland Winters, George Ives.

When the Hucksters' Club names Darrin one of the advertising men of the year, Sam claims he won't be affected by such a title. To prove otherwise, Endora intensifies Darrin's likability so that everyone who comes within a few feet of him is charmed.

Samantha, Darrin, and Tabitha in "Splitsville." (Columbia Pictures Television/Gary Matheson.)

Later, when Darrin envisions himself as the president of another company, Samantha realizes that her mother has been at it again, and demands that Endora remove the spell.

No. 140

"Splitsville" (5-16-68)

Written by Richard Baer. Directed by William Asher. Guest cast: Arthur Julian.

When Gladys leaves Abner, Samantha invites her to stay with Darrin and her. Darrin is not happy about the situation. To bring the Kravitzes back together, Samantha casts a spell over the butcher, Mr. Hogersdorf, and makes him fall for Gladys so that Abner will get jealous. Happily, Gladys returns to her beloved. Note: Remake of No. 32.

Darrin, having been cast into a miniature man by Endora, finds himself in an oversize condiment jar in "Samantha's Wedding Present." (Elizabeth Montgomery/William Asher collection.)

THE FIFTH SEASON: 1968 to 1969

No. 141

"Samantha's Wedding Present" (9-26-68)

Written by Bernard Slade. Directed by William Asher. Guest cast: Dick Wilson, Art Metrano.

After giving Samantha a belated wedding present, Endora decides to make peace with Darrin, but only becomes furious with him and shrinks him down in size. Unable to find her husband, Samantha thinks he's been eaten by a dog. Meanwhile, Darrin has crawled into a liquor bottle that is found by a drunk, who thinks the little Darrin is a leprechaun. The drunk offers to free Darrin only if he's granted three wishes. Darrin then persuades the drunk to take him home, where Sam will twitch up the requests.

No. 142

"Samantha Goes South for a Spell" (10-3-68)

Written by Ed Jurist. Directed by William Asher. Guest cast: Jack Cassidy, Isabel Sanford.

Brunhilda, a jealous witch-wife of one of Serena's boyfriends, thinks Sam is the "other woman" in her husband's life and sends her back to old New Orleans of 1868. There Aunt Jenny takes Sam

Elizabeth with Jack Cassidy as Rance in "Samantha Goes South for a Spell." (Columbia Pictures Television/Dan Weaver.)

to the home of Rance, who falls immediately in love with the lost witch. Meanwhile, Serena sends Darrin back in time to the rescue. When Darrin arrives, Sam doesn't recognize him and refuses to kiss him (Serena had said kissing Darrin would restore Sam's memory of him). After a duel with Rance, Darrin finally persuades Sam to pucker up; she remembers everything and they return home.

No. 143

"Samantha on the Keyboard" (10-10-68)

Written by Richard Baer. Directed by Richard Michaels. Guest cast: Jonathan Harris, Fritz Feld.

Endora transforms Tabitha into a virtuoso at the piano, while Samantha accepts Darrin's challenge to learn how to play the mortal way. However, when Sam's piano teacher, Mr. Monroe, hears Tabitha's playing, he brings a world-famous conductor to hear her play. Unfortunately, the maestro is upset when, without the benefit of magic, Tabitha produces only random chords. Later, Sam finds a real child prodigy for the maestro and impresses Darrin by learning the song "Born Free" on the keyboard, minus the magic.

Note: Remade as No. 246.

No. 144

"Darrin Gone and Forgotten" (10-17-68)

Written by Lila Garrett and Bernie Kahn. Directed by William Asher. Guest cast: Mercedes McCambridge, Steve Franken.

Witch Carlotta holds Darrin captive as she reveals that eons before, Endora promised Samantha to her son Juke. As part of a plan to get Darrin back, Sam tells Carlotta she will marry Juke because her mortal marriage is a strain. Juke then follows Sam's instructions to defy his overprotective mother. When Juke does side with Sam, Carlotta calls off the wedding and returns Darrin to Sam.

No. 145

"It's So Nice to Have a Spouse Around the House" (10-24-68)

Written by Barbara Avedon. Directed by William Asher. Guest cast: Fifi D'Orsay, Dick Wilson.

Darrin mistakenly takes Serena on a second honeymoon, thinking she's Sam, who's presiding over a Witches' Council meeting. At Moonthatch Inn, Serena is alarmed at Darrin's affectionate mood, and Darrin is angry at what he thinks is Sam's standoffish

Mercedes McCambridge and Elizabeth in the mist in "Darrin, Gone and Forgotten." (Columbia Pictures Television.)

Mercedes McCambridge and Steve Franken in "Darrin, Gone and Forgotten." (Columbia Pictures Television.)

behavior. Later, back at home, Tabitha mentions she saw Serena, and Darrin figures out his mistake.

No. 146

"Mirror, Mirror on the Wall" (11-7-68)

Written by Lila Garrett and Bernie Kahn. Directed by Richard Michaels. Guest cast: Herb Voland, Sara Seegar.

Endora zaps Darrin into the most self-centered person in the world, just as Larry is dealing with the very conservative Hascomb account. At a Tate dinner party, Darrin and Samantha arrive in dazzling outfits. This intrigues Mrs. Hascomb, who's won over by Sam's argument that her company should go after the youth market. Later Endora removes the vain spell from Darrin, only to have Larry insist Darrin dress wildly to attract more clients.

No. 147

"Samantha's French Pastry" (11-14-68)

Written by Richard Baer. Directed by William Asher. Guest cast: Henry Gibson, Dort Clark, J. Edward McKinley.

When Uncle Arthur tries to make napoleons for dessert, he accidentally zaps up the emperor himself. Samantha passes Napoleon off as her cousin from Paris when Larry wants him to be in a TV detergent commercial. Samantha then persuades Napoleon to blow the TV spot. Unfortunately, Arthur doesn't know how to send Mr. Bonaparte back. When Samantha casually utters the correct incantation, the emperor is zapped back to the past.

Samantha and Uncle Arthur in "Samantha's French Pastry." (Columbia Pictures Television/Nancy Noce/E. Ben Emerson.)

Elizabeth and Henry Gibson as Napoleon in "Samantha's French Pastry." (Roy Cummings.)

No. 148

"Is It Magic or Imagination?" (11-21-68)

Written by Arthur Julian. Directed by Luther James. Guest cast: Dick Wilson.

Darrin is depressed when Barton Industries uses one of Samantha's ideas for its diaper division. Hoping to compensate, Sam leaves Darrin's portfolio—with his slogans enclosed—on Mr. Barton's desk. Darrin and Samantha learn that a computer program has turned down Samantha's campaign, which had been entered in a national contest.

No. 149

"Samantha Fights City Hall" (11-28-68)

Written by Rick Mittleman. Directed by Richard Michaels. Guest cast: Arch Johnson, Vic Tayback, Art Metrano.

Samantha finds out that a neighborhood playground is being torn down and a supermarket will replace it. At first Darrin encourages her to organize a protest until he finds out that the park's owner, Mr. Mossler, is a client. When Sam realizes that Darrin's job is at stake, she withdraws from a rally to stop bulldozers from destroying the park. Yet Darrin insists she keep up the fight, even after Larry fires him. In the end, Sam brings the park's statue of Col. Mossler to life to change Mr. Mossler's mind and Larry gives Darrin his job back.

No. 150

"Samantha Loses Her Voice" (12-5-68)

Written by Lila Garrett and Bernie Kahn. Directed by William Asher.

While Samantha comforts Louise, who's had a fight with Larry, Uncle Arthur switches Sam's and Darrin's voices. The Stephenses frantically try to keep the Tates from discovering what's happened. After many attempts, Uncle Arthur finally removes the spell on Darrin and Sam, and Larry and Louise make up.

No. 151

"I Don't Want to Be a Toad" (12-12-68)

Written by Doug Tibbles. Directed by Richard Michaels. Guest cast: Maudie Prickett, Art Metrano, Paul Sorenson.

When Phyllis enrolls Tabitha in the Delightful Day Nursery School, the little witch changes classmate Amy into a butterfly. Later Samantha chases Amy (the insect) into and up a tree, and then up a skyscraper, before Tabitha changes her friend back. Meanwhile, Tabitha's teacher, Mrs. Burch, is exhausted from what she thinks she sees during these escapades, and goes on a long vacation.

No. 152

"Weep No More, My Willow" (12-19-68)

Written by Michael Morris. Directed by William Asher. Guest cast: Paul Sorenson, Jean Blake.

Dr. Bombay chants a spell to restore Samantha's ailing willow tree and makes it weep with every breeze. This incantation goes awry and instead of the tree, Samantha cries. After many tears, Bombay answers Sam's call and reverses the spell. Darrin comes home and finds Sam and Larry (who thinks the Stephenses are having marital problems) now laughing hysterically. Sam calls Bombay again; he returns to stop the silliness and restore the willow tree.

No. 153

"Instant Courtesy" (12-26-68)

Written by Arthur Alsberg. Directed by R. Robert Rosenbaum. Guest cast: Mala Powers, Herb Voland, Sharon Vaughn.

Endora turns Darrin into a perfect gentleman, which causes client Mrs. Sebastian to be impressed with Darrin's chivalry. In fact, she offers to set him up in his own agency. Later, however, Mrs. Sebastian suspects Darrin's behavior was a ploy to trick her into signing with McMann and Tate. Sam zaps her into changing her mind.

No. 154

"Samantha's Super Maid" (1-2-69)

Written by Peggy Chantler Dick and Douglas Dick. Directed by R. Robert Rosenbaum. Guest cast: Nellie Burt, Virginia Gregg, Nora Marlowe.

Phyllis persuades a reluctant Samantha to hire a maid, and after many applicants are turned down, the sweet, good-hearted Amelia is chosen. However, the Stephenses know she can't stay because of the supernatural state of affairs, yet neither Sam nor Darrin can find the courage to fire her. Samantha then makes certain that Phyllis's very social friend, Mrs. Otis, steals Amelia away from the Stephens household.

No. 155

"Serena Strikes Again" (Part 1, 1-9-69)

Written by Ed Jurist. Directed by Richard Michaels. Guest cast: Nancy Kovack.

Sexy client Clio Venita plays up to Darrin, and Serena thinks the woman is out to make a fool of Samantha. Serena then makes a monkey out of Venita. Very angry, Darrin orders Serena to change Clio back, and then leaves the house. When Serena pops off she leaves the lady a chimp.

Dick York and Nancy Kovack as Miss Vanita in "Serena Strikes Again." (Columbia Pictures Television/Memory Shop/ Dan Weaver.)

No. 156

"Serena Strikes Again" (Part 2, 1-16-69)

Written by Ed Jurist. Directed by Richard Michaels. Guest cast: Nancy Kovack, Cliff Norton, Richard X. Slattery.

Serena returns, but Clio the monkey escapes and has adventures with a boy and his mother, an organ grinder, and the police. After Serena finally changes Clio back, Samantha presents the organ grinder to Ms. Venita in Larry's office, and announces Darrin's slogan: "Don't monkey around with anything but the best. Drink Vino Venita."

No. 157

"One Touch of Midas" (1-23-69)

Written by Jerry Mayer and Paul Friedman. Directed by Richard Michaels. Guest cast: Meg Wyllie, Cliff Norton.

As a favor to Samantha, Endora assists Darrin by conjuring up a foolproof marketing scheme featuring the Fuzz Doll, which automatically charms mortals. When the doll becomes amazingly successful, it looks as if Darrin will become a millionaire. Before he finds out that Endora is behind the "Fuzz," he tenderly promises Samantha that he'll now be able to buy her all the things he couldn't before. Endora then removes the spell at Samantha's request, and Sam confirms she already has everything she wants.

No. 158

"Samantha the Bard" (1-30-69)

Written by Richard Baer. Directed by Richard Michaels. Guest cast: Larry D. Mann, Dick Wilson, Sara Seegar.

Samantha finds herself involuntarily speaking in rhymes when the Stephenses are invited to dinner with the Tates and client Mr. Durfee and his wife. As the night goes on, Larry warns Sam to stop rhyming, as Mr. Durfee has used jingles for years and is reluctant to change. After many tries for an antidote with Dr. Bombay, Sam is cured and announces she spoke in rhymes to prove how irritating they can be. Won over, Durfee asks Larry and Darrin to plan a new campaign.

No. 159

"Samantha, the Sculptress" (2-6-69)

Written by Doug Tibbles. Directed by William Asher. Guest cast: Cliff Norton.

While Darrin and Larry entertain a client, Endora has zapped up a couple of living clay busts of the two ad men, and she places them in the Stephens home. Though Darrin and Samantha fight over who's to blame for her mother's antics, the client, despite this lunacy, quickly signs a contract with McMann and Tate. Endora is then disgusted when Darrin offers his gratitude for help landing the account.

No. 160

"Mrs. Stephens, Where Are You?" (2-13-69)

Written by Peggy Chantler Dick and Douglas Dick. Directed by Richard Michaels. Guest cast: Ruth McDevitt, Hal England.

Resenting Phyllis's catty remarks about Samantha and her family, Serena turns her into a cat. After a dog then chases her up a tree, next-door neighbor Miss Parsons, who has many cats, rescues Phyllis the cat. Samantha finally tracks down her mother-in-law, while Serena entertains Darrin's dad, who's come for his wife. Picking out Phyllis from Miss Parson's batch of cats, Samantha then returns home and asks Serena to change Phyllis back.

Note: A non-Darrin episode.

No. 161

"Marriage, Witches Style" (2-20-69)

Written by Michael Morris. Directed by William Asher. Guest cast: Lloyd Bochner, John Fiedler.

Serena decides she wants to marry a mortal as Samantha has, and she consults a computer dating service. The service matches her with Franklyn Blodgett, who (unknown to Serena) is a warlock and is also looking for a mortal love. Later, when both decide to reveal their true identities, they envision a lifetime of wedded witches' bliss, until Franklyn belittles Serena's magic style.
Note: A non-Darrin episode.

No. 162

"Going Ape" (2-27-69)

Written by Lila Garrett and Bernie Kahn. Directed by Richard Michaels. Guest cast: Lou Antonio, Paul Smith, Danny Bonaduce, Gail Kobe.

Tabitha turns a chimp into a man named Harry, and client Evelyn Tucker names him as the model for her men's cologne line. Later, after posing all morning for commercials, Harry decides that being a man isn't any fun, and the only way he can get out of the contract is to turn the TV studio upside down. Then, before Tabitha changes him back, Samantha explains that he was just launching Darrin's campaign based on wild emotions.
Note: A non-Darrin episode.

No. 163

"Tabitha's Weekend" (3-6-69)

Written by Peggy Chantler Dick and Douglas Dick. Directed by R. Robert Rosenbaum.

To please Phyllis, Frank asks that Tabitha be allowed to spend a weekend at their home. Samantha reluctantly agrees. Later Phyllis is annoyed when Endora pops in and begins to argue with her. Endora then convinces Samantha that Tabitha has turned herself into a cookie because she feels responsible for all the adult fighting. Sam finds her daughter on the table, and makes her change back.
Note: A non-Darrin episode.

No. 164

"The Battle of Burning Oak" (3-13-69)

Written by Pauline and Leo Townsend. Directed by R. Robert Rosenbaum. Guest cast: Edward Andrews, Glenda Farrell, Harriet MacGibbon.

Darrin is being considered for membership in an exclusive club. Endora turns him into a supersnob, and he becomes very enthusiastic about wanting to join. Sam's lunch with the ladies' screening committee doesn't go well. When she realizes Darrin's under a spell, she finds skeletons in every member's closet, and this leads to a relaxation of the rules.

No. 165

"Samantha's Power Failure" (3-20-69)

Written by Lila Garrett and Bernie Kahn. Directed by William Asher. Guest cast: Ron Masak.

Uncle Arthur singing "Dry Bones" in "Samantha's Power Failure." (Elizabeth Montgomery/William Asher collection.)

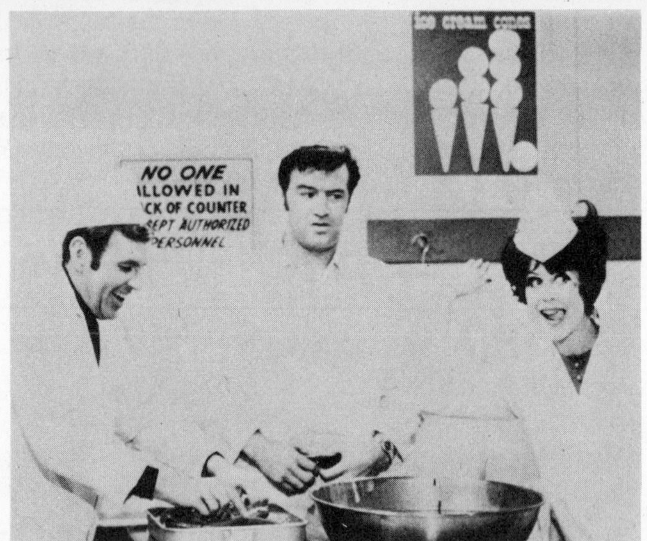

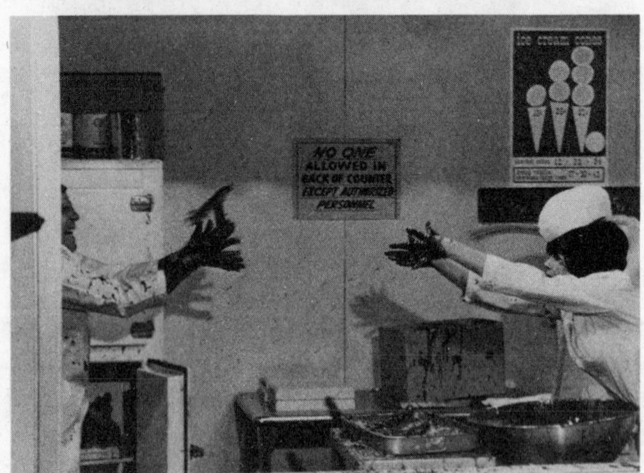

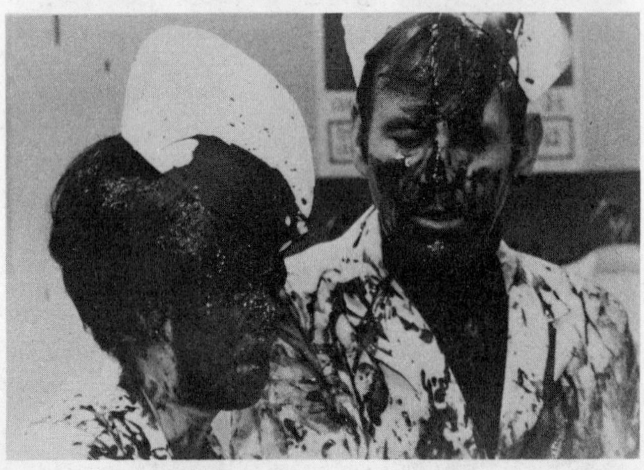

Elizabeth (as Serena), Paul Lynde, and Ron Masak in "Samantha's Power Failure." (Columbia Pictures Television/Nancy Noce.)

Herb Voland as Mr. Haskell in "Samantha Twitches for UNICEF." (Columbia Pictures Television.)

Samantha loses her powers when she refuses to obey the Witches' Council's demand that she give up Darrin. Uncle Arthur and Serena side with her and forfeit their witchcraft as well; then they get mortal jobs at an ice cream store to pass the time. The results are disastrous, and Sam pleads her case before the council, saying that the members are being just as ignorant as those who condemned the innocent of Old Salem who were accused of witchery. Later, power is restored to all supernaturals.
Note: A non-Darrin episode.

No. 166

"Samantha Twitches for UNICEF" (3-27-69)

Written by Ed Jurist. Directed by William Asher. Guest cast: Herb Voland, Sara Seegar, Bernie Kopell (his first episode), Howard Dayton.

Samantha spooks Mr. Haskell, a millionaire, into making good on his $10,000 pledge to UNICEF. Larry thinks Haskell has problems with his very demanding (financially) fianceé. Endora joins in Samantha's plight when she puts a spell on Lila, Haskell's girl friend, so she confesses about another man. Mr. Haskell breaks up with her and gives Sam a check for UNICEF.
Note: A non-Darrin episode.

No. 167

"Daddy Does His Thing" (4-3-69)

Written by Michael Morris. Directed by William Asher. Guest cast: Karl Lukas, Mercedes Moliner.

Maurice turns Darrin into a mule when he refuses a birthday gift of a magical lighter. After Endora refuses to help Maurice change Darrin back, Sam flies to Paris to meet with her father. On returning home, she finds Darrin has been taken to an animal shelter. Sam finally finds Darrin and Maurice changes him back.

No. 168

"Samantha's Good News" (4-10-69)

Written by Richard Baer. Directed by Richard Michaels. Guest cast: Murray Matheson, Janine Gray.

Maurice pops in with a beautiful young witch who claims to be his secretary. Jealous, Endora pops out and returns with John Van Millwood, a warlock who is also a Shakespearean actor. John and Maurice then compete in reciting Shakespeare, and Endora consoles her husband by declaring him the best. Later Sam reveals she's to have another baby.
Note: A non-Darrin episode.

No. 169

"Samantha's Shopping Spree" (4-17-69)

Written by Richard Baer. Directed by Richard Michaels. Guest cast: Steve Franken, Dave Madden, Herb Ellis, Jonathan Daly, Herb Anderson, Jack Collins.

While Samantha, Endora, Tabitha, and Cousin Henry are shopping in a department store, Henry turns a floor salesman into a mannequin. Henry then takes offense and pops off to the moon. When he is located, he refuses to change the dummy back. However, Tabitha remembers the spell Henry used and Endora reverses the trick.

Note: A non-Darrin episode.

No. 170

"Samantha and Darrin in Mexico City" (4-24-69)

Written by John L. Greene. Directed by R. Robert Rosenbaum. Guest cast: Thomas Gomez, Victor Millan.

To introduce client Carlos Aragon's product to the American market, the Stephenses fly to Mexico. While on the plane, Endora casts a spell on Darrin that causes him to disappear every time he speaks Spanish. Sam has her mother remove the spell, but warns Darrin not to speak the language. Later Endora reverses the spell so that Darrin vanishes each time he speaks English. Before Endora removes the zap for good, Samantha magically improvises by allowing Darrin to present a great speech at an ad luncheon meeting with both Spanish and American guests.

Note: Last episode with Dick York.

THE SIXTH SEASON: 1969 to 1970 (Beginning with Dick Sargent as Darrin)

No. 171

"Samantha and the Beanstalk" (9-18-69)

Written by Michael Morris. Directed by Richard Michaels. Guest cast: Ronald Long, Bobo Lewis, Johnny Whitaker, Deacon Jones.

Tabitha becomes jealous of the new baby and switches places with Jack in her storybook, *Jack and the Beanstalk*. While Phyllis is miffed at Jack in the Stephenses' living room, Samantha follows her daughter into the story. Once there, she finds that Tabitha has, among other things, shrunk the tale's giant. Sam then orders Tabitha to return the story to its original form, and Sam, Tabitha, and Jack return to their proper homes.

No. 172

"Samantha's Yoo-Hoo Maid" (9-25-69)

Written by Ed Jurist. Directed by William Asher. Guest cast: J. Edward McKinley.

Endora introduces Esmeralda to Samantha, claiming her daughter needs a maid for the new baby. Against Darrin's objections, Larry brings his client, Mr. Hampton, to the Stephenses' to look over some ad layouts. When Esmeralda sneezes up a unicorn, Darrin incorporates it into the Hampton Motors new car campaign. Later Sam tells Darrin that Esmeralda will show up only when called.

No. 173

"Samantha's Caesar Salad" (10-2-69)

Written by Ed Jurist. Directed by William Asher. Guest cast: Jay Robinson, Herb Ellis, Joyce Easton.

When Larry comes over to discuss ideas for a beauty account, Esmeralda accidentally conjures up Julius Caeser while making a Caeser salad, and she can't send him back. It seems that Caeser does not want to return. Sam conjures up Cleopatra to lure him back. When the client, Mrs. Charday, sees the two historic figures, she approves the ad slogan, "The Great Romances of History," for her beauty line.

No. 174

"Samantha's Curious Cravings" (10-9-69)

Written by Fred Freeman and Lawrence Cohen. Directed by Richard Michaels. Guest cast: William Schallert.

Samantha develops an unusual food problem; it appears whenever she thinks of it. When Dr. Bombay treats her, she ends

Alice Ghostley with Jay Robinson as Caesar in "Samantha's Caesar Salad." (Elizabeth Montgomery/William Asher collection.)

up going to the food instead of making it come to her. Once she calls Darrin from the ballpark with a hot dog in her hand. Bombay confers with Sam's obstetrician, Dr. Anton, and they argue over their diagnoses. Eventually Sam returns home cured.

No. 175

"And Something Makes Four" (10-16-69)

Written by Richard Baer. Directed by Richard Michaels. Guest cast: Art Metrano, Pat Priest, Bobo Lewis.

Samantha and Darrin have a boy, and to make sure that everyone takes to the infant, Maurice casts a love spell around him. Larry then insists the baby is perfect for the label of Berkley Baby Foods and proceeds to bring a camera crew to the hospital for a screen test. When Endora arrives, she helps to convince Maurice that the baby's publicity will not please the Witches' Council, causing Maurice to remove the spell.

No. 176

"Naming Samantha's New Baby" (10-23-69)

Written by Ed Jurist. Directed by William Asher.

Upset that the boy will be named after Frank Stephens, Maurice zaps Darrin into the hall mirror. Both Frank and Phyllis are then astounded when they see their son's reflection in the mirror, which prompts Sam to explain that Maurice has invented a new kind of photo-mirror that retains images. During a money-making discussion over this invention, Frank and Maurice discuss the baby's name. Darrin solves the problem by tricking Maurice into naming the baby Adam. Darrin says he dislikes this name but really prefers it.

Samantha on Halloween in "To Trick or Treat or Not to Trick or Treat." (Columbia Pictures Television.)

No. 177

"To Trick or Treat or Not to Trick or Treat" (10-30-69)

Written by Shirley Gordon. Directed by William Asher. Guest cast: Larry D. Mann, Paul Sorenson, Judy March, Jean Blake.

Darrin and Endora argue over the importance of Halloween, and she transforms him into the stereotypical image of a witch: an old hag with warts and a big nose. Later Darrin apologizes to his mother-in-law, and she leaves and removes the spell. Then, to help save an account, Darrin, Samantha, and the kids go trick-or-treating for UNICEF, whose local chairman happens to be a client. In a solemn moment, Endora realizes that millions of hungry children are more important than her magical whims.

No. 178

"A Bunny for Tabitha" (11-6-69)

Written by Ed Jurist. Directed by William Asher. Guest cast: Bernie Kopell, Carol Wayne, Dick Wilson, Danny Bonaduce.

When Uncle Arthur does a magic trick for Tabitha's birthday party, he conjures up a *Playboy* bunny instead of a rabbit. Client Mr. Sylvester then falls for the bunny and the two secretly leave. Sam and Uncle Arthur show the two are unlikely to get along. The next day, Mr. Sylvester is back with an old girl friend and accepts Darrin's ideas.

No. 179

"Samantha's Secret Spell" (11-13-69)

Written by Ed Jurist. Directed by Richard Michaels. Guest cast: Sid Clute, Bernie Kopell.

When Darrin and Endora argue, she threatens to turn him into a mouse at midnight unless he apologizes. To prevent this, Samantha consults the witch-apothecary, who gives her a spell she must perform without witchcraft. After completing the procedure, Sam avoids having a mouse for a husband.
Note: Remake of No. 39.

No. 180

"Daddy Comes for a Visit" (11-20-69)

Written by Rick Mittleman. Directed by Richard Michaels. Guest cast: John Fiedler, J. Edward McKinley.

Maurice gives Darrin a magic watch in honor of Adam's birth, but Darrin refuses it. Later, however, Maurice persuades him to try the magic life for just one day. Then, when the watch helps

Darrin gather information about a prospective client, he becomes hooked on witchcraft, much to Samantha's dismay.
Note: Part 1 of 2.

No. 181

"Darrin the Warlock" (11-27-69)

Written by Rick Mittleman and Ed Jurist. Directed by Richard Michaels. Guest cast: J. Edward McKinley, John Fiedler, Irene Byatt.

Darrin's newfound powers have Samantha worried, as he continues to enjoy his supernatural ways. Yet when he really becomes power mad at the office with Larry, Darrin decides to give the magic watch back to Maurice. He then presents some original ideas for a campaign he created (without witchcraft); this causes Larry to fire him. In the end Darrin, Sam, and even Maurice agree that Darrin is better off a mortal.
Note: Part 2 of 2

No. 182

"Samantha's Double Mother Trouble" (12-4-69)

Written by Peggy Chantler Dick and Douglas Dick. Directed by David White. Guest cast: Jane Connell.

While reading to Tabitha, Esmeralda sneezes up Mother Goose. At that moment Phyllis arrives, saying she's left Frank. Shortly afterward, Frank comes for his wife, sees Mother Goose, and is charmed, which prompts Samantha to use the "jealous wife" routine to reunite the elder Stephenses. Esmeralda then works on returning Mother Goose to her proper place. Mother Goose does a slow fade-out before Phyllis's eyes.

No. 183

"You're So Agreeable" (12-11-69)

Written by Ed Jurist. Directed by Luther James. Guest cast: Charles Lane, J. Edward McKinley, Bernie Kuby.

Darrin tries to be nice to Endora, but instead gets on her nerves (he's too agreeable). This makes her cast a spell which has him agreeing to everything. Now a real yes-man, Darrin gets fired, so Endora reverses the spell and makes him very disagreeable. When Larry later wants him back, Darrin throws his boss out of the house. However, Sam makes her mother remove the spell just as Darrin is about to accept a new job.

R*oy Roberts and Mabel Albertson as Darrin's parents in "Samantha's Double Mother Trouble." (Elizabeth Montgomery/ William Asher collection.)*

No. 184

"Santa Comes to Visit and Stays and Stays" (12-18-69)

Written by Ed Jurist. Directed by Richard Michaels. Guest cast: Ronald Long.

Esmeralda sneezes up Santa Claus after Tabitha's friend says he doesn't believe in old St. Nick. Then, after Samantha succeeds in getting Gladys and Larry out of the house, she conjures up Santa's elves to help with toys. And when Larry and the Kravitzes see Santa's sleigh on the Stephenses' front lawn, Sam explains it as a Christmas decoration. In further keeping with the spirit, Sam convinces a grouchy Larry that he has the heart for Christmas, which causes him to buy Louise a mink.

No. 185

"Samantha's Better Halves" (1-1-70)

Written by Lila Garrett and Bernie Kahn. Directed by William Asher. Guest cast: Richard Loo, Frances Fong, Debbie Wong.

The Stephenses recall the time when Endora split Darrin in two so that he was able to stay at home and go on vacation at the

Samantha, Darrin, and Larry get into the spirit of Christmas in "Santa Comes to Visit and Stays and Stays." (Columbia Pictures Television.)

same time. This happens again: while Darrin No. 1 takes care of Samantha and attends to her every need, Darrin No. 2 talks business with Mr. Tanaka. Later Mr. Tanaka finally meets the total Darrin.

Note: First episode Dick Sargent filmed. Remake of No. 69.

No. 186

"Samantha's Lost Weekend" (1-8-70)

Written by Richard Baer. Directed by Richard Michaels. Guest cast: Pat Priest, Bernie Kopell.

Samantha accidentally drinks a glass of milk hexed by Esmeralda, who intended it to help Tabitha's poor appetite. Now Sam can't stop eating. With the help of Dr. Bombay, she breaks the overeating habit, but then continually falls asleep. Once Bombay and Esmeralda confer, the apothecary prescribes the proper antidote.

No. 187

"The Phrase Is Familiar" (1-15-70)

Written by Jerry Mayer. Directed by Richard Michaels. Guest cast: Jay Robinson, Cliff Norton, Todd Baron.

At the same time that Endora causes Darrin to speak in clichés, she introduces Sam and Darrin to a warlock-tutor, who conjures up the Artful Dodger from *Oliver Twist*. Making matters worse, Larry threatens to fire Darrin unless he comes up with more original ideas for a campaign. The situation is solved by Samantha's pretend-it-never-happened plan after Darrin and client Mr. Sommers are seen in Mets uniforms.

No. 188

"Samantha's Secret Is Discovered" (1-22-70)

Written by Lila Garrett and Bernie Kahn. Directed by William Asher. Guest cast: Bernie Kopell, Nydia Westman.

After Phyllis sees Samantha and Endora work some magic with the living room furniture, she thinks she's losing her mind. Samantha then decides to tell her mother-in-law that she is a witch. At first, Phyllis is calm, but when Frank arrives, she can't wait to tell him. Samantha then tries to spill the magic beans to Frank as well, but the Witches' Council has taken her powers away. This time, Phyllis really thinks she's gone off the deep end, and she commits herself to a nursing home. Sam then convinces Phyllis that she was taking hallucinogens instead of tranquilizers.

No. 189

"Tabitha's Very Own Samantha" (1-29-70)

Written by Shirley Gordon. Directed by William Asher. Guest cast: Sara Seegar, Parley Baer, Kay Elliott.

Tabitha is upset because she now has to share Samantha with Adam, so she creates her "very own mother," one who gives her undivided attention. During a disastrous dinner party with a client and his wife and both "mothers," and after Gladys encounters Tabitha and the duplicate Sam at the park, Sam persuades her daughter to zap away the other "mommy" and explains she loves her equally as much as Adam.

No. 190

"Super Arthur" (2-5-70)

Written by Ed Jurist. Directed by Richard Michaels. Guest cast: Paul Smith, Bernie Kuby.

Despite Darrin's pleas, Uncle Arthur pops in and out of every mirror in the house, breaking each one. Sam then decides Arthur is ill and calls Dr. Bombay, who prescribes a pill that has dreadful side effects: everything Arthur thinks of, he becomes—specifically, Superman. As Super Arthur flies around the neighborhood, Darrin and Larry arrive, and Samantha suggests it's all a stunt to promote Darrin's new slogan.

No. 191

"What Makes Darrin Run" (2-12-70)

Written by Lila Garrett and Bernie Kahn. Directed by William Asher. Guest cast: Leon Ames, Arch Johnson, Jeanne Sorel, Jerry Rush.

Endora casts an ambition spell on Darrin, causing him to become obsessed with work. He tries to undermine Larry's position in the firm before Endora finally removes the spell. Consequently, Darrin has to do some fast talking to restore Mr. McMann's faith in Larry.

No. 192

"Serena Stops the Show" (2-19-70)

Written by Richard Baer. Directed by Richard Michaels. Guest cast: Tommy Boyce, Bobby Hart, Art Metrano.

As chairperson for the Cosmos Cotillion, Serena seeks to hire Darrin's clients, the musicians Boyce and Hart, for the witches' annual dinner dance. However, when she approaches the duo, they decline, which prompts her to cast a spell making them unpopular. As a result, they're desperate for business and comply with Serena's request. Then, after they play the cotillion, Samantha demands that Serena send them back to Earth and restore their success.

Note: This was the first segment with the Pandora Spocks credit listing.

No. 193

"Just a Kid Again" (2-26-70)

Written by Jerry Mayer. Directed by Richard Michaels. Guest cast: Ron Masak, Pat Priest, Lindsay Workman.

Hearing that department store salesman Irving Bates wants to be a kid again, Tabitha twitches him into a nine-year-old boy. Once Samantha finds this out, she orders her daughter to reverse the spell. Unfortunately, Irving is enjoying his new youth, and the incantation is useless. Sam then persuades Irving to return to adulthood and his adult girl friend.

Serena discusses the Cosmos Cotillion with Boyce and Hart's music manager in "Serena Stops the Show." (Columbia Pictures Television.)

No. 194

"The Generation Zap" (3-5-70)

Written by Ed Jurist. Directed by William Asher. Guest cast: Melodie Johnson, Arch Johnson (not related).

Unaware that Endora cast a spell to make a client's daughter, Dusty Harrison, fall in love with Darrin, Samantha becomes jealous. In the meantime, Dusty's father cancels his account with McMann and Tate. After Endora removes the love spell, the Stephenses learn from a TV newscast that Mr. Harrison has been indicted for embezzlement.

Note: Partial remake of No. 8.

No. 195

"Okay, Who's the Wise Witch?" (3-12-70)

Written by Richard Baer. Directed by Richard Michaels.

A vapor lock caused by Samantha's nonuse of her powers seals the Stephenses, Endora, Esmeralda, and Dr. Bombay in the house. There is a cure, but it must be performed outside the home. Consequently, Sam magically photographs Dr. Bombay and slides his picture under the front door. Once on the outside, Sam three-dimensionalizes Bombay, who incants a spell releasing the house and everyone in it.

No. 196

"A Chance on Love" (3-19-70)

Written by John L. Greene. Directed by Richard Michaels. Guest cast: Jack Cassidy, Molly Dodd, and Bernie Kuby.

When client Mr. Dinsdale falls for Serena, he thinks she's Samantha. Later, Sam insists that Serena explain their relationship to Dinsdale, who refuses to believe it. As a result, he takes Darrin off his account. Later, on a visit to the Stephenses, he encounters both Sam and Serena. Now convinced of the truth, Dinsdale puts Darrin back on his campaign.
Note: Remake of No. 3. Remade as No. 196.

No. 197

"If the Shoe Pinches" (3-26-70)

Written by Ed Jurist. Directed by William Asher. Guest cast: Henry Gibson.

Endora sends a leprechaun to make trouble for Darrin. The leprechaun makes Darrin's nose grow and gives him ears like a donkey's. After the little green man gives Darrin a pair of shoes that makes him lazy, Sam concocts a potion to gain control over leprechauns.

No. 198

"Mona Sammy" (4-2-70)

Written by Michael Morris. Directed by William Asher.

When Larry and Louise see a *Mona Lisa* type of painting of Samantha, the Stephenses claim Darrin was the artist. It's actually a gift from Endora, who says the picture is of Sam's grand-aunt Cornelia. Meanwhile, Louise asks Darrin if he'll paint a portrait of her. That night at the Tates', Sam zaps Darrin into an artist, only to have Endora appear and counter-zap his hands into creating an unsightly rendering of Louise. After tears and much confusion, the Stephenses give Louise a more flattering portrait.

No. 199

"Turn on the Old Charm" (4-9-70)

Written by Richard Baer. Directed by Richard Michaels. Guest cast: John Fiedler.

Samantha gives Darrin a magic amulet that causes Endora to be extremely courteous in his company. But when Endora finds out about the charm, she punishes both of them, making them constantly bicker. This does not sit well with Larry or client Mr.

Samantha's portrait in "Mona Sammy." (Columbia Pictures Television/Milton T. Moore, Jr.)

Sunshine, who owns a greeting card company, as both are unimpressed with the Stephenses' steady arguing. Later, after Endora removes the spell, Sam presents a new way to sell cards: use insults instead of poetry.

No. 200

"Make Love, Not Hate" (4-16-70)

Written by Ed Jurist. Directed by William Asher. Guest cast: Sara Seegar, Charles Lane, Cliff Norton.

Dr. Bombay concocts a potion to help Esmeralda find a man, but ends up creating havoc at the Stephenses' dinner party when Samantha accidentally pours the serum into some clam dip. Consequently, a warlock falls for Sam, the client's wife falls for Larry, and the once-shy Esmeralda falls for Darrin. Later, Sam corrects the love-fest fiasco.

Samantha and Darrin balance themselves after Hepzibah casts a spell in "To Go or Not to Go, That Is the Question." (Columbia Pictures Television.)

THE SEVENTH SEASON: 1970 to 1971

No. 201

"To Go or Not to Go, That Is the Question" (9-24-70)

Written by Michael Morris. Directed by William Asher. Guest cast: Jane Connell.

Despite Endora's warning, Samantha refuses to go to the Witches' Convention in Salem unless Darrin is allowed to accompany her. This infuriates Hepzibah, the High Priestess of All Witches, who then pops in and dethrones Darrin in his own home. After a time, Hepzibah learns to tolerate the mortal of the house, and decides to observe the mixed marriage rather than dissolve it, as she had originally planned.

Note: Part 1 of 2.

Endora and Hepzibah in "To Go or Not to Go." (Columbia Pictures Television.)

No. 202

"Salem, Here We Come" (10-1-70)

Written by Michael Morris. Directed by William Asher. Guest cast: Jane Connell, Cesar Romero, Ray Young.

During her study of the Stephenses' marriage, Hepzibah chooses to observe Darrin at work. While remaining invisible at McMann and Tate, she takes a liking to client Ernest Hitchcock, who owns an airline. She feels Hitchcock is a vastly superior mortal and begins to date him. Sam uses this situation to her advantage and persuades Hepzibah to allow Darrin to come to Salem with her.

Note: Part 2 of 2.

David White and Cesar Romero in "Salem, Here We Come." (Columbia Pictures Television.)

No. 203

"The Salem Saga" (10-8-70)

Written by Ed Jurist. Directed by William Asher. Guest cast: Joan Hotchkis, Ron Masak, Richard X. Slattery.

During a tour of the House of the Seven Gables in Salem, a spooked bed warmer begins to follow the Stephenses. It takes a particular liking to Samantha and seems to despise Darrin. When Samantha tries to find out more about the haunted antique piece, she pulls it aside and begins to talk to it, puzzling the tour guide. The bed warmer then follows Sam and Darrin to their hotel room, and Darrin is accused of stealing it.
Note: Part 1 of 2.

No. 204

"Samantha's Hot Bed Warmer" (10-15-70)

Written by Ed Jurist. Directed by William Asher. Guest cast: Noam Pitlik, Dick Wilson, Ron Masak, Joan Hotchkis.

Desperate for answers about the bed warmer while Darrin sits in jail, Samantha learns that the piece is actually a warlock who was transformed by Serena centuries earlier. Consequently, Sam calls upon her cousin to review the steps leading up to the transformation. Serena then goes back in time to old Salem, where she meets Newton, a warlock, who pesters her into zapping

Samantha at the witches' convention in "Sam's Hot Bed Warmer." (Columbia Pictures Television.)

him into the bed warmer. On returning to present-day Salem, she remembers how to turn the bed warmer back into Newton, just in time to release Darrin from jail.
Note: Part 2 of 2.

No. 205

"Darrin on a Pedestal" (10-22-70)

Written by Bernie Kahn. Directed by William Asher. Guest cast: Robert Brown.

While in Gloucester, Massachusetts, Serena becomes upset with Darrin and turns him into a statue of the famed Helmsman, whom she brings to life. When Larry notices the statue's resemblance to Darrin, Samantha denies it, claiming it has different facial features. In the meanwhile, Serena is off gallivanting with her man from the sea until Samantha persuades her to defreeze Darrin and return the statue.

Bill Asher and Robert Brown between takes of "Darrin on a Pedestal." (Photo courtesy of Robert Brown.)

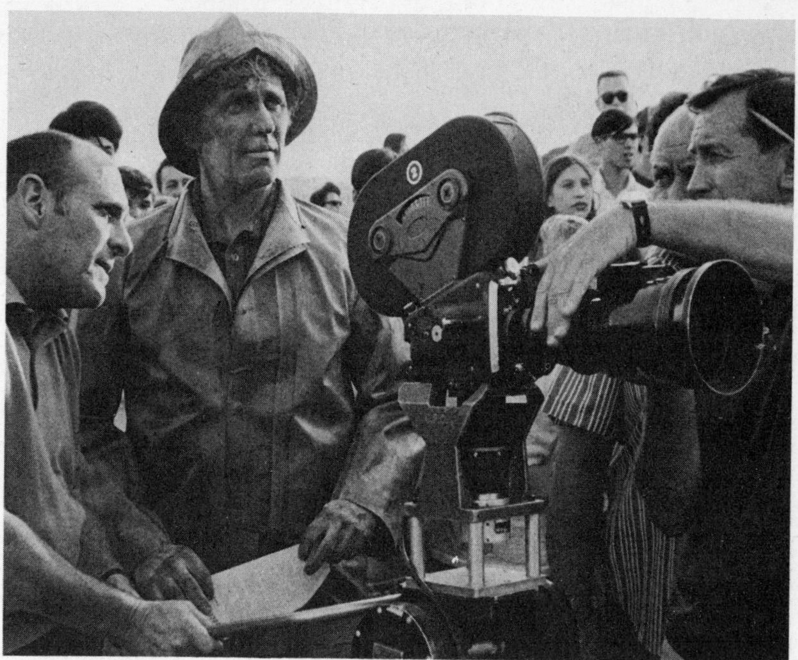

No. 206

"Paul Revere Rides Again" (10-29-70)

Written by Philip and Henry Sharp. Directed by Richard Michaels. Guest cast: Bert Convy, Jonathan Harris, Parley Baer, Ron Masak.

When Samantha asks Esmeralda to return a classic Paul Revere teapot to Salem—it had mistakenly been zapped to Connecticut—the witch-maid conjures up the historical figure. This does not sit well with Darrin, who is meeting with client Sir Leslie Bancroft. When Paul and his horse appear in the Stephenses' hotel room, Darrin convinces Sir Leslie that the silversmith-patriot is part of a campaign.

No. 207

"Samantha's Bad Day in Salem" (11-5-70)

Written by Michael Morris. Directed by William Asher. Guest cast: Hal England, Anne Seymour, Bernie Kuby.

The Stephenses' marriage is again threatened by Samantha's childhood warlock friend Waldo, who still has a mad crush on her. When Sam rejects his affections, Waldo zaps up a robotlike replica of her. Larry sees this robot and thinks that Sam and Darrin are breaking up. In the meantime, Waldo has turned Darrin into a crow, and is doing the same to Larry when Sam explains that the robot was, in fact, Serena.

No. 208

"Samantha's Old Salem Trip" (11-12-70)

Written by Ed Jurist. Directed by Richard Michaels. Guest cast: Maudie Prickett, Ronald Long, James Westfield.

The Stephenses return home to Connecticut, but Esmeralda feels Samantha should have stayed in Salem. She accidentally sends Sam back to the seventeenth century. Darrin has to retrieve his wife, and Esmeralda then whisks him into the past as well. On his arrival, Sam does not recognize him. And when he tries to write her a note with a modern ballpoint pen, he's accused of being a witch. After he persuades Sam to follow a certain magic recall procedure explained by Esmeralda, he and Sam return to the present.

No. 209

"Samantha's Pet Warlock" (11-19-70)

Written by Jerry Mayer. Directed by Richard Michaels. Guest cast: Edward Andrews, Noam Pitlik, David Huddleston.

An egotistical former boyfriend of Samantha's, a warlock named Ashley, pursues her and tries to persuade her to run away with him. When she rejects his amorous advances, he turns himself into a dog. At first this animal upsets Darrin and complicates his efforts to convince client Mr. Gibbons, a dog food manufacturer, that he really loves man's best friend. This changes later, as Ashley helps Darrin win the account.

Note: Partial remake of No. 70.

No. 210

"Samantha's Old Man" (12-3-70)

Written by Michael Morris. Directed by Richard Michaels. Guest cast: Ruth McDevitt, Edward Platt.

To prove to Samantha that her love for Darrin is a temporary thing, Endora turns him into a seventy-three-year-old man. When Larry and Louise come over, Sam and Darrin convince them that they are meeting Darrin's grandfather, Grover Stephens. This prompts Louise to fix Grover up with her aunt Millicent. After a disastrous outing at the drive-in with the Stephenses, the Tates, and Millicent, Endora changes Darrin back—however, not before Samantha convinces Darrin that she will grow old with him the mortal way.

Note: Emmy nomination for makeup.

Darrin and Samantha in "Samantha's Old Man." (Columbia Pictures Television.)

No. 211

"The Corsican Cousins" (12-10-70)

Written by Ed Jurist. Directed by Richard Michaels. Guest cast: Ann Doran, Barbara Morrison.

After Sam's negative reaction to Darrin's client-induced suggestion to join a country club, Endora tries to persuade her to be more fun loving like Serena. When Samantha rejects this idea, Endora casts a Corsican Brothers type of spell on both cousins, allowing Sam to experience everything Serena does. This creates trouble when the wife of a club member (also a client) pays a visit to inspect the Stephens home life and finds Samantha acting a little bizarre. Endora then removes the act-alike spell from the cousins.

Dr. Bombay assists Sam and Darrin in "Samantha's Magic Potion." (Columbia Pictures Television/ Memory Shop.)

No. 212

"Samantha's Magic Potion" (12-17-70)

Written by Shirley Gordon. Directed by William Asher. Guest cast: Charles Lane.

Darrin thinks that Endora's black magic is at work when he experiences a slump at work. When he finds out the truth, he decides to finally surrender to his wife's witchy lifestyle. Sam then tricks him with a bogus confidence-building potion. Later, after winning over a grouchy client, he realizes that it isn't any fun to be the master of every situation. At this point, Sam admits that he won the account all on his own—without the help of witchcraft.

No. 213

"Sisters at Heart" (12-24-70)

Teleplay by Barbara Avedon and William Asher; Story by Fifth Period English class, Thomas Jefferson High School, 1970.

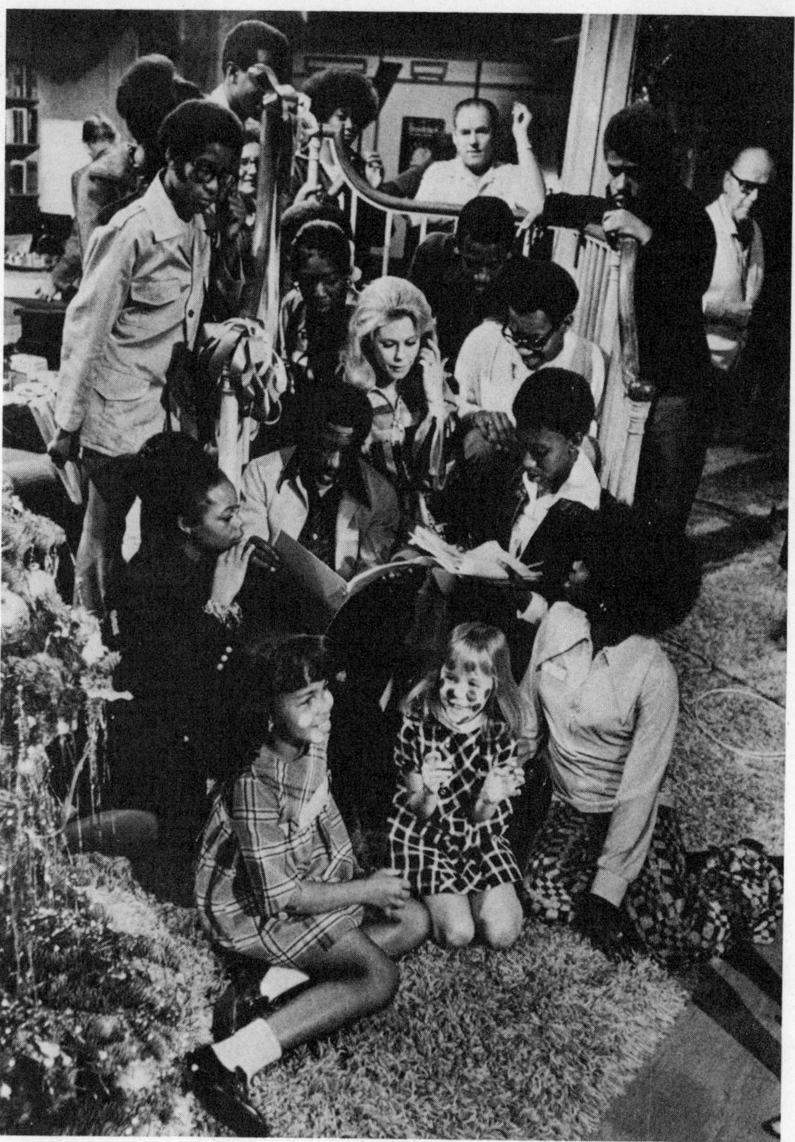

Elizabeth, Erin Murphy, and the cast and crew of "Sisters at Heart." *(Courtesy of* TV Guide.)

Directed by William Asher. Guest cast: Don Marshall, Parley Baer.

Hurt by a negative remark heard in the park, Tabitha and her friend, Lisa, who is black, wish they could be sisters. Tabitha then twitchingly obliges by accidentally placing black and white polka dots on herself and Lisa. As Samantha calls Dr. Bombay, the bigoted client Mr. Brockway is on his way over to make sure Darrin runs a tight ship. Later, after Brockway shows his ignorance, Samantha convinces Tabitha and Lisa that they don't have to look like each other to be sisters.

No. 214

"Mother-in-Law of the Year" (1-14-71)

Written by Philip and Henry Sharp. Directed by William Asher. Guest cast: John McGiver, Jim Lange, Robert Q. Lewis.

Endora promotes herself as the ideal spokesperson for the Bobbins Candy Company campaign that Darrin is arranging. As a result, she is chosen Mother-in-Law of the Year. However, when she fails to show up for a TV commercial advertising Bobbins Bonbons, Samantha impersonates her. This infuriates Endora, who materializes as Samantha during the commercial shoot. Now everyone at the studio is seeing double while Darrin is seeing red. Finally Darrin convinces his client that the ad spot should be considered a special effect.

No. 215

"Mary, the Good Fairy" (1-21-71)

Written by Ed Jurist. Directed by William Asher. Guest cast: Imogene Coca.

Mary, the Good Fairy, an old friend of Samantha's, comes by the Stephens home to collect Tabitha's lost tooth. As she and Sam reminisce about old times, Mary explains that she caught a cold

Elizabeth and Imogene Coca as the good fairy in "Mary, the Good Fairy." (Elizabeth Montgomery/ William Asher collection.)

while flying over a wheat field. To warm up a bit, Mary then has a shot of brandy. Unfortunately, she has a little too much to drink, and Samantha ends up collecting coins in Mary's place.
Note: Part 1 of 2.

No. 216

"The Good Fairy Strikes Again" (1-28-71)

Written by Ed Jurist. Directed by William Asher. Guest cast: Imogene Coca, Vic Tayback, Herb Voland, Howard Smith.

As Samantha tires of donning wings and having the nightly job of placing money under children's pillows after they lose their teeth, she tries to persuade Mary to return to her "Good Fairy" chores. In the meantime, Darrin is working on a slogan for a "Reducealator," a contraption that Sam uses to cover her wings. Fortunately for all, Mary helps Darrin win the account and then flies away.
Note: Part 2 of 2.

Samantha as the good fairy in "The Good Fairy Strikes Again." (Elizabeth Montgomery/William Asher collection.)

Dick Sargent as Darrin's great ancestor in "Return of Darrin the Bold." (Columbia Pictures Television/Memory Shop.)

No. 217

"Return of Darrin the Bold" (2-4-71)

Written by Ed Jurist. Directed by Richard Michaels. Guest cast: David Huddleston, Gordon Jump, Richard X. Slattery.

Endora and Serena retrieve a potion from a wise old warlock so as to transform Darrin into a warlock. The spell requires Serena to travel to fourteenth-century Ireland, pluck the beard of Darrin's ancestor, Darrin the Bold, and mix his hairs in the potion. Back in the twentieth century, Darrin starts wishing things away, in particular a bush belonging to next-door neighbor Mr. Ferguson. Samantha then returns to the fourteenth century, and restores her husband's mortality and Ferguson's bush.

No. 218

"The House that Uncle Arthur Built" (2-11-71)

Written by Bernie Kahn. Directed by Richard Michaels. Guest cast: J. Edward McKinley, Barbara Rhoades, Ysabel MacCloskey.

To win the heart of his snobbish girl friend, the witch Aretha, Uncle Arthur transfers all practical jokes into the Stephens house. Some tricks include a floating boxing glove that punches Larry and a bunch of monkeys that unsettle a client and his wife. Later, to the delight of all, Samantha convinces Uncle Arthur that Aretha is not worth his efforts, and persuades him to return the house to normal.

Note: The last Uncle Arthur episode.

No. 219

"Samantha and the Troll" (2-18-71)

Written by Lila Garrett and Joel Rapp. Directed by William Asher. Guest cast: Robert Cummings, Nan Martin.

While Samantha goes in for her 10,000-spell checkup, Serena takes her place at home. When Darrin fails to derail a party with Larry and hair tonic client Mr. Berkley, Serena brings Tabitha's toys to life. Sam returns and introduces one of the animated creatures, a troll, as Harry. Berkley then assumes Harry is part of Darrin's campaign.

No. 220

"This Little Piggie" (2-25-71)

Written by Ed Jurist. Directed by Richard Michaels. Guest cast: Herb Edelman, Ysabel MacCloskey.

When Endora thinks Darrin is being pigheaded, she casts a spell that makes him indecisive and gives him the head of a pig. This all happens at a most inopportune time, as client Colonel Brigham, who specializes in spareribs, comes to the house with Larry. As they arrive, Darrin has been zapped to the top of the house by Endora. Thinking quickly, Samantha explains that Darrin is modeling a new way to advertise Brigham's ribs, and the client loves the idea.

No. 221

"Mixed Doubles" (3-4-71)

Written by Richard Baer. Directed by William Asher. Guest cast: Natalie Core.

Samantha spends a restless night worrying about Louise, who she thinks may be having trouble with Larry. The next day Sam finds herself in bed with Larry, while Louise is in bed with Darrin. Larry sees Sam as Louise, while Darrin sees Louise as Sam, and Sam is the only one who's aware of this. Then, as Dr. Bombay is summoned to relieve the situation, Sam convinces Darrin of what's happened, and the "real" Stephenses invite the Tates over for a small party. Dr. Bombay finally resolves the confusion, explaining that it was caused by a dream inversion. Sam becomes Sam and Louise becomes Louise.

No. 222

"Darrin Goes Ape" (3-11-71)

Written by Leo and Pauline Townsend. Directed by Richard Michaels. Guest cast: Herb Vigran, Sid Clute, Allen Jenkins, Paul Smith, Janos Prohaska, Ysabel MacClosky.

Posing as Samantha, Serena turns Darrin into a gorilla, and he runs amok in the neighborhood. At her wits' end, Gladys calls the police, who notify the Johnson brothers of Johnson's Jungle Isle. Fortunately, Samantha rescues Darrin from this circus show just as Tillie, a fellow female ape hitched up with the Johnsons, is getting romantic with Darrin.

No. 223

"Money Happy Returns" (3-18-71)

Written by Milt Rosen. Directed by Richard Michaels. Guest cast: Arch Johnson, Karl Lukas, Allen Jenkins.

When Darrin finds thousands of dollars in a taxi, he thinks Endora has zapped it up for him. When she denies it, he doesn't believe her. Consequently, he and Samantha have a fight, and she leaves. Later Sam returns only to find Darrin in trouble with thieves who had left their stolen money in the cab. And while Larry thinks Darrin is negotiating with a new ad firm, Sam tricks the crooks into being hauled off by the police.

No. 224

"Out of the Mouths of Babes" (3-25-71)

Written by Michael Morris. Directed by Richard Michaels. Guest cast: David Huddleston.

When Endora transforms Darrin into a ten-year-old boy, he meets a youngster named Herbie, who inspires a new ad campaign for Mother Flanagan's Irish Stew. When Endora gets wind of this, she is disgusted and returns Darrin to adulthood. However, Her-

bie later needs the young Darrin's basketball skills to play against a winning neighborhood team. With Darrin's consent, Samantha magically obliges by making him a child again to play.
Note: Remake of No. 46.

No. 225

"Sam's Psychic Slip" (4-1-71)

Written by John L. Greene. Directed by William Asher. Guest cast: Irwin Charone, Irene Byatt.

After Darrin gives Sam a bracelet to celebrate thirty days without witchcraft, Samantha feels guilty when she develops a magic case of the hiccups—every time she hiccups, bikes of all kinds appear. Even though Dr. Bombay supposedly treats her, a department store necklace disappears when she passes by it while shopping with Darrin's mother. As a result, both ladies are accused of shoplifting. Serena then helps Darrin contact Dr. Bombay again, who, in turn, helps to find Sam. Dr. Bombay finally offers the correct cure.

No. 226

"Samantha's Magic Mirror" (4-8-71)

Written by Ed Jurist. Directed by Richard Michaels. Guest cast: Tom Bosley, Nancy Priddy.

Esmeralda asks Samantha to help her with magic so she can impress her boyfriend Ferdy, a warlock, so that he will marry her. Without Esmeralda's knowledge, Sam zaps up a more attractive mirror double to boost Esmeralda's ego. When Ferdy arrives, his powers prove just as deficient, and the couple find humor in their situation and comfort in each other's arms.
Note: Remake of No. 47.

No. 227

"Laugh, Clown, Laugh" (4-15-71)

Written by Ed Jurist. Directed by William Asher. Guest cast: Charles Lane, Ysabel MacCloskey, Marcia Wallace.

Endora makes Darrin such an obnoxious humorist that Larry sends him home. Samantha then demands that Endora take the spell off. She does so, only to replace it with another spell, one that makes Darrin tell a joke whenever he hears something sad. This does not sit well with the ever-serious insurance client Mr. Jameson, who takes offense at Darrin's inappropriate humor. However, Sam and Darrin later convince him that his approach to selling insurance is too serious, and that he should lighten up.

Agnes Moorehead as Endora in "Laugh, Clown, Laugh." (Columbia Pictures Television.)

No. 228

"Samantha and the Antique Doll" (4-22-71)

Written by Ed Jurist. Directed by Richard Michaels.

When Phyllis sees Tabitha and Adam using their powers, Samantha leads her to believe that her subconscious willed the magic to happen. Later, when Frank questions his wife's sanity, Samantha makes Phyllis think she's turned her husband into a mule. Then, during a séance, Samantha persuades her mother-in-law to give up her powers, since it is the only way to transform Frank back. When Phyllis complies, Sam changes Frank back to a man.

THE EIGHTH SEASON: 1971 to 1972

No. 229

"How Not to Lose Your Head to King Henry VIII" (Part 1, 9-15-71)

Written by Ed Jurist. Directed by William Asher. Guest cast: Ronald Long, Ivor Barry, Laurie Main.

As the Stephens begin a European business-pleasure trip, they first visit the Tower of London, where Samantha notices a nobleman trapped in a portrait. When she frees him, Malvina, the witch who imprisoned him there via a curse, gets angry and zaps

Ronald Long guest stars in "How Not to Lose Your Head to King Henry VIII." (Columbia Pictures Television.)

Samantha and Darrin in King Henry's court in "How Not to Lose Your Head . . ." (Columbia Pictures Television/Dan Weaver collection.)

Samantha back to the court of King Henry VIII. As part of a traveling minstrel show, Sam then attracts the attention of the King himself. Back in the twentieth century, Darrin and Endora worry about Sam, who could literally lose her head, so Endora zaps Darrin back to save his wife.

No. 230

"How Not to Lose Your Head to King Henry VIII" (Part 2, 9-22-71)

Written by Ed Jurist. Directed by William Asher. Guest cast: Ronald Long, Ivor Barry, Henry Oliver.

Darrin arrives at the King's court just as Samantha is about to be married (and possibly beheaded). Due to the time change, and the fact that she's under a spell, Samantha doesn't recognize her husband. However, when he is later hurt during a wrestling match with the King, she offers him a sympathetic kiss, thus restoring his memory and breaking the spell. Darrin, Sam, and Endora, who's also zapped herself back to the sixteenth century to help, return to the present.

No. 231

"Samantha and the Loch Ness Monster" (9-29-71)

Written by Michael Morris. Directed by William Asher. Guest cast: Steve Franken, Don Knight, Bernie Kopell.

While at Loch Ness, Scotland, the Stephenses meet up with the legendary Loch Ness Monster, who's really an old friend of Serena's, a warlock named Bruce, whom she had transformed ages ago because he was getting on her nerves. All is almost forgiven when Serena changes Bruce back to his original form, but then he makes her a mermaid. To trick Bruce into ridding Serena of her fish garb, Samantha leads him to believe that Serena the Mermaid will be more popular than the Loch Ness Monster. This causes Bruce to remove Serena's fins and return to the lake as his alter ego.

No. 232

"Samantha's Not-So-Leaning Tower of Pisa" (10-6-71)

Written by Ed Jurist. Directed by William Asher. Guest cast: John Rico, Steve Conte.

When Sam and Darrin are in Pisa, Italy, Esmeralda appears from home to report some mishaps with the children. She then

Samantha with Alice Ghostley as Esmeralda and Robert Casper in "Samantha's Not-So-Leaning Tower of Pisa." (Columbia Pictures Television/Dan Weaver collection.)

begins to recollect that it was she who caused the famous Italian city's tower to lean. Reliving a depressing encounter with the tower's builder, Bonano Pisano, Esmeralda restores the historic landmark, causing havoc in Pisa. To make it lean again, Sam and Esmeralda return to Pisano's time and make the tower lean.

No. 233

"Bewitched, Bothered and Baldoni" (10-13-71)

Written by Michael Morris. Directed by William Asher. Guest cast: Francine York, Michael Taylor, Al Molinaro, Lou Krugman.

While in Rome, Endora brings a statue of Venus alive to test Darrin's love for Samantha. The figure, now a woman named Vanessa, persuades Darrin to hire her as his and Sam's villa maid. To counter her mother's work, Sam then brings an Adonis statue to life, now a man called Alberto. And after a very confusing house meeting with a client and his wife, Endora and Sam return the two lifelike statues to their original form, though not before Darrin has proved his love for Sam.

No. 234

"Paris, Witches Style" (10-20-71)

Written by Michael Morris. Directed by William Asher. Guest cast: Maurice Marsac, Carl Don.

While in Paris, Sam fears her father's anger when Maurice discovers his daughter has been traveling in Europe without seeing him. As a result, he sets out to punish Darrin, whom he blames for the situation. In a rare turn, Endora decides to protect Darrin by zapping up a duplicate version of him, one that is pleasant and charming to Maurice. All goes well until the real Darrin shows up. Maurice is furious and zaps Darrin to the top of the Eiffel Tower. However, Darrin's client, Mr. Sagan, of Europa Tours, is later convinced that a picture of Darrin on the tower is part of a wonderful campaign for his company.

No. 235

"The Ghost Who Made a Spectre of Himself" (10-27-71)

Written by Ed Jurist. Directed by William Asher. Guest cast: Patrick Horgan, Maurice Dallimore.

When the Stephenses spend the weekend with the Tates in a haunted English castle, an amorous ghost causes problems for Samantha when he zaps himself into Darrin's body and refuses to leave. Louise believes the Stephenses are having an argument and thinks Darrin is flirting with *her* (it's the ghost). The argument actually consists of Sam demanding that the specter vacate her husband's body. He refuses, so she conjures up a former girl friend of the ghost's, and that straightens things out.

No. 236

"TV or Not TV" (11-3-71)

Written by Bernie Kahn. Directed by William Asher. Guest cast: Wanda Hendrix, Robert Q. Lewis.

Sam and Darrin worry that Tabitha may become a television star when she makes an unexpected appearance on a children's show. In fact, she's so impressive, she's asked to be a regular. When Tabitha tires of the daily grind of television work, Samantha

Samantha and Tabitha in "TV or Not TV." (Columbia Pictures Television/Milton T. Moore, Jr.)

suggests that she flub her lines. Sam then looks for a replacement for the show, and finds the daughter of a client, who also happens to be the show's sponsor.

No. 237

"A Plague on Maurice and Samantha" (11-10-71)

Written by Ed Jurist. Directed by Richard Michaels. Guest cast: Bernie Kopell, J. Edward McKinley, Susan Hathaway.

When Sam loses her powers (because of her frequent contact with mortals), Dr. Bombay explains that any witch or warlock who kisses her will be infected as well. Problems arise when Maurice visits, and he falls ill to the disease. Dr. Bombay finds a cure—but not before Maurice kisses Endora and infects her. But he saves half the antidote for her.

No. 238

"Hansel and Gretel in Samanthaland" (11-17-71)

Written by Michael Morris. Directed by Richard Michaels. Guest cast: Bobo Lewis, Billie Hayes, Eric Chase, Cindy Henderson.

Tabitha zaps the classic fairy tale characters Hansel and Gretel into her parents' life, while she disappears into their storybook. Meanwhile, Larry and Louise are visiting, and they become confused about these two odd children. Samantha then pops into the story and confronts Hansel and Gretel's archrival, the Wicked Witch, who has captured Tabitha. Samantha rescues her daughter, and they both return to real life; Tabitha sends the two make-believe children back to the book.

No. 239

"The Warlock in the Gray Flannel Suit" (12-1-71)

Written by John L. Greene. Directed by Richard Michaels. Guest cast: Bernie Kopell, Charles Lane, Samantha Scott.

Angry because Darrin won't let Sam attend her cousin Panda's wedding, Endora enlists the aid of a hippie warlock named Alonzo. He poses as a copywriter at McMann and Tate and puts Darrin's job in jeopardy. Alonzo then casts a spell over Larry to make him fall for his bogus slogan for the Monticello Carpet account. With Samantha's help, Darrin opens his own ad agency and persuades Larry to see through Alonzo's lousy ideas.

No. 240

"The Eight-Year Witch" (12-8-71)

Written by Ruth Brooks Flippen. Directed by Richard Michaels. Guest cast: Julie Newmar, Ron Russell, Parley Baer, Samantha Scott.

Endora decides to prove to Samantha that Darrin is eyeing other ladies and summons catwitch Ophelia to seduce him. While Darrin, Larry, and a client are away on a business trip, Ophelia arranges to be involved with the account, and tries to seduce Darrin in his hotel room. However, Samantha pops in just in time to keep Ophelia's claws from sinking into Darrin, who had remained faithful to his wife through it all.

Note: Remake of No. 11.

No. 241

"Three Men and a Witch on a Horse" (12-15-71)

Written by Ed Jurist. Directed by Richard Michaels. Guest cast: John Fiedler, Hoke Howell, Scatman Crothers.

Darrin's conservative nature leads Endora to cast a gambling spell on him, which allows Darrin to win a bundle at the races. By

Julie Newmar as the catwitch Ophelia, in "The Eight-Year Witch." (Columbia Pictures Television.)

the time Samantha finds out what's happened, Larry and client Mr. Bengler try their luck with Darrin's tips, one of which is bad—thanks to Endora. Knowing that magically fixing the race would be wrong, Sam encourages the losing horse to win, saving Darrin's reputation.

No. 242

"Adam, Warlock or Washout" (12-29-71)

Written by Ed Jurist. Directed by William Asher. Guest cast: Diana Chesney, Maryesther Denver, Bernie Kuby.

The Witches' Council sends Grimalda and Enchantra to the Stephenses' to test young Adam's supernatural powers. If it is determined that he is not a warlock and is just an average mortal, Samantha and Darrin's marriage will be dissolved. This prompts Sam to call for her father's assistance. All is well when Adam proves to have amazing magical ability for his age.
Note: The last episode with Maurice.

No. 243

"Samantha's Magic Sitter" (1-5-72)

Written by Phillip and Henry Sharp. Directed by Richard Michaels. Guest cast: Richard X. Slattery, Jeanne Arnold.

Just as Esmeralda is again experiencing failure as a witch, Larry suggests her services for client Mr. Norton and their wife,

Darrin, Endora, and Enchantra and Grimalda observe Adam's witchcraft in "Adam, Warlock or Washout." (Columbia Pictures Television.)

who cannot find a baby-sitter. Though Samantha reluctantly complies, Esmeralda does the job. Unfortunately, she ends up telling the Norton child that she's a witch. And not until Samantha arranges a party—complete with a magic show—does she make everyone understand what Esmeralda meant.
Note: Remake of No. 27.

No. 244

"Samantha Is Earthbound" (1-15-72)

Written by Michael Morris. Directed by Richard Michaels. Guest cast: Sara Seegar, Jack Collins, Molly Dodd.

Samantha develops a condition that makes her weigh exactly 518 pounds. The cure turns out to be worse than the disease when Dr. Bombay prescribes a potion that makes her lighter than air. This all happens just as she is about to be a model at a charity bazaar for Mr. Prescott, a client of Darrin's. Yet Samantha's light-as-air approach to modeling benefits the account, as Darrin is inspired to create the slogan: "With Prescott Shoes, you don't walk, you float."

No. 245

"Serena's Richcraft" (1-22-72)

Written by Michael Morris. Directed by William Asher. Guest cast: Peter Lawford, Bernie Kuby.

Serena's witchcraft is stricken from her when she is caught with the fiancé of Contessa Pirhana, a very powerful witch. In the meantime, she amuses herself with wealthy client Harrison Woolcott, who falls hard for her and sweeps her off her feet. Darrin then becomes nervous, thinking the Woolcott account is in jeopardy because of Serena's involvement. Fortunately, the contessa finally restores Serena's magic, and everything returns to normal, with the Woolcott account under Darrin's control.
Note: Remake of Nos. 3 and 196.

No. 246

"Samantha on Thin Ice" (1-29-72)

Written by Richard Baer. Directed by William Asher. Guest cast: Alan Oppenheimer, former Canadian Olympic skating champ Robert Paul.

Samantha agrees that Tabitha should learn to ice-skate the mortal way. However, Endora becomes infuriated when she learns her granddaughter is performing poorly at a local rink, so she then zaps Tabitha into a fantastic skater. Consequently, Tabitha cap-

Peter Lawford and Serena in "Serena's Richcraft." (Columbia Pictures Television.)

tures the eye of Olympic officials who set out to take her on tour. These plans later change, as Samantha persuades her mother to remove the spell from Tabitha's feet.
Note: Remake of No. 143.

No. 247

"Serena's Youth Pill" (2-5-72)

Written by Michael Morris. Directed by E. W. Swackhamer. Guest cast: Ted Foulkes, David Hayward.

While baby-sitting for Tabitha and Adam, Serena decides to liven things up a bit by giving Larry a youth pill when he comes over looking for Darrin. When he first starts feeling and looking more youthful, Larry want to put the capsule on the market. Then, however, he starts getting younger and younger, becoming a ten-year-old boy, then an infant, and finally . . . Both Samantha

and Darrin become furious with Serena, who at last offers an antidote.
Note: The last Serena episode.

No. 248

"Tabitha's First Day at School" (2-12-72)

Written by Ed Jurist. Directed by Richard Michaels. Guest cast: Maudie Prickett, Jeanne Arnold, Nita Talbot.

The authorities discover that Tabitha is not attending school, and Samantha is forced to enroll her daughter in a local school. However, Sam is afraid Tabitha will use her powers in the classroom, and her fears are well founded when a bully in her class is turned into a frog. When the child's mother discovers that her son is missing, she traces him to the Stephenses', where Tabitha then returns her classmate to his original form.

No. 249

"George Washington Zapped Here" (Part 1, 2-19-72)

Written by Michael Morris. Directed by Richard Michaels. Guest cast: Will Geer, Jane Connell, Dick Wilson.

To help Tabitha with a school project, Esmeralda mistakenly conjures up George Washington. While Samantha and Darrin think of what to do about the situation, Esmeralda dematerializes the president. But he leaves his shoes behind, and when she tries to send them back, Mr. Washington returns instead—with his wife, Martha!

No. 250

"George Washington Zapped Here" (Part 2, 2-26-72)

Written by Michael Morris. Directed by Richard Michaels. Guest cast: Will Geer, Jane Connell, Herb Vigran, Jack Collins, Herb Voland.

Before long, George Washington has caused himself to appear in court to defend his identity. This inspires Larry to envision George as a part of the Whirlaway Washing Machines campaign. George complies, only because he feels he's doing Darrin a favor, but when he meets with the client, Mr. Washington is so honest the agency loses the account. After his inherent truthfulness is demonstrated in court, all charges against him are dropped. And when Esmeralda remembers how to send both George and Martha back to their own time, Darrin is sorry to see them go.
Note: No. 249 and No. 250 are remakes of No. 87 and No. 88.

Sam and Darrin welcome Will Geer and Jane Connell as George and Martha Washington in "George Washington Zapped Here." (Columbia Pictures Television.)

No. 251

"School Days, School Daze" (3-4-72)

Written by Michael Morris. Directed by Richard Michaels. Guest cast: Maudie Prickett, Charles Lane.

Samantha learns that Endora has cast a spell on Tabitha that's made her an authority on everything from Shakespeare to Einstein. School officials notice Tabitha's genius, and this leads them to discover the family's witchcraft. Samantha derails this truth by explaining that she, Darrin, and the children were once a nightclub act called The Witches.

No. 252

"A Good Turn Never Goes Unpunished" (3-11-72)

Written by Bernie Kahn. Directed by Ernest Losso. Guest cast: J. Edward McKinley.

Samantha and Darrin fight over her alleged use of witchcraft to create an advertising campaign slogan for Mr. Benson, a mattress manufacturer. Samantha, who firmly professes she did not use her powers in the campaign, grows so angry with Darrin that she flies off to Cloud Nine with Endora. Later Darrin realizes that he was wrong in accusing his wife and apologizes, so she happily returns.

Note: Remake of No. 5.

Samantha and Darrin in "Samantha's Witchcraft Blows a Fuse." (Columbia Pictures Television.)

No. 253

"Sam's Witchcraft Blows a Fuse" (3-18-72)

Written by Leo Townsend. Directed by Richard Michaels. Guest cast: Paul Smith, Richard X. Slattery, Herb Vigran, Bernie Kopell, Reta Shaw, Janos Prohaska, Benson Fong.

Samantha seems doomed to go through life with bright red stripes crisscrossing her face after she consumes an exotic drink at a Chinese restaurant. Consequently she, Darrin, and Aunt Hagatha, who's been watching the children, call upon the assistance of Dr. Bombay, who at first seems to prescribe an antidote. However, it is learned he left one ingredient out: the tail feather of a dodo bird, a creature Tabitha has secretly zapped up in her room. Dr. Bombay retrieves the final ingredient and Samantha is cured.

Note: Remake of No. 42.

No. 254

"The Truth, Nothing but the Truth, So Help Me, Sam" (3-25-72)

Written by Ed Jurist. Directed by William Asher. Guest cast: Parley Baer, Sara Seegar, Bernie Kuby.

Endora tests Darrin's devotion to Samantha one last time, as she casts a spell on a pin that causes the wearer to tell the absolute truth. This first causes trouble for Darrin at the office, but later the problem escalates at home, when Larry and a client and his wife visit the Stephenses. However, Samantha catches on to her mother's scheme just in time to save the evening, and Samantha and Darrin profess their love for each other.

Note: Remake of No. 50.

BEWITCHED TRIVIA

Samantha

Samantha is a level-headed witch who keeps her cool. Except, of course, when Aunt Clara's or Esmeralda's spells create havoc. Then she simply utters "Oh, my stars!" with the slightest trace of hysteria in her voice. In fact, when she sees Mother Goose in Episode No. 182, she exclaimed, "Oh, my goose, it's Mother Stars!"

Other Samantha specifics include her first meeting with Darrin in the pilot episode, in a revolving door of the Clark Building in New York City. Also it should be noted that Sam and Darrin live in a furnished rented house in Episodes No. 1 and No. 2, before buying their home (in No. 2) at 1164 Morning Glory Circle in Westport, Connecticut (Hopkins Realty is the agent).

Their home phone numbers are 555-7328 (No. 9 and No. 73), 555-2134 (No. 106), and 555-2368 (No. 141).

In the summer of 1968 they have new plumbing installed in the house, or so says Sam in No. 126, "Snob in the Grass."

Sam had her first date with Darrin on January 23, 1963, at Sorrento's Restaurant (No. 157). On April 2, 1963, they ate at the Automat, because Darrin forgot to make reservations at The Lobster. Samantha wore a pink wool dress (No. 198).

More specific Samantha facts are as follows:

In No. 13 she says: "All my friends are witches. We're just waiting to swoop down on Morning Glory Circle and claim it in the name of Beelzebub." She's only half serious but is very mad at Darrin.

In No. 84 it's learned that she knew she was a witch when she was only nine months old. Endora tells her: "You were very precocious."

In No. 86 it's established that Sam and Endora lived in Boston (apparently sometime in the nineteenth century) on the same block as the Farnsworths. Sam had one date with Clyde Farnsworth, who later asked Sam's Aunt Enchantra to transform him into a chair (using the spell without the oxtails) when she rejected him.

In No. 132 Samantha mentions she knew Shakespeare (who died in 1616); Henry VIII (who died in 1547, and whom she would meet again under the influence of a spell in No. 229); and Bluebeard, who, as she told Darrin, "was more of a gentleman than you've been tonight."

In No. 147 Sam explains how Napoleon arrived at the Stephenses' ("It's sorta technical"): "When a witch, or a warlock, casts a spell involving an object . . . the name of which may also be used to indentify a human being, the kinetic vibrations run the risk of zonking across the atmospheric continuum, and the ectoplasmic manifestations that might not ordinarily occur . . ."

In No. 158 Sam finds herself speaking in rhyme from a witch disease (primary vocabularyitis): "There once was a mommy named Sam, whose speech got her into a jam. Though she tried not to show it, she talked like a poet; if you think I'm unhappy, I am." During dinner with a dog food client: "Who, me? Boop dopp de dee" and "Me too. Fiddle de doo" and "I feel groovy. Anyone seen a good movie?" Other rhymes include: "I hate to burst your bubble, but I think I'm in trouble"; "In case I'm cured by a last-minute miracle, I have to be ready, don't I, dearicle?"; and "There must be a logical answer, or my name is not Samansar." She then tests Dr. Bombay's cure with "how now, brown horse."

In No. 163 Sam and Endora have one of their rare disputes, in this case over whether or not Tabitha should be disciplined for turning herself into a raisin cookie. Endora: "I always tell the truth . . . as I see it." Sam: "Mother, you are an incorrigible witch." Endora: "And you are an insensitive, selfish, mortal-marrying child." Sam: "You don't have to get that huffy about it." (Endora pops out angrily.) Sam: "I guess she does have to get that huffy about it. Oh, well . . . Mom?"

In No. 175 it's noted that Sam was born on the eve of the Galectic Rejuvenation and Dinner Dance (Maurice was on Venus at the time).

In No. 186 Sam thought she had contracted the witch-disease voracious ravenousitis, but she didn't. She was accidentally under Esmeralda's eating spell. However, some of the many witch-diseases Sam did acquire include: square green spots disease (No. 42), primary vocabularyitis (No. 158), metaphysical molecular disturbance (No. 221), gravititus inflammitis (No. 244), and bright red stripes disease (No. 253).

In No. 188 Samantha imitated Darrin's aunt Madge, who thought she was a lighthouse (mentioned in No. 1 and No. 14). The strange behavior of this never-seen relative was one of Sam's defenses against Darrin's tirades about her own unique family.

In No. 198 it's made known that Samantha's grandaunt Cornelia's portrait (which had been cluttering up Endora's attic for centuries) was painted by Leonardo da Vinci. Cornelia looked a great deal like Samantha.

In No. 204 it's revealed that when Sam was a little girl, Endora brought Sir Walter Raleigh home for dinner. Since Raleigh died in 1618, that gives us some idea of just how old Samantha really is. (In No. 203, however, she claims she was just a child during the Salem witch trials of 1692.)

In No. 224 Sam calls Endora with: "Boil and bubble, toil and trouble, Mother, get here on the double." Also, Sam explains the Unicorn Handicap: "It's like the Kentucky Derby, only with unicorns." And when Endora asks her what the happiest day of her life was, Sam says: "The day I married Darrin." To which Endora responds, "I didn't say insanely happy."

In No. 226 Sam explains to Esmeralda: "When you look into the mirror you see the image that you project . . . your reflection casts back your inner glow and your charisma comes to the fore, because, after all, beauty is in the eye of the beholder, isn't it? Do you understand?" Esmeralda: "No." And she also explains to Larry in the same segment: "When you don't respect someone, when you treat him as if he doesn't exist, he just disappears from your consciousness. He fades away. Follow me?" Larry: "No." But her best lines from No. 226 are said to Esmeralda again: "What did you have in mind? A little plastic sorcery?" and "I cook by mortal methods."

In No. 228 she says: "Supernatural powers have a tendency to come and go, mostly go. This will probably never happen again." And Phyllis, who's listening to this explanation, says: "Samantha . . . this is one subject you know nothing about."

In No. 237 it's learned that Samantha first flew when she was three years old, and that when she was a child, she frequently changed herself into a polka-dotted unicorn (a favorite of both Samantha and Elizabeth Montgomery).

Also, when Sam was a little girl, she turned herself into a postage stamp because Maurice and Uncle Arthur were arguing over who would take her to be introduced at court. She wound up in Istanbul, and as she recalls in No. 163, "Those Turks are kinda rough."

Let it also be known that Samantha is a very intelligent witch. She's fluent in Italian, Spanish, and French, and also speaks very well the frog, mule, horse, and goose languages, among others.

Serena's World

Serena likes to sing. For example, she sings two songs in No. 128, and in No. 192 she tries to get her tune, "I'm Gonna' Blow You a Kiss in the Wind," introduced at the Cosmos Cotillion.

In No. 160 she tells Sam's neighbor, Miss Parsons, that she came from the cabbage patch, but it's a known fact that she's originally from Babylon (No. 222). Also in No. 160 she says she's Sam's cousin on her father's side. And she tells Phyllis Stephens: "Well, Samantha's always had unusual taste. In people, too; Darrin for instance, is extremely unusual." And she tells her cousin: "Oh, Sammy, you used to be so much fun before you caught mortalitis."

In No. 196, when Sam tells Serena not to "play innocent with me" regarding Serena's flirtation with a client, Serena replies: "Innocence is not my bag. . . . He's very good-looking, and I happen to turn him on." Sam: "Well, turn him off!!" Serena: "Okay, okay. Don't bust your broom."

In No. 205 Sam refers to Serena: "I have a cousin that makes Lucrezia Borgia look like Shirley Temple."

In No. 245 Serena says: "There's not much difference between witchcraft and richcraft . . . except maybe you fly a little slower."

And in No. 247, when Sam calls Serena to baby-sit, Serena says: "Do I look like Mary Poppins to you?" and "Do you realize that the French fleet of St. Tropez was about to crown me Miss Navel?"

Darrin's Double Play

According to the *Bewitched* pilot, Darrin is a vice-president of McMann and Tate (rather than account executive), and as noted in No. 247, he joined the firm in 1961, while No. 107 says it was 1964.

Endora's spells turn him into a chimp, a mule, a werewolf, a goose, a pony, a parrot, a goat, a gorilla, a toad, a statue, a crow, a dog, and an invisible man.

Darrin's favorite dishes are beef stew, Irish stew, and corned beef and cabbage. His favorite breakfast is eggs Benedict, but he likes waffles also. His favorite pie is lemon meringue.

Darrin calls Endora "Mom" in No. 41 and No. 50.

Darrin's office is located in the International Building on the thirty-second floor. Darrin doesn't know how to swim (No. 68).

In No. 103 Darrin kisses Endora upon entering the living room, to help convince his parents that he and Samantha are not having an argument. In this segment it is also learned that Darrin was named for his grandfather, a statement later contradicted in No. 210, wherein Grover Stephens, a guise Darrin takes when Endora turns him into an old man, is said to be his grandfather.

Darrin's ancestor, Darrin the Bold, first appears in No. 79, and was played by York. He appears again in No. 217, portrayed by Sargent.

York's Darrin is zapped into the mirror in No. 122 by Lord Montdrako; the same thing happens to Sargent's Darrin by Maurice in No. 176.

York's Darrin is turned into a little boy by Endora in No. 46, "Junior Executive"; the same thing happens to Sargent's Darrin in No. 224, "Out of the Mouths of Babes."

York's Darrin says he went to college at Missouri, class of 1950 (No. 20); he graduated cum laude and was student body president (No. 99).

Sargent's Darrin went to Missouri (class of 1953, according to No. 191) and Missouri State (No. 224), where he was an all-star forward. Also, Darrin's best time for the 100-yard dash was 10.3 (or so he claims in No. 191, "What Makes Darrin Run").

Dick York did 156 shows as Darrin; Dick Sargent filmed 84 segments. No. 89 was the first episode York missed. He missed a total of fourteen before leaving in 1969.

Darrin's Double-Talk

In No. 2 Darrin says "Welcome, Mother" to Endora. However, by No. 72 he tells her: "This is my house, you're not welcome, and I want you out of here on the next broom." Yet a semitruce is called in No. 41, when Darrin greets her with "Hi, Mom." And she replies: "How are you, *Darrin*?" He's understandably amazed, but she says: "I'll make an agreement with you. I'll try to remember your name if you promise never to call me 'Mom.'" Darrin holds up his end of the bargain, but Endora does not.

Words return to normal in No. 75, when Darrin says: "Hi, Endora. When did you swoop in?" (He also says this in No. 141.)

In No. 81 he says to Sam: "It's been Halloween around here for the past week, what with your mother, Uncle Arthur, houses appearing and disappearing. . . ."

In No. 120 Endora gives Tabitha a pony and says: "The pony is on me." Darrin then responds: "That I'd like to see."

In No. 126 Darrin says to Sam (regarding Endora): "How is the old war wagon?"

In No. 131 Darrin says (about Endora): "Well, that's the *last* time I try to be nice to her."

In No. 153 Darrin says of Endora: "She never knocks. All of a sudden she's here, like the flu." This was also used in No. 254.

In No. 159 Darrin greets Endora: "It's the queen of sick jokes," and later says to her: "We eat at seven thirty. You take your broom to a drive-in or something," and "What can you expect from a crotchety old bat who learned to read from the Dead Sea Scrolls?" And he also states later about Endora: "Oh, yes, it's amazing how much help we get around here from Sam's mother."

In No. 170 Darrin calls Endora "The Old Lady of the Sea."

Also in No. 170 York speaks his last lines as Darrin to Sam about Endora: "Yeah, I know your mother. She's every inch a mother-in-law."

Dick Sargent's first line as Darrin is in No. 171: "Sam, how many times have I told you, never talk in the middle of somebody's backswing." Also in No. 171 Sam wonders if Darrin is sorry he married her. "Between this big witch and the little witch upstairs," she says, "and that witch of a mother of mine, you're really up to your neck in witches." But Darrin loves Sam and Tabitha. Sam: "And Mother?" "Well, two out of three," he says, "that's not bad."

In No. 172 Darrin says to Sam (about Endora): "Show me another mother who sharpens her teeth in the morning."

In No. 187 he tells Endora: "If you're able to drop in tomorrow morning, I certainly hope not." And later, during much magic goings-on, he says to his boss: "Crawl in the window? Come on, Larry . . . what are you trying to do, *Gaslight* me?"

In No. 191 he's at it again with Endora: "Ah, the cloud in my silver lining." After he asks her if Sam has told her about his "trip," meaning a business trip, Endora replies: "Yes, and I hope you do."

In No. 203 Darrin asks, after Endora flies on the wing of a plane and the top of the backseat in his convertible: "Must your mother ride on the outside of everything?" And later, after Endora says, "We saw those sights years go," he responds with: "Let's face it, Endora. Hundreds of years ago you *were* one of the sights."

In No. 211 he offers his best left hook with: "Sam, don't expect your mother to be gracious. She doesn't do imitations." And no matter how rattled Endora may have caused Darrin to be over the years, or how much trouble he finds himself in because of Samantha's magic, he still garners the strength to mention lightly to Larry in the same segment: "Don't tell anybody, but I'm married to a witch."

And in No. 223 Darrin says to Endora: "Hello, El Moutho," and later, "The bad fairy strikes again."

Endora

In No. 108, while Darrin is drowning his sorrows at a bar, Endora says to Sam: "Look, if he comes back, he comes back. If he doesn't, we'll open a bottle of champagne. . . . Well, I thought that was rather a good idea." When Darrin returns, she says: "Samantha . . . bad news, he's back." And after Darrin insults her, she says: "Samantha, I will not stand here and be insulted by something which is ninety-four percent water," only to have Darrin reply: "Oh, yeah! Well, what about something which is a hundred percent hot air?" And when Sam refuses to be Queen of the Witches, Endora says to Ticheba: "We do our best, but sometimes we fail."

In No. 118, Endora explains that she always has eggs over easy for breakfast, while her favorite dish is *coq au vin* (No. 159).

In No. 120 she apologizes to Darrin: "I regret my slight transgression of this morning, however deserved." (Darrin: "That's an apology?" Sam: "For Mother it is.")

And in No. 121, when Sam says, "Marriage is a poor excuse for snooping," Endora replies: "Well, if you ask me, this is a poor excuse for a marriage." In No. 125 Endora gets a taste of her own medicine, as she accidentally falls under her own love spell, which she had intended for Samantha, who was to become bewitched by Rollo, an old warlock boyfriend.

In No. 157 she gives the witches' honor sign with her mitten on (which probably doesn't count). And after Sam asks if she's "sure," Endora responds with: "Samantha, have I ever lied to you?"

And in No. 158, after she catches the rhyme bug from her daughter, she says: "This is absolutely outrageous; you must have been contagious." Then when Darrin gloats about it, she says: "Durwood, I do not like the way you gloat, so I'm turning you into a billy goat." And when Sam begs her to change him back she says: "I will, I will, but when I'm cured, and not until." Her other rhymes include: "Hello, Darius, the pleasure of seeing you is rather vicarious" and "That's absurd, I'll not rhyme a single word."

Further noting her witchy wit, in No. 177 she says to Samantha: "You took your vows for better or for worse and you certainly are getting the worse." Later, however, she uncharacteristically retreats with "You win. I'm bored with all this trivia."

In No. 195, when Dr. Bombay says, "Durwood is totally irrelevant," Endora responds with "I'll buy that." Then Bombay one-ups her with "It's not for sale."

In No. 197 Endora explains the leprechaun: "It was a test to see where the breaking point is in this mortal marriage . . . it was sponsored by the Witches' Council." Sam: "Who suggested it to the Witches' Council?" Endora: "I believe the suggestion came from the floor . . . all right, I suggested it!"

In No. 198, when Darrin says Endora "majored in cruelty with the Marquis de Sade," she says: "It's not true. He was just a classmate." And in No. 201 she tells Darrin: "Aren't we the terrible tiger this morning!" And to Sam: "Oh, this room—oh, it's all *you*."

Her cutest spell occurred in No. 139: "Edgeful, eyeful, trifle, tree; this removes the spell 'round thee." Her least imaginative spell appeared in No. 153, which was "disappear courtesy."

In No. 240, when Darrin throws a good-bye kiss, Endora makes a face and says: "Eucchh." And via skywriting in the tag: "I, Endora, promise never, never again to bug what's his name" (also in No. 164); in No. 251 she writes: "Endora promises not to interfere" 500 times (sort of) on a blackboard.

And in No. 246 she asks Darrin: "How would you like to be a carrot growing in a field of rabbits?" (See also No. 159.) Then after more bickering has given her a headache, she says: "And now that you've made a perfectly marvelous person sick . . . she's leaving."

Larry

Generally, when Larry was at his worst, the Stephenses' situation would work out for the best, or they would at least get the best of Larry.

In No. 134 Larry states: "I'm the one with a vivid imagination; I can see five hundred thousand dollars flying out the window." At this moment Samantha zaps up a winged bag of money that proceeds to fly out the window. Larry then says to Sam: "If you love Darrin, get him out of the advertising business—while there's still time."

All this from a man who, according to No. 35, spent seven years in analysis. Maybe a little sympathy is in order, as Larry does, on occasion, display his true feelings.

In No. 50 he admits he can't get along without Darrin, which he also confesses in No. 254. Of course, in both cases he is under a truth spell.

Larry's questionable behavior is also evident in these episodes:

In No. 104 he actually admits his desire for money after Darrin says: "You know, your eyes light up when you talk about money." Larry: "Of course, I'm a greedy person."

In No. 128 Larry tells Darrin: "I didn't get to be the head of an advertising agency without stretching the truth now and then. I might honestly say that I'm one of the best truth stretchers in the business."

In No. 135, when Larry realizes that Sam's a witch (in a dream sequence), he gets a bit out of hand: "Samantha . . . with my brains and your voodoo, we can control the world. . . . Today the nation, tomorrow the world!" Darrin: "Larry, take it easy." Larry: "I can't. I'm mad with power!" Sam: "But we're not. We don't want to use my witchcraft to rule the world." Darrin: "Right. And I'm sure when you've had time to think it over you'll decide—" Larry: "I'll decide I want to rule the world. I've wanted to rule the world ever since I was a little kid." Much of this dialogue is repeated almost verbatim in No. 181.

In No. 153 Larry tells Darrin: "I've got radar. I get a ping when something's wrong." And then he professes his "word of honor. My *real* word of honor." Only to state later: "I'm going home to celebrate all over again with . . ." Sam: "Louise." Larry: ". . . Louise."

And in No. 175, after Maurice has removed a spell from a just-born Adam that's made everyone think he's the best baby in the world, Larry, who was all set to use Adam in an ad, is out to look for another baby at the hospital: "You mean to tell me in a place like this we can't borrow a . . . Maybe we could borrow a camera and take a picture in the nursery and then . . . Listen! That's a two-million-dollar account!" Finally, Sam calls it: "Oh, Larry . . . you son of a gun."

Sam captures Larry's essence further, as in No. 138, where she states: "That's just Larry's way. The hardest thing for him to give, is in."

In No. 178, when Darrin asks: "What do you want me to do—cut my throat?"

after nearly losing an account, Larry says: "I'm thinking it over." And later (to his secretary): "Remind me to put Stephens on the 'B' list for Christmas."

In No. 158 he says: "That's not bad character, it's my character."

And in No. 181 he says: "Darrin, if I've told you once, I've told you a thousand times—integrity doesn't feed the bulldog."

In No. 224 Larry offers many moments of insight into his character. On planning to stay at the Stephenses': "It's either here or going home and listening to Louise and her string quartet murder Bach." And later: "I didn't become the president of McMann and Tate without bending my integrity occasionally, and this is one of those occasionallys." And to a client: "At McMann and Tate, Sunday is just the day before Monday."

In No. 247 it's learned that Larry lived at 1432 Elm Drive when he was a child, and he originally had red hair, played ice hockey for his school team, and served in the navy. How did all this come to be known? Serena gives him a youth pill, and the rest is Larry's history.

Aunt Clara

Aunt Clara always had the best intentions, but she usually brought about the worst disasters. For example, in No. 116, "Out of Synch, Out of Mind," Clara accidentally casts a spell causing Samantha to speak out of synch. She moves her lips and then her voice is heard later.

Other Clara catastrophes appear in the following episodes:

No. 124, "Samantha's Da Vinci Dilemma": she summons legendary artist Leonardo da Vinci to paint Samantha's house.

No. 119, "Samantha's Thanksgiving to Remember": she accidentally transfers herself, the Stephenses, and Mrs. Kravitz to seventeenth-century Plymouth on Thanksgiving Day, where *Darrin* finds himself accused of witchcraft.

No. 137, "Samantha's Secret Saucer": she transports a spaceship with two doglike aliens into Samantha's backyard.

No. 78, "Accidental Twins": she turns the Tates' son into twins.

No. 87, "My Friend Ben" (Part 1 of 2): she summons Benjamin Franklin to help Samantha fix a light bulb.

In No. 100, "Aunt Clara's Victoria Victory," she mistakenly beckons Queen Victoria for a present-day stay with the Stephenses. Yet her biggest flub probably appeared in No. 83, "The Short Happy Circuit of Aunt Clara," which dealt with a blackout of the entire Eastern Seaboard, apparently caused by her misguided witchcraft. (The real-life New York blackout was one year earlier, on November 9, 1965.)

Uncle Arthur

In No. 80 Uncle Arthur and Endora have a running battle over Tabitha's care, at Sam's expense. Eventually they zap a house on and off a vacant lot across the street.

In No. 81 Uncle Arthur has some great lines. "Anybody who'd knock anybody else out of a tree is sick!" and "Endora, you decorate the way you do everything else—in superstupendous, glorious bad taste," and "She's joking. She's not very good at it, but that's what she's doing."

In No. 41, Arthur convinces Darrin he can protect himself from Endora's wrath with this phrase: "Yagazuzi, yagazuzi, yagazuzi, zim [cowbell, duck call]; Zoomazoozi, zoomazoozi, zoomazoozi, bim [cowbell, duck call]; Zuzzi, hi! Zuma Huga Pits." This incantation, however, is bogus.

Endora's Halloween party takes place at the Stephens home, and as she begins to recite, "'Twas the night before Halloween, and all who were witches were sipping champagne . . ." Arthur then cuts in and says, "They'd been stoned for a week." Endora: "The witches and warlocks in Rome by the score with their ladies attired in their best by Dior . . ." Arthur: "Checking their warts as they came through the door." Endora: "And the odd little mortals all snug in their beds, while visions of trick-or-treat danced in their heads. Our children were practicing spells and their chants . . ." Arthur: "And even the poltergeists pulled off their pants."

In No. 138 Arthur first appears in a stewpot. "I'm a stewaway," he explains. Then he puts a pocket watch into the stew ("It could use a pinch of thyme") and says "it's a watched pot."

He also zaps up a cow when Tabitha wants more milk. Sam: "What's wrong with getting it from the refrigerator?" Arthur: "I never milked a refrigerator." Later Sam wonders how to cheer Darrin up. Arthur offers some advice: "How about a hotbed . . . same as a hotfoot, only we do it to the whole bed." Sam gets really worried about Darrin: "He might not get through the day alive," she says. To which Arthur replies, "That is a problem; black isn't one of your best colors." (Sam is wearing black in the scene.)

One last bit from No. 138: Arthur: "Knock, knock." Darrin: "Who's there?" Arthur: "Chester." Darrin: "Chester who?" Arthur: "Chester gigolo, everywhere I go . . ."

In No. 147, when Arthur ruins Sam's angel food cake, he decides to replace it with a fancier dessert, reasoning: "Oh, no, not an angel food cake; that's so cafeteria." And later Arthur says to Napoleon: "Okay, Emperor. Stand up. All the way." Later still, Darrin threatens to break Arthur's neck. Arthur: "Just try it, buster, and I'll turn you into a tiny Eiffel Tower." Napoleon: "That I'd like to see." Near the segment's end, Darrin tells Arthur, "You're a lousy warlock." To which Arthur replies, "How would you know?"

In No. 150 Arthur says: "Excuse me for not getting up, but my feet are killing me" (pistols on his shoes fire at him). Also, Arthur gives Tabitha a puppy: "I got him in a thunderstorm. It was raining cats and dogs." Sam: "And you stepped in a poodle." Arthur: "Not bad, Sammi. Been funnier if I'd said it." More puppy talk: Sam: "I hope he's trained." Arthur: "Only to kill." Later Sam says to Darrin: "Uncle Arthur came to give Tabitha something." Darrin: "What? A hotfoot?" Arthur: "Sammi, I feel another pout coming on."

Also in No. 150 Arthur is scheduled to ride the favorite in the Ostrich Derby. It seems that long ago Arthur taught Sam how to make her first pony.

Esmeralda

In her first appearance in No. 172, Esmeralda sneezed up a unicorn by accident, which was later used as a symbol for Darrin's new car campaign.

In No. 195 Ramon Verona, Esmeralda's true love (he's the salad chef at the Interplanetary Playboy Club and was at the Warlock Club in No. 200) has finally asked her out on a date. They're going dining and dancing on Jupiter, and she notes: "Ramon is no gentleman. That's why I'm so anxious to go out with him."

In No. 226, however, her other warlock boyfriend, Ferdy, whom she hasn't dated in over 400 years, makes an appearance. She's a little nervous to meet him because her powers are failing. But as it happens, his witchcraft isn't that great either. So they romantically console each other.

In No. 232 Samantha says *"Buffa, buffa,"* in reference to Esmeralda's odd behavior. This is an Italian word that means trick or jest and is related to *buffone*, meaning clown or buffoon. Also here, she calls Samantha Sam. Esmeralda's really nervous because she's just straightened the Leaning Tower of Pisa; she was around when it was constructed (1174) and tells Samantha that she's the reason why it leaned in the first place.

On ordering a tower sandwich for its architect, she said: "One tower, and make it lean." It did. Fortunately, she returns the tower to its leaning position, but she still contemplates turning herself "into something harmless; maybe a bird, or a zebra . . . I've always looked good in stripes."

Esmeralda says she "couldn't have been more than one hundred" when she made the tower lean, and in No. 172 she says she was once a lady-in-waiting to a wife of Henry VIII (who ruled from 1509 to 1547), so she's no spring "witchen."

Dr. Bombay

Dr. Bombay used a bevy of witch-nurses and supernatural medicinal devices to heal the witch-ills of the world. Some of these metaphysical contraptions included the atmospheric oscillator (from No. 195), a witch hunter (No. 225), and an amber corpuscular evaluator (No. 158).

In general, his first diagnosis of any ailment is usually wrong, as was the case in his first appearance on the show in No. 107. Here, Endora threatens to replace him with Dr. Agraphor because Dr. Bombay is reluctant to assist in the matter at hand—which, by the way, includes treating mortals. And not just any mortal, but Darrin, who has a cold. While Samantha's away, Endora has called for Dr. Bombay, who gives Darrin, and later Larry and a client, who also both have colds, pills that have unpleasant side effects—high-pitched voices.

Initially, Dr. Bombay is referred to as a warlock doctor by Samantha, but later on, Samantha usually tells a doubtful Darrin something like: "He's the only witch doctor we have."

Actually, in No. 118, Sam says Dr. Bombay is "just our practitioner; you should see our specialist" (though we never do). In No. 253 Sam asks Hagatha to talk to the Witches' Council about replacing Bombay, whom she calls a "quack-pot."

In No. 152 it's learned that Dr. Bombay was riding entry No. 7 in the Ostrich Derby in Sydney, Australia, but he came in last. But the good witch doctor has always remained a very active fellow—witness his escapades with his nurses. Also, he plants a flag on the summit of Mount Everest, alongside flags of England, Switzerland, and the United States. And he climbs the Matterhorn in No. 174.

In No. 158, after Endora misdiagnoses Samantha's condition as Venetian verbal virus, Dr. Bombay also miscalls it as secondary vocabularyitis, finally making the proper diagnosis of primary vocabularyitis, using his amber corpuscular evaluator (which, according to Darrin, "no home should be without"); treatment is by sound wave injection. Of his first diagnosis, Bombay says: "Same family as verbal virus, but the cure is completely different."

In No. 221 Bombay describes the transcendental transplant potion: "Marrow of tooth of saber-toothed tiger, eye of newt, toe of frog, wool of bat, and dietetic cola." It's also learned that his favorite tongue twister is: "Willy Warlock walked away with Wally Walrus."

In No. 225 there is a wealth of Bombay's puns: "I must get back to my nurse, Hazel . . . cute little witch . . . get it? Witch . . . Hazel . . . witch Hazel . . ." and "Thursday? So am I; let's have another drink." And during his prognosis of Samantha's hiccup-related-various-cycle-appearances disease, he says, "You showed a lack of wheel power" and "Your problem is not only logical, but cycle-logical." And after Sam comments on his athletic attire with "That's what you wear when you play golf?" he replies: "It is when I'm playing a round with my nurse."

And in No. 253 Bombay's nurse says: "Bomb's away. I call him Bomb." Sam: "What does he call you?" Nurse: "Often. He calls me often." And she also says: "I'm his receptionist. I'm very receptive." And later, after Sam says: "I'm running out of patience," Bombay adds: "You and me both. [patients]"

Also in No. 253 (which is the next-to-last show), an abundance of vintage Bombay material runs rampant. His antidote potion consists of: eye of condor, powdered snakeskin, fig newts ("That's the way the cookie crumbles"), one pint nonfat unicorn milk, a toasted cheese sandwich on rye ("That's for me; I'm starved"), the tail feather from a dodo bird (but the computer overlooked this ingredient and Bombay left it out), and a Himalayan cinnamon stick. Unfortunately, Bombay forgets to mention the latter ingredient. "Of course I did; it's the most important ingredient; it's not only essential to the potion, it provides the necessary antitoxin." But Sam has a witness; so Bombay admits, "In that case, it's obvious I didn't mention it."

Tabitha

In No. 75 Tabitha drives famous baby photographer Diego Fenman out of his tree, when she levitates all her of her toys during a photo session.

In No. 131 her pediatrician is Dr. McDonald; in No. 75, it was Dr. Koblin.

In No. 151 she asks: "Is this one of those things that's called a problem?"

In No. 156 she says: "I want to stay and hear you scream, Daddy."

In No. 159: "You're a good yeller, Daddy."

In No. 175 Tabitha says about Adam: "He's very nice. How long is he going to stay here?" But later she magically gives him a rattle: "It's my being-born present." (Endora: "Oh, isn't that sweet." Sam: "Yes . . . and no.")

For her party in No. 178 Tabitha wears one of the dresses Samantha bought her at Hinkley's Department Store in No. 169—the $5 number with the red flowers and blue windowpane checks.

In No. 184 she says about her playmate Sidney: "He kept saying, 'There's no Santa . . . there's no Santa . . .' so I turned him into a mushroom."

In No. 189 Tabitha's chin is bandaged (Erin Murphy really hurt herself on a pony ride) and Sam tells her: "Maybe next time I tell you you're too young to fly, you'll pay attention to me." After Tabitha leaves, Darrin says: "Women start to get difficult early in life, don't they?"

In No. 211 Sam explains that "Tabitha" is an international name.

In No. 215 Tabitha says, "Gee whiz, everything good that happens around here is a secret."

In No. 246 she asks her mother: "Is he [Darrin] mad at us?"

In No. 248, when Darrin asks her how school was, she replies: "Oh, it's still there."

Overall, Tabitha is really just like any other kid; her favorite dessert is chocolate ice cream (No. 163) and she wears Poughkeepsie woolen socks (No. 55), though Gladys calls them "Kapoopsie."

Adam

Adam was born in No. 175, "And Something Makes Four," airing on October 16, 1969. David Lawrence made his first appearance as Adam in No. 203, "The Salem Saga," airing October 8, 1970. He was born at 4:45 A.M. (No. 175), and Sam and Darrin originally planned to name him Frank Maurice Evans (No. 176).

Further regarding Adam's name, Maurice says in No. 176: "That was my great-grandfather's name." Darrin: "Adam was your great-grandfather?" Maurice: "Not *that* Adam." And Tabitha comments: "I like him the way he is."

In No. 202 Adam makes a no-no on Hepzibah, prompting Darrin to say: "Darn, I wish I'd thought of that."

In No. 242 Adam's powers are revealed, and Darrin says to the gathered witches and warlocks who've come to find out if he was mortal or a warlock: "The way you're carrying on [which is very happily], you'd think he'd just taken his first step." Sam: "But . . . that's exactly what he did."

Maurice

Samantha's father, Maurice, is a very powerful warlock and is probably the one seriously threatening supernatural force on *Bewitched* (besides the Witches' Council). Darrin may have been ruffled here and there by Endora, but he is definitely not safe around Maurice, who constantly places his mortal son-in-law at the mercy of some very temperamental mood swings.

Resplendent in top hat and tails (and noted for his eye for the ladies), Maurice had a tendency to quote classic soliloquies in a Shakespearean, if bombastic, fashion.

He resides in London (somewhere), but materializes in his Rolls-Royce, or has the winds blow at zephyr speeds before making his entry. Like Endora, he arrives at the Stephenses' only to see his daughter and grandchildren, all of whom he loves very much. As to how he feels bout Darrin? Well, he refers to him in much the same way as his estranged wife Endora does . . . hardly at all.

Yet Maurice is endearing, as he loves the theater, and has a penchant for the dramatic.

In No. 77 he's on his way to Vienna, and states: "They're doing *Faust* [which includes various devilish references], and I always get a million laughs out of that."

In No. 167 he mentions that he prefers his martinis made with Spanish gin, Italian vermouth, and a Greek olive. Actually, that's exactly how Endora prefers her martinis, but if Maurice knew that, it would not sit well with him. He and Endora have a kind of semiseparation, but down deep they really love each other, as Endora finds it very difficult to resist his charms. Some of them are displayed in No. 175.

Here Maurice blesses his newly born grandchild Adam: "Special baby, full of grace . . . so tiny and so new; whatever mortal sees your face . . . will fall in love with you." Yet that's kind of a blessing in disguise, as that incantation causes much mayhem at the hospital. But his intentions are always good where Sam, Tabitha, and Adam are concerned.

The Kravitzes

Abner and Gladys—what a pair! In love, but ever at odds. How long have they been married, anyway? Well, Gladys says in No. 32 (first shown on May 6, 1965) that she and her husband have been together for thirty years, but by No. 140 (which aired on May 16, 1969), the Kravitz marriage has been reduced to twenty-two years. They became engaged while in college, but each would have been too old for college in 1946 (according to calculations), so their earlier date (married in 1935) seems to make more sense.

At any rate, through the years they managed to stay together, and by the time that Samantha and Darrin come to live in the neighborhood, it may have proved more challenging than ever to keep their relationship on an even keel.

Even though Gladys always gets very nervous after seeing something strange going on next door, Abner is never too mystified by his wife's reactions. If anything, he is quite the wit when it comes to his reactions to her reactions, which many times may have bordered on the maniacal, from his perspective.

Now let's take a look at some of their interactions:

In No. 29 Gladys starts things off with "I *have* no imagination" and (to Samantha): "You're from Venus, aren't you?" And later, to Abner, "Guess what I've got?" He replies, "Heartburn." Then Gladys says: "Abner, I've got the power!" Abner: "Well, take some lemon juice and hot water—that'll knock it out." Gladys: "It's nothing to joke about." Abner: "All right, until you get over it, I'll sleep in the den."

In No. 31 she says to Abner: "You've had your nose stuck in that book all day." Abner: "I want to see how it turns out." Gladys: "It's about the Civil War; the North won." (This is also used in No. 152.)

In No. 40 Abner professes that he "got mugged in the tunnel of love."

In No. 42 Gladys refers to Samantha (who's come down with square green spots disease): "I bet she has some strange disease and we could catch it. You want to wake up with something strange?" Abner: "I've been doing that for twenty years."

In No. 47 Gladys says: "Abner, there's a wizard at the Stephenses' house." Abner: "Good for the lawn. It eats the mosquitoes." Gladys: "Not a lizard, a *wizard*." Abner: "Wizard, lizard . . . as long as it eats the mosquitoes."

In No. 60 it's made known that Abner and Gladys honeymooned on the S.S. *Sorrento*, and it sank. Abner: "During all the time we were floating around in our life belts, I kept thinking, 'Somebody's trying to tell me something.'"

In No. 83 Abner says to Gladys: "Have you got that buzzing in your head again?" and "You'll be all right, dear, just as soon as the swelling goes down." Abner again: "Gladys, it's dangerous to stand by the window. Somebody might throw a rock at you." Gladys: "Who would do a thing like that?" Abner: "Me, if you don't sit down and shut up."

In No. 101 Gladys is on the phone to Samantha: "I have a visitor here, and I have a feeling that she's your kind of people." Later Abner says: "You'll say anything to get me up."

In No. 118 Gladys says: "Tabitha Stephens just made a newspaper fly through the air like it had wings. Do you know what that proves?" Abner: "Mmmhmm. News travel fast."

In No. 137 Abner is having a dream, and Gladys wakes him up because there are spacemen (whom Aunt Clara accidentally conjured up) next door. Abner to Gladys: "I think your curlers are wound too tight."

In No. 140, when Abner and Gladys split up, she ends up staying with the Stephenses, which in itself is a very strange development that gets stranger . . . for Samantha and Darrin, as Gladys proves to be quite the obnoxious houseguest. She's demanding and selfish and she almost runs the household, so Darrin almost yearns for a visit from Endora.

Also in No. 140 Gladys cakes her face with a mud pack, which introduces the Stephenses to her health-oriented lifestyle. As her visit continues, she prepares the following dishes for her host and hostess: alfalfa soup, organic vegetable loaf, kumquat pudding, and soybean brownies. In the meantime, Abner is as happy as a lark, singing, whistling, and dancing while mowing the lawn.

Contrary to the way he has often been perceived, he is not without energy. His wit is ever rampant and always evident.

In No. 158, after he witnesses Samantha's (bespelled) rhyming, he says to Gladys, who pushes him out the door: "Don't shove, my love." In No. 184 he states: "Gladys, let's play house. You be the door, and I'll shut you." And in No. 189 he says: "Great news. Hurricane Gladys is right off your starward bound."

In No. 167 Gladys says to Abner: "I tell you it *is* a jackass and she is feeding it eggs Benedict for breakfast." Abner: "Lucky jackass—all I ever get is lumpy oatmeal."

In No. 189 Gladys shows concern more than curiosity for once, when she reacts to what she sees as strange behavior by Samantha, who replies: "There's nothing wrong with me." Gladys: "That's what they *all* say." And Gladys to Darrin: "She keeps insisting she's fine. That what they *all* say, you know." Darrin by phone in the tag: "She's fine, Mrs. Kravitz. Of course, that's what they *all* say." (From the couch, Sam mouths the last few words along with Darrin.)

And in No. 222, after Gladys makes a phone call ("Hello, operator; get me the corpse—I mean the cops"), Abner sums up what could have been the answer to everybody's problem: "Gladys," he says, "if you had any compassion for your fellow neighbor, you'd move."

Louise

Larry and Louise each appear for the first time in the third episode, "It Shouldn't Happen to a Dog," which also happens to be the first show that features a McMann and Tate client (Rex Barker).

Like Samantha, Louise is very supportive of her husband, and she puts up with many business-oriented meetings, luncheons, and dinner parties. Unlike Samantha, however, she is more prone to talk back to her husband, and to speak in a snippy fashion.

For example, in No. 64 when it's explained how Larry and Louise got engaged, she explains in this way: "One night he blew a smoke ring. I stuck my finger in it and said, 'I do.'" And she also spars with Larry; after he says, "I've got news for you, Tinted Top—I run my business the way I see fit, and I don't need any suggestions from the corset crowd," she comes back with: "Be my guest, Snow White."

But when push comes to shove, Louise stands by her man, as in No. 76. Here Samantha and Darrin try to persuade the Tates to leave so that they will not see any of Tabitha's newly discovered magic. Consequently, the Stephenses lead Larry to believe that he's drunk by making him take a sobriety test ("Say Chrysanthemum." "Oh, daffodils," Larry replies), an equilibrium test (which he fails, prompting Louise to call: "Taxi!"), and a test in which he is supposed to walk a straight line (Darrin: "Why don't you walk from where you spilled the champagne to where you burned the table?"). Through it all, Larry still turns to Louise in the end. "Is that you, Louise?" he asks after all the embarrassment. "Are Darrin and Sam still here? Would you say good night to them for me, please?"

In all, Louise (who according to No. 238 belongs to the Women's League, whose auditorium seats 300) is a sensitive soul who goes through some slight badgering.

In No. 78, when Sam creates a double birthday party for the Tates' son, Louise has these reactions to the parties: "I'm beginning to feel like a yoyo" and "Is this a birthday party, or am I training for the Olympics?"

In No. 226 it's made known that Louise has been on the phone all day. Larry says: "I wonder how Miss AT&T managed to squeeze me into her schedule." Sam then says: "You and Louise should take a little vacation." Larry: "You mean from each other?" However, Larry later gets on the phone and says: "Hello, Teddy Bear [that's Louise] . . . how would you like to pack your toothbrush and your chin strap and come to Chicago?"

In No. 235 Larry says of his wife: "Louise has a pretty tough hide. . . . When it comes to handling ugly moods, Louise is a specialist. She's been handling mine for years."

No. 235 includes dealings with a sex-starved ghost who has possessed Darrin's body. Louise: "He asked me to go to the gardener's cottage with him." Larry:

"What for?" Louise: "What do you think?" Larry: "Oh. It's obvious he's having a nervous breakdown." Louise: "Why is he acting [Darrin is flirting] so ridiculous?" Larry: "Because you're old enough to be Darrin's . . . sister." Larry finally defends his wife and says to Darrin (who now is depossessed): "The soufflé fell, and you're next." But Louise still sniffles about it all: "What you're all saying is that unless somebody's out of his mind, he couldn't possibly be interested in me."

Louise also sheds tears in No. 150 when she and Larry are fighting. He does console her, though, and he does most every time. In fact, in Christmas segment No. 184 he's wondering if he should buy her an expensive mink coat. Infected with the spirit, he lovingly gives in. The audience is led to believe that he truly cares for Louise and that he appreciates all of her support.

Phyllis and Frank Stephens

Darrin's parents were married thirty-five years as of November 2, 1967, the air date of No. 116. However, in No. 19 Phyllis says they have been married for forty years. They don't know their daughter-in-law is a witch, so anything supernatural must be kept from them whenever they visit.

Consquently, Phyllis is convinced she is going crazy more often than not during these visits. And when she does have bizarre experiences at her son's house, she usually begins feeling ill and complains to her husband, "Frank, I'm getting a sick headache."

Frank was named for his grandfather (No. 176); Darrin was named for *his* grandfather (No. 103); so where did Grover Stephens (named as Darrin's grandfather in No. 210) come from? It's simple. Three episodes, three different writers, three different directors. Those are the vagaries of television sitcoms.

Darrin's aunt (Phyllis's sister Madge), who thought she was a lighthouse, is initially mentioned by Darrin on his honeymoon in No. 1, then in No. 14 (and also in No. 51 in recut form), and finally in No. 188, when Samantha demonstrates the way she turned this way and that.

In No. 58 Phyllis and Frank see Tabitha for the first time. Their next visit comes fourteen months later in No. 103. However, Tabitha stays with them in No. 60 and No. 68; they live some distance away at this point in the series. Frank's get-rich-quick scheme in No. 58 is the same one he later discusses in No. 163.

In No. 116, after Darrin calls his father although his mother said not to, Phyllis states: "Darrin Stephens, you do that again and I'll box your ears." Dr. Bombay is called in to fix a hex on Sam, but he thinks Phyllis is the patient and says: "You've got a very sick witch here . . . oh . . . well, she's not too warm for a mortal."

While talking with Serena in No. 160, Phyllis mentions the fact that she and Frank have never met Samantha's father. They finally do meet him (for the first and only time) in No. 176. Also in No. 160, Phyllis discusses Uncle Arthur at length with Serena, but nowhere in the series do Darrin's parents meet Arthur.

Further in No. 160, due to a mis-spell, Phyllis says: "My, that sherry was strong" (she is turned into a cat). Frank then asks her: "Phyllis . . . what is that around your neck?" She replies, "My bell to warn birds."

In No. 163 Mabel Albertson does the voice of Black Bart, the mynah bird owned by Phyllis. The bird says, "I'm Black Bart," "Hello there, baby," and "Frank, I'm getting a sick headache." Samantha also tells Endora (about Phyllis): "Most grandparents don't have grandchildren who can turn them into toads." And after Phyllis says: "Now that we're all here, I have an idea," Endora takes a shot at her: "Oh, beginner's luck." They have been feuding since No. 19, "A Nice Little Dinner Party."

In No. 228 Phyllis, thinking she has supernatural powers, says to her daughter-in-law: "Samantha . . . this is one subject you know nothing about." She scolds Darrin: "This is a private conversation. . . . Out!" And then she asks Sam: "Do you know what a 'familiar' is?" Sam: "A what?" Earlier, Phyllis had shown her childhood doll (which Samantha leads her to believe possessed inspirational powers) to Frank, saying, "It's my familiar." Frank: "Well, it should be familiar—you've had it since you were a child." Phyllis later believes she's turned Frank into a mule during a séance rigged by Samantha. But she really hasn't—it's just all part of Sam's plan to reunite Phyllis and Frank.

AN ENCHANTED LEXICON

Abner!: The primal scream of Gladys Kravitz anytime after she has witnessed anything unusual at the Stephenses', or with regard to Samantha's magic.

Bewitched: A general term referring to someone or something that has been supernaturally manipulated by a witch or warlock.

Cosmos Cotillion, The: A very hip function held annually for only the coolest of witches and warlocks. The affair included fine intergalatic entertainment. In fact, Serena once employed the mortal rock duo Boyce and Hart to perform a song she wrote ("I'm Gonna Blow You a Kiss in the Wind") at the ball.

Cotton Top: Serena's playful nickname for Larry Tate.

Darwin, Durwood, Dagwood, Donald, Dennis, Dum-Dum, Dumbo, Derek, Darwood, Durweed, Darius, David, Dobbin: Names Endora calls Darrin. Maurice also calls him *Dobbin*, while Serena usually refers to him as "tall, dark, and nothing."

Dematerialize/Dematerialization: Terms used whenever a given person, place, or thing disappears because of a spell.

Freeze (also known as *Deep Freeze*): A spell cast by a witch or a warlock that completely halts the physical, verbal, and conscious movement of a particular subject.

"Ha ha . . . ha ha . . . nothing": Dr. Bombay's self-comforting response to his less than funny (and often disappointing) attempts at humor.

"Hiya, Sammi": A greeting to Samantha, used by both Uncle Arthur and Serena.

"I have a sick headache": A claim made many times by Darrin's mother, Phyllis, to her husband, Frank, after she witnesses strange goings-on at her son's house.

"I love you very much": A response Samantha uses whenever she thinks Darrin is really mad (mostly in the later years of their marriage).

"I wish you wouldn't call him that" (or *"say that"*): A phrase used by a doubtful Darrin whenever Samantha tells him that Dr. Bombay is the only witch doctor available.

"Larry!": Louise Tate's plea for her husband to act more appropriately.

"Louise!": Larry Tate's plea for his wife to act more appropriately.

Materialize/Materialization: Terms used whenever a something or somebody appears because of a spell.

Metaphysical: A term used in the witch/warlock world that means beyond physics. This is often used to explain their existence.

Metaphysical Continuum: The energy field measured by the witches and warlocks; it can also be used when discussing their source or center.

"Mother!"/"Mom?": Samantha's scream heard around the witch world whenever havoc strikes the Stephens household. This is usually due to Endora's interference with Darrin's personality, looks, position, or situation. If Endora fails to appear, Samantha uses a softer voice and shortens the plea with "Mom?"

"Oh, my stars!": A phrase Samantha utters whenever the situation at hand seems a little out of hand.

"Oh, dear!": A phrase employed by Esmeralda just prior to slowly fading out because of her nerves, a condition brought about by either her witchy mistakes or Darrin's arrival.

"Oh, Samantha . . . really!": A turn of the tongue employed by Endora whenever she seems a little disconcerted with Samantha's words or behavior. (And after speaking her mind, Endora usually pops off in a huff.)

"One, two, three, four, five . . .": The counting sequence Samantha applies whenever Endora takes longer than usual to appear; used many times between *"Mother!"* and *"Mom?"*

"Paging Dr. Bombay! Paging Dr. Bombay! Emergency! Emergency! Come right away!": A verbal appeal given by Samantha whenever she's in need of the warlock medicine man, Dr. Bombay. (Also heard as: *"Calling Dr. Bombay! Calling Dr. Bombay!"*)

Pop: A colloquial term for casting a spell.

"Sam!": A scream usually heard only around the Stephens home whenever Darrin becomes very upset about the magic goings-on in his life.

"Sam, Can I See You?" "When?" "Now." "Oh!": Samantha and Darrin's beginning dialogue that takes place either immediately or shortly after some magical interference in their lives.

"Son of a Gun": A phrase usually employed by Larry whenever he is impressed with or approves of Darrin's advertising skills; once spoken a record seven times (in No. 31); also once stated by Samantha (in No. 174) and by Endora (No. 120).

"Uh-oh . . . Uh-oh . . . Uh-oh!": An extensive exclamation made by Samantha when it looks as if trouble is in the magic-making.

"Weeeeellll": A phrase Samantha employs whenever trouble really begins and she is unable to think of an answer to one of Darrin's queries of "What's going on?"

"Why did I say that?" A phrase various mortals use whenever witchcraft makes them say things against their will or things that they cannot have known.

"Witchcraft got you into this mess; I see no reason why witchcraft shouldn't get you out of it": A logic Samantha applies to Darrin's predicament in many instances.

Witches' Honor Sign, The: Samantha occasionally makes this galactic gesture to signify the absolute truth; an oath that Samantha usually asks of her mother, though Sam occasionally uses it to assure Darrin things are as she says they are. The correct *Witches' Honor Sign:* index and middle fingers of the left hand on either side of the nose with fingertips pointing toward the eyes. While giving the sign, the witch intones, "Witches' Honor." It can be done with the right hand as well. (In No. 144 Samantha asks Endora for the sign, with the added phrase: "Spiders that crawl, bats that fly, silence my tongue if I'm telling a lie.")

Zap: A colloquial term for casting a spell.

McMANN AND TATE'S ADVERTISING ACCOUNTS

EPISODE NO.	ACCOUNT	CLIENT
3	Barker Baby Food	Rex Barker
5	Caldwell Soup	Philip Caldwell
7	(Halloween candy)	Mr. Brinkman
8	————	Mr. Austen
11	Jasmine Perfume (Miss Jasmine campaign)	————
18	Margaret Marshall Cosmetics	Margaret Marshall
20	Woolfe Bros. Department Store	————
21	Jewel of the East (jewelry)	Mr. Pickering
23	Slegershamer's Dairy	————
30	Feather Touch Typewriters	————
35	Perfect Pizza Parlors	Linton Baldwin
36	Shelley's Shoes	————
38	Stanwyck Soap	Mr. Martin
41	E Z Open Flush Door	Mr. Foster
42	————	Howard Norton
43	party favors	Jack Rogers
44	Mother Jenny's Jam	Charles Barlow
45	Jarvis account; Slater account; Murphy Supermarket	————
46	toy ship models	Mr. Harding

EPISODE NO.	ACCOUNT	CLIENT
49	Harper's Honey	————
50	Hotchkiss Appliance Company	Ed Hotchkiss
52	Kingsley Potato Chips	————
53	————	H. J. Simpson
58	Hockestedder Toy Company	————
59	————	Randolph Turgen
60	————	J. T. Glendon Aubert of Paris
62	Naisley's Baby Food	————
63	Westchester Consolidated Mills	James Dennis Robinson
64	detergent	J. K. Kabaker
65	————	Osgood Rightmire
66	Robbins Baby Food Company	————
67	Robbins Baby Food Company	————
68	Stern Chemical Company	Sanford Stern
71	United Cosmetics	Toni Devlin
73	Waterhouse Thumbtack Company	————
75	Robbins Truck Transmissions	Mark Robbins
82	Wright Pens	————
83	MacElroy Shoes	Mr. MacElroy
85	————	Randolph Parkinson, Jr.
86	————	Max Cosgrove
87	Franklin Electronics	Bernie Franklin
89	Super Soapy Soap	Tom Scranton
92	Solow Toy Company	————
93	Sheldrake Sausage	Mr. Sheldrake
94	Morton Milk	C. L. Morton
95	Ganzer Garage Doors	————
96	Tropical Bathing Suits	————
97	————	Ed Pennybaker

EPISODE NO.	ACCOUNT	CLIENT
98	Cunningham Perfume	Mr. Cunningham
100	———————	Mr. Morgan
101	Warbell Dresses	Jay and Terry Warbell
102	Baldwin Blankets	Horace Baldwin
	Mayor Rocklin	Frank Eastwood
104	Madame Maruska Lipstick	Madame Maruska
105	———————	unnamed client
106	Saunders Soups	———————
107	Hornbeck Pharmaceutical	———————
108	Rohrbach Steel Company	———————
109	———————	Bob Chase
110	Chef Romani Foods	———————
112	Bigelow Tires	Mr. Bigelow
113	Carter Bros. Industrial Products (anti-smog device)	———————
114	Baxter Sporting Goods	Joe Baxter
117	Springer Pet Foods	Alvin Springer
120	Gregson Home Appliances	Mr. Gregson
121	———————	Mr. Grayson
122	Chappell Baby Foods	Roy Chappell
123	Mortimer Instant Soups	Jesse Mortimer
124	Mint Brite Toothpaste	J. P. Pritchfield
125	Autumn Flame Perfume	Bo Callahan
126	Webley Foods	J. P. Sommers
127	Prune Valley Retirement Village	Leroy Wendell
	———————	Jonathan Broadhurst
128	Giddings Tractors	———————
129	Abigail Adams Cosmetics	Mr. Blumberg
132	———————	Dwight Sharpe
134	Baker Foods	Edgar Baker

EPISODE NO.	ACCOUNT	CLIENT
136	Mishimoto TV Sets	Kensu Mishimoto
138	Omega National Bank	R. H. Markham
139	Hercules Tractors	Charles Gilbert
	Slocum Soup	O. J. Slocum
	Angel Coffee	————
146	Hascomb Drug Company	Whitney Hascomb
147	Zoom Detergent	H. L. Bradley
148	Barton Industries (Tinker Bell Diapers division)	Mr. Barton
149	E Z Way Rent-a-Car/Sav-Most Markets/Mossler Enterprises	Harlan Mossler
152	————	Mr. Stewart
153	Adrienne Sebastian Cosmetic Products	Adrianne Sebastian
155	Vino Vanita	Clio Vanita
157	"Fuzz Doll"	————
	Hanley's Department Store	Jim Hanley
	————	Mr. Henderson
158	Durfee's Dog Food	Oscar Durfee
159	Campbell Sporting Goods	Waldon R. Campbell
160	Struthers account	————
162	Brawn Cologne	Evelyn Tucker
164	————	J. Earl Rockeford
170	Bueno/aka Zap	Raul Garcia
172	Hampton Motors	Mr. Hampton
173	Top Tiger Cologne	Evelyn Charday
174	a detergent account	Mr. Paxton
175	Berkley Baby Foods	————
177	Bartenbach Beauty Products (dental creme, hair tonic, wart remover)	————
178	————	Alvin J. Sylvester
179	Illinois Meat-Packers	————

EPISODE NO.	ACCOUNT	CLIENT
180	Bliss Pharmaceutical	Silas Bliss, Sr., and Jr.
181	Bliss Pharmaceutical	Silas Bliss, Sr., and Jr.
183	Shotwell Pharmaceuticals	———
185	Tanaka Electronics (a division of Tanaka Enterprises)	Mr. Tanaka
187	Multiple Industries	H. B. Summers
189	———	Mr. Nickerson
190	Top Pop	———
191	Braddock Sporting Goods	Bob Braddock
192	Breeze Shampoo	———
194	Harrison Industries	John J. Harrison
195	a housing development	———
196	Dinsdale Soups	George Dinsdale
197	Barber Peaches	———
199	Sunshine Greeting Card Company	Augustus Sunshine
200	———	George Meiklejohn
201	Gotham Industries	———
202	———	Ernest Hitchcock
205	Barrows Umbrellas	———
206	British Imperial Textile Mills	Sir Leslie Bancroft
207	Blakely account	———
209	Gibbons Dog Burgers	Charlie Gibbons
210	Beau Geste Toiletries	Jennings Booker
211	Bigelow Industries	J. J. Langley
212	Harmon Savings and Loan	———
213	———	Mr. Brockway
214	Bobbins Candy Company/Bobbins Buttery Bonbons	Bernard Bobbins
216	Reducealator	Mr. Ferber
218	Rockfield Furniture	Lionel Rockfield
219	Berkley Hair Tonic	Roland Berkley

EPISODE NO.	ACCOUNT	CLIENT
220	Colonel Brigham Spareribs	Colonel Brigham
222	Cushman Cosmetics	————
223	Patterson account	————
	Bradwell account	————
	Cushman's Restaurant	————
224	Mother Flanagan's Irish Stew	Sean Flanagan
226	a client in Chicago—unnamed	————
227	Mount Rocky Mutual	Harold Jameson
232	Count Bracini's Olive Oil	————
233	House of Baldoni	Ernesto Baldoni
234	Europa Tours	Henri Sagan
235	Regal Silverware	————
236	Silverton Toy Company	Lester Silverton
237	Benson's Chili Con Carne	————
239	Monticello Carpets	Mr. Cushman
240	Tom Cat Tractors, Inc.	Mr. Buckeholder
241	————	Mr. Spengler
243	————	Mr. Norton
244	Prescott Shoes	Wilbur Prescott
245	Woolcott Towers	Harrison Woolcott
250	Whirlaway Washing Machines	Hector Jamison
252	Benson Sleep-Ezy Mattress	Mr. Benson
253	Ah Fong's Restaurant	Mr. Ah Fong
254	Cora May Sportswear	Cora May Franklin Mr. Franklin

EMMY AWARDS AND NOMINATIONS

(*denotes winner)

1965–66
Outstanding Comedy Series

BEWITCHED
The Dick Van Dyke Show (CBS)*
Batman (ABC)
Get Smart (NBC)
Hogan's Heroes (CBS)

Outstanding Continued Performance by an Actress in a Leading Role in a Comedy

ELIZABETH MONTGOMERY, *BEWITCHED*
Mary Tyler Moore, *The Dick Van Dyke Show**
Lucille Ball, *The Lucy Show* (CBS)

Outstanding Performance by an Actress in a Supporting Role in a Comedy

ALICE PEARCE, *BEWITCHED**
AGNES MOOREHEAD, *BEWITCHED*
Rose Marie, *The Dick Van Dyke Show*

Outstanding Directorial Achievement in a Comedy

WILLIAM ASHER, *BEWITCHED**
Paul Bogart, *Get Smart*
Jerry Paris, *The Dick Van Dyke Show*

1966–67
Outstanding Comedy Series

BEWITCHED
The Monkees (NBC)*
The Andy Griffith Show (CBS)
Hogan's Heroes

Outstanding Continued Performance by an Actress in a Leading Role in a Comedy Series

ELIZABETH MONTGOMERY, *BEWITCHED*
AGNES MOOREHEAD, *BEWITCHED*
Lucille Ball, *The Lucy Show**
Marlo Thomas, *That Girl* (ABC)

Outstanding Performance by an Actress in a Supporting Role in a Comedy

MARION LORNE, *BEWITCHED*
Frances Bavier, *The Andy Griffith Show** (CBS)
Nancy Kulp, *The Beverly Hillbillies* (CBS)

Outstanding Directorial Achievement in a Comedy

WILLIAM ASHER, *BEWITCHED*
James Frawley, *The Monkees**

1967–68
Outstanding Comedy Series

BEWITCHED
*Get Smart**
Family Affair (CBS)
Hogan's Heroes
The Lucy Show

Outstanding Continued Performance by an Actor in a Leading Role in a Comedy Series

DICK YORK, *BEWITCHED*
Don Adams, *Get Smart**
Richard Benjamin, *He and She* (CBS)
Sebastian Cabot, *Family Affair* (CBS)
Brian Keith, *Family Affair*

Outstanding Continued Performance by an Actress in a Leading Role in a Comedy Series

ELIZABETH MONTGOMERY, *BEWITCHED*
Lucille Ball, *The Lucy Show**
Barbara Feldon, *Get Smart*
Paula Prentiss, *He and She*
Marlo Thomas, *That Girl*

Outstanding Performance by an Actress in a Supporting Role in a Comedy Series

MARION LORNE, *BEWITCHED**
AGNES MOOREHEAD, *BEWITCHED*
Marge Redmond, *The Flying Nun* (ABC)
Nita Talbot, *Hogan's Heroes*

1968–69
Outstanding Comedy Series

BEWITCHED
*Get Smart**
Family Affair
The Ghost and Mrs. Muir (NBC)
Julia (NBC)

Outstanding Continued Performance by an Actress in a Leading Role in a Comedy Series

ELIZABETH MONTGOMERY, *BEWITCHED*
Hope Lange, *The Ghost and Mrs. Muir**

Diahann Carroll, *Julia*
Barbara Feldon, *Get Smart*

Outstanding Performance by an Actress in a Supporting Role in a Series
AGNES MOOREHEAD, *BEWITCHED*
Barbara Anderson, *Ironside* (NBC)
Susan St. James, *The Name of the Game** (NBC)

1969–70
Outstanding Continued Performance by an Actress in a Leading Role in a Comedy Series
ELIZABETH MONTGOMERY, *BEWITCHED*
Hope Lange, *The Ghost and Mrs. Muir** (ABC)
Marlo Thomas, *That Girl*

Outstanding Performance by an Actress in a Supporting Role in a Comedy Series
AGNES MOOREHEAD, *BEWITCHED*
Karen Valentine, *Room 222** (ABC)
Lurene Tuttle, *Julia*

1970–71
Outstanding Performance by an Actress in a Supporting Role in a Comedy Series
AGNES MOOREHEAD, *BEWITCHED*
Valerie Harper, *The Mary Tyler Moore Show* (CBS)*
Karen Valentine, *Room 222*

Outstanding Achievement in Makeup (A single program of a series or a special program)
ROLF J. MILLER, *BEWITCHED* ["SAMANTHA'S OLD MAN"]
Robert Dawn, *Mission Impossible* ["Catafalque] (CBS)*
Marie Roche, *Hamlet, Hallmark Hall of Fame* (NBC)
Perc Westmore, Harry C. Blake, *The Bill Cosby Show* [*The Third Bill Cosby Show*] (CBS)

ALSO: Bewitched **episode No. 213, "Sisters at Heart," received the Governor's Award at the 1971 Emmy Award Ceremony.**

The "*Bewitched* Theme" Lyrics (never used)

Bewitched, bewitched, you've got me in your spell.
Bewitched, bewitched, you know your craft so well.
Before I knew what you were doing, I looked in your eyes.
That brand of woo that you've been brew-in' took me by surprise.

You witch, you witch, one thing is for sure—
That stuff you pitch—just hasn't got a cure.
My heart was under lock and key—but somehow it got unhitched.
I never thought my heart could be had.
But now I'm caught and I'm kinda glad to be—
Bewitched. Bewitched—witched.

Words and music by Howard Greenfield and Jack Keller.

MEMORABILIA

***Bewitched* Merchandise**

Stymie Card Game [Milton Bradley, 1964]
Jigsaw Puzzle (painting) with enclosed photo of Samantha [Milton Bradley, 1964]
The Samantha and Endora Board Game [Game Gems, 1965]
Fun and Activity Book [Treasure Books, 1965]
Story Book [Grosset and Dunlap, 1965]
Bewitched (Paperback Novel) by Al Hine [Dell, February 1965]
Comic Book Series Nos. 1 through 14 [Dell, April 1965 to October 1969]
Elizabeth Montgomery Paper Dolls [1966]
Tabitha (spelled "Tab*a*tha" on box)—The "Bewitched Baby" Paper Dolls [Magic Wand Corporation, 1966]
Samantha Doll [1966]
Tabitha Doll [1966]
Plastic Play Dishes for Tabitha Doll [1968]
Hardcover Novel: *The Opposite Uncle* by William Johnston [Whitman, 1970]

Elizabeth Montgomery gazing into a Bewitched *comic book, 1965. (Columbia Pictures Television.)*

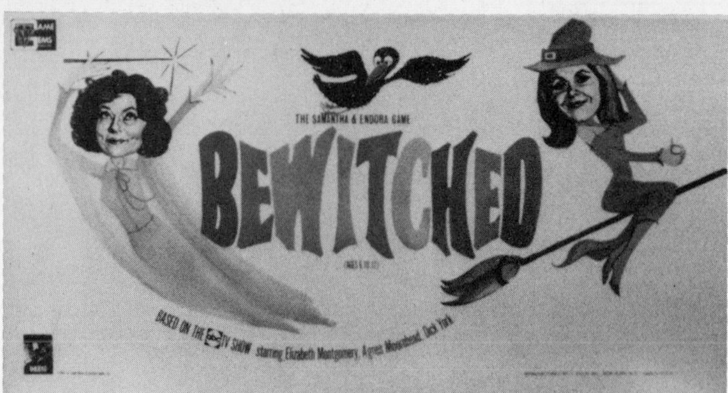

The Samantha/Endora board game by Game Gems.

"Along for the Ride" jigsaw puzzle by Milton Bradley.

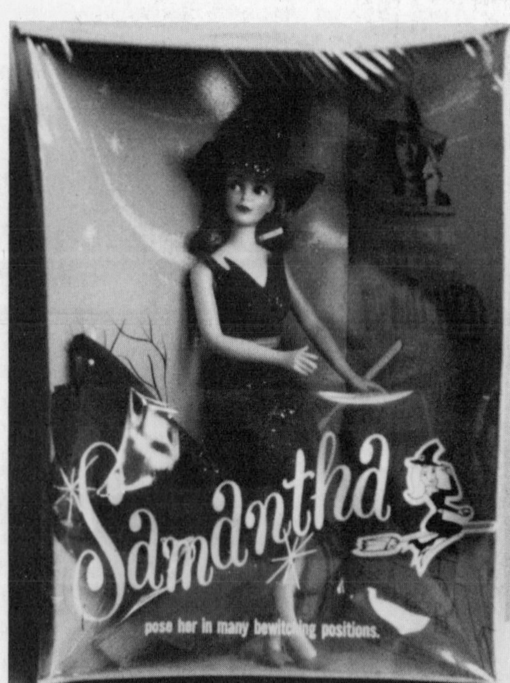

The Samantha Bewitched *posing doll by Ideal.*

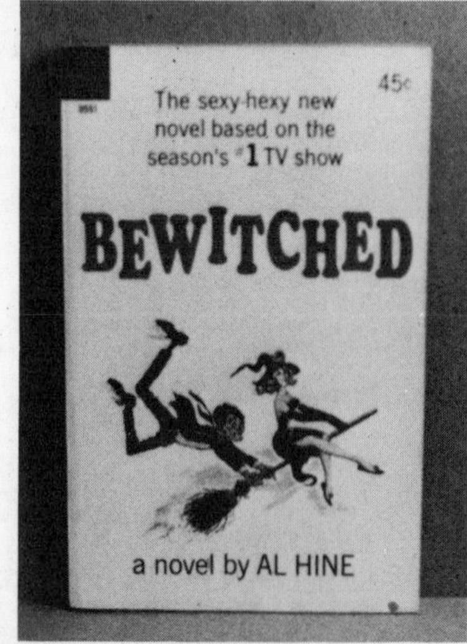

Bewitched *paperback by Al Hine/Dell.*

BEWITCHED DISCOGRAPHY

Albums

Milton DeLugg and His Orchestra: *Music For Monsters, Munsters, Mummies and Other TV Fiends* (Epic LN-24125 mono/BN-26125 Stereo) 1965.

Frank Devol: *TV Potpourri—Themes from Top Television Shows* (Audio Fidelity AFLP 2146 mono/AFSD 6146 Stereo) 1965. [Note: This LP also rereleased through Realistic/Audio Fidelity Boxed Set: *The Wonderful World of Music*, 50-2003, 1968.]

Peggy Lee: *Pass Me By* (Capitol T-2320 mono/ST-2300 Stereo) [Vocal] 1965.

Jimmy Smith: *Monster* [Arranged and Conducted by Oliver Nelson] (Verve V-8618 mono/V6-8618 Stereo) 1965.

Lawrence Welk: *My First of 1965* (Dot DLP 3616 mono/DLP 25616 Stereo) 1965.

45rpm Singles

Billy Costa (Colpix 750) 1965.

Paul and Mimi Evans (Epic 5-9726) [Vocal] 1965.

Steve Lawrence (Columbia 4-43192) [Vocal] 1965.

Peggy Lee (Capitol 5404) [Vocal/same as album] 1965.

Frankie Randall (RCA 47-8434) [Vocal] 1965.

Foreign (Albums)

The Castle Music Orchestra/Conducted by Eric Cook: *Castle Music, Volume 1* (Castle Music LTD YPRX-1409 Stereo) [Australia], no date.

Additions (Albums)

Various Artists: *Television's Greatest Hits, Volume II* (TeeVee Toons TVT-1200) 1986. [Note: no artist credited on all these recreations (including "Bewitched" theme).]

Emily Yancy: *Yancy* (Mainstream 56046 mono/S 6046 Stereo) [Vocal] 1965.

Irene Reid: *Room for One More* [Arranged and conducted by Oliver Nelson] (Verve V-8621 Mono/V6-8621 Stereo) 1965.

"OH, MY STARS, STAFF, AND CREW"— BIOGRAPHIES

Elizabeth Montgomery (Samantha)

Elizabeth Montgomery made her professional debut in a drama called "Top Secret" on her father's television series, *Robert Montgomery Presents*, December 3, 1951. She played her father's daughter.

She later became a regular featured player on her father's show and also appeared in a number of other television anthology series, including *Studio One, The Twilight Zone, Kraft Theater, G.E. Theater, Alcoa Presents, One Step Beyond,* and *Armstrong Circle Theater.*

Elizabeth also appeared on Broadway in plays such as *The Loud Red Patrick* with Arthur Kennedy and David Wayne, and *Late Love,* which featured Arlene Francis and Cliff Robertson. The latter was Elizabeth's first Broadway play, in the 1953–54 season, and she received the Theatre World Award for Most Promising Newcomer.

After a brief marriage in 1954 to Frederick Gallatin Gammann, the son of an old and socially prominent New York family, Elizabeth married the late actor Gig Young and semiretired from acting. Her marriage to Young lasted six years (1957–63), and she returned to acting full throttle, making three films in a row. The first was *Johnny Cool* (1963). On that film she met and married future *Bewitched* associate William Asher, who directed and produced *Cool.*

Elizabeth also appeared in *Who's Been Sleeping in My Bed?* which was released in 1964 and starred Dean Martin and her good friend Carol Burnett, and *The Court Martial of Billy Mitchell* (1955), featuring Gary Cooper (and Robert F. Simon, who later played her father-in-law on *Bewitched*).

When *Bewitched* ended its run in 1972, Liz took one year off and returned to television in a movie-of-the-week, entitled *The Victim.* It was her first dramatic performance since before *Bewitched.* Other television films followed, including *Mrs. Sundance* (1974) and the chilling *Legend of Lizzie Borden* (1975).

Her shattering portrayal of a sexually and emotionally abused woman in *A Case of Rape* (1974) earned her an Emmy nomination. *A Case of Rape* received one of the ten highest ratings for a made-for-television film in the medium's history.

Other small-screen movies included *Dark Victory* (a 1976 remake of the Bette

Elizabeth Montgomery. (Courtesy of Elizabeth Montgomery.)

Davis 1939 film classic about a woman with a brain tumor), *A Killing Affair* (a 1977 interracial love story also starring O. J. Simpson), *The Awakening Land* (a 1978 miniseries), *An Act of Violence* (1979), *When the Circus Comes to Town* (a 1981 romantic comedy), *The Rules of Marriage* (a two-part movie with Elliott Gould made in 1982), and *Missing Pieces* (1983).

There were also *Second Sight: A Love Story* (1984), *Amos* (with Kirk Douglas in 1985), *From the Darkness Till the Dawn* (also in 1985), *Face to Face* (which aired in 1990 and also starred Elizabeth's longtime love, Robert Foxworth—of *Falcon Crest* fame—whom she had met some years before on *Mrs. Sundance*), and *Sins of the Mother* (based on the true-crime book *Son* [1991]).

Each of these films has shown a different side of the actress's talents. "They all have different kinds of 'feels' to them," says Elizabeth, "and that's probably one of the reasons why I've done them. I get letters from people saying one of the things they like best about what I've done since *Bewitched* is that they never know what I'm going to do next."

E*lizabeth Montgomery. (Herbie J Pilato collection.)*

With all her experience as an actress, Elizabeth Montgomery has had dreams of being a criminal lawyer, a jockey, and an artist for Walt Disney Studios. Of the last-named aspiration, she adds with a smile, "But for some reason, I was never asked to be on the payroll. Certainly ruined Walt's career, didn't I?"

However, her artistic talent has been highly praised. "One gift I'll always treasure," says *Bewitched* director R. Robert Rosenbaum, "is the painting of a man sitting in a director's chair that Elizabeth created for me."

Besides her acting career Elizabeth remains active as a political advocate for many causes, including the AIDS Project, Amnesty International, and the peace movement. Of her involvement with these interest groups, she says: "There are times when I know I could still be doing more, as there are many other things in life that are certainly more important than acting."

Elizabeth lives in Los Angeles with actor Robert Foxworth. Besides painting, Elizabeth also enjoys tennis, gardening, and cooking. Her children are Robert Asher, Bill Asher, Jr., and Rebecca Asher.

Dick York (Darrin)

Born on September 4, 1928, in Fort Wayne, Indiana, Dick York had always possessed social awareness and concern for others, and was an advocate for the homeless and the less fortunate. He believed the seeds of his acting career were sown in his Depression-era childhood in Chicago, a city where he began in radio in the late 1930s.

He appeared in many network and local shows, including *Junior Junction* (a children's show), *Jack Armstrong: The All-American Boy* (in 1948), and *That Brewster Boy.*

A student of St. Paul University, Dick moved to New York in 1950 and began acting on television in many live productions. When television began to move west, so did York, and he started a commuting routine between New York and the West Coast that ended when he finally moved his family to Hollywood in 1961.

York met his wife, Joan, whom he called Joey, when he was fifteen and she was twelve and they were both acting in a Chicago radio show. He practically ignored her at first, but years later they met again, courted, and in 1952, married. Five children followed.

Years before his move to California, York was asked to read for Broadway director Elia Kazan, who cast him in *Tea and Sympathy* in 1953. This brought York a nomination for the Best Supporting Actor Award from the New York Drama Critics. He was also nominated for an Emmy in 1968 for *Bewitched,* as Outstanding Continued Performance by an Actor in a Leading Role in a Comedy Series.

Dick York. *(Copyright 1968 Columbia Pictures Television.)*

York appeared in numerous other television shows, including guest spots on *Playhouse 90*, *The Twilight Zone* (two episodes), *Alfred Hitchcock Presents* (as a hired killer), *Route 66*, *Thriller*, *Rawhide*, *Wagon Train*, *Goodyear Playhouse* (*Visit to a Small Planet*, 1955), *The U.S. Steel Hour*, *Father Knows Best*, and *Kraft Theatre*.

After *Bewitched*, he appeared on *Simon and Simon*, *Fantasy Island*, and *Our Time*, a mid-1980s NBC summer show hosted by Karen Valentine (of *Room 222* fame). York appeared on the *Tonight Show* to promote *Our Time*. His guest shot with Valentine was his final on-air acting appearance (on August 10, 1985).

York's film credits include *My Sister Eileen* (1955), *Cowboy* (1958), *They Came to Cordura* (1959), during the filming of which he developed a back ailment, and *Inherit the Wind* (1960).

York lived in Rockford, Michigan, suffering from a deteriorating spine and emphysema. Despite his physical condition, the actor established Dick York's Acting for Life, an organization dedicated to feeding the homeless. This is evidence that York was a most amazing man: not only a master of his craft, but of his heart.

Not one for sympathy, he had said: "I'm going to keep on doing what I'm doing, no matter what happens. . . . And whether or not *Bewitched* had given me the opportunity to become a 'known personality,' I still would have pursued the path I'm on now.

"There are so many young people who cut their teeth on *Bewitched*," he had continued, "that I'm more amazed every day at the show's response. I guess you never know the impact you're going to have."

York died on February 21, 1992, at sixty-three years of age.

Dick Sargent (Darrin)

Dick Sargent was literally born into show business. His mother, Ruth McNaughton, was an actress who had supporting roles in films like *Four Horsemen of the Apocalypse* (1961) and *Hearts and Triumphs* (1962). And his father, Colonel Elmer Cox, was the business manager of Douglas Fairbanks, among others.

Sargent was enrolled at San Rafael Military Academy in San Rafael, California (near San Francisco), and at the Menlo School in Menlo Park. During his years at Stanford University, he starred in some twenty-five plays with the Stanford Players Theater. He was born Richard Cox, and upon his graduation, he won a bit part in MGM's *Prisoner of War* (1954) and changed his name to Sargent.

As a struggling actor he sustained his hopes and needs with a variety of nontheatrical jobs. He even dug ditches. Leaving a position as a department store salesman, he journeyed to the colonial city of San Miguel Allende in Mexico to enter the import-export business. He later began collecting Mexican art.

He returned to Hollywood and TV roles in *Medic*, *Playhouse 90*, *Gunsmoke*, *Ripcord*, *West Point*, and *Code 3*.

His first major role in a motion picture was as Fo Fo Wilson in *Bernardine* in 1957, for which he received a Laurel Award from the nation's film exhibitors. His other movies include *Operation Petticoat* (1959), *The Ghost and Mr. Chicken* (1966), *Captain Newman, M.D.* (1963), *The Great Impostor* (1961), *That Touch of Mink* (1962), and *For Love or Money* (1964).

D*ick Sargent. (Dick Sargent collection.)*

Sargent has made dramatic appearances on TV's *Fantasy Island*, *Vegas*, *Trapper John, M.D.*, etc., and in films like *Hardcore* (1979) with George C. Scott. He credits his age and his ability to draw upon a larger experience of life as contributory to his expansion as an actor.

His other television appearances have included *Family Ties* and an episode of the revived *Columbo* series. In that appearance, Dick played himself sitting in on a poker party with actress Nancy Walker and other celebrities. Peter Falk's character quizzes the game players about a particular mystery. Falk recognizes Dick from *Bewitched* and says something to the effect of "Hey, I loved that show."

In all, Sargent has appeared in twenty-three motion pictures, four made-for-television movies, and five series of his own. In the most recent, *Down to Earth*, instead of having a witch for a wife, he had an angel (Carol Mansell as Ethel) for a maid.

Involved with such organizations as the Special Olympics and World Hunger, Sargent is constantly on the go. He travels from one American city to the next in promotion of the unique Olympic program. His dedication to ridding the world of hunger and offering hope and support in places where there is little of either has also taken him from continent to continent.

The Special Olympics, he says, "has been one of the most rewarding experiences of my life. There are so many of these athletes who can tell me the plots of every *Bewitched* episode. No matter what they're going through, the show seems to be one of the things their minds cling to.

"And this makes me happy to know that the power of television has been put to good use. And that the accident of celebrity can be used for something besides filling up scrapbooks."

Dick Sargent has recently revealed that he is homosexual. The high rate of suicide among young homosexuals, Sargent says, is the reason for his coming out of the closet. His message is that gay and lesbian people "are just like everybody else."

Agnes Moorehead (Endora)

Of Protestant Irish background, Agnes Robertson Moorehead was born on December 6, 1906, in Clinton, Massachusetts, the only child of Reverend John Henderson Moorehead, a minister. Her mother, Mary Mildred MacCauley, had been reared in rural Pennsylvania. Soon after the birth of Agnes, the Mooreheads moved to St. Louis, Missouri, where Mr. Moorehead had been assigned to a new pastorate.

At age ten, Agnes spent her summers performing in the theater and also worked with the St. Louis Municipal Opera Company for four years. After completing high school in 1919, Agnes attended Muskingum College in New Concord, Ohio, a coeducational institution founded by an uncle. While there, Agnes majored in biology, performed in the glee club, and was an active member of the Girls' Athletic Association and the Student Volunteer Group.

After receiving her B.A. degree, she remained at Muskingum for an additional year of postgraduate work, majoring in education, speech, and English. The following year she transferred to the University of Wisconsin to be closer to home. There she earned her master's degree in English and public speaking. She later received a Ph.D. in literature from Bradley University in Illinois.

While at Wisconsin, she began teaching English and public speaking at the Central High School in nearby Soldiers Grove, Wisconsin, and coaching the local drama club. Shortly thereafter, in 1926, she enrolled in the American Academy of Dramatic Arts in New York, where she met John Griffith Lee, whom she married on June 6, 1930. It was not long before she began winning Broadway and radio roles. Soon she was one of radio's most active performers. She took part in such programs as *The March of Time*, *Cavalcade of America*, and *Mayor of the Town*. One of her most notable performances was in the radio play *Sorry, Wrong Number*. Her comedy credits were *The Fred Allen Show*, *The Phil Baker Show* (in which she worked with *Bewitched* executive producer Harry Ackerman), and stints with Bob Hope and Jack Benny.

Yet it was her longtime association with Orson Welles's historic Mercury Theatre Company in New York City where she received the most rigorous training.

Agnes Moorehead. (Columbia Pictures Television.)

This was an ensemble with a theatrical hierarchy including Welles himself and other acting greats such as Joseph Cotten and Everett Sloan as well as director John Houseman.

When the Mercury Players made their first film, *Citizen Kane*, in 1941, Agnes made her screen debut as Kane's mother. Other movies with the Welles troupe included *The Magnificient Ambersons* (1942)—she was nominated for an Oscar for her role as Aunt Fanny—as well as *Journey into Fear* (1943) and *Jane Eyre* (1944).

In addition to her role in *Ambersons*, Agnes was nominated for an Academy Award for three other films (though she never won): *Mrs. Parkington* (1944), *Johnny Belinda* (1948), and *Hush . . . Hush, Sweet Charlotte* (1964). Her other films included *Dark Passage* (1947), *The Revolt of Mamie Stover* and *The Conquerer* (1956), which was filmed near St. George, Utah. Ironically, *The Conqueror* is now in the midst of a controversial investigation. Moorehead, Dick Powell, John Wayne, and Susan Hayward, all members of the cast, have died of cancer. Many claim these deaths were attributable to the film's location shooting, which was close to a nuclear testing site, and to the fact that tons of Utah's red soil was brought back to the studio sets for matching purposes.

Moorehead's numerous television appearances include *The Twilight Zone*, *Shirley Temple Theater*, *Studio One*, *Night Gallery* (she played an old crone of a witch), and *The Wild, Wild West* (for which she won an Emmy for her role as Emma Valentine in the episode titled "Night of the Vicious Valentine"). In the early fifties she toured the U.S. and Europe in readings of *Don Juan in Hell*. Moorehead took many stage bows with the Mercury Players, but later, during the filming of *Bewitched*, she toured the country with her one-woman show, *An Evening with the Fabulous Redhead*.

However, her favorite color wasn't red . . . it was lavender. In fact, she was nicknamed the "Lavender Lady" by one of the many maids of her Beverly Hills home because she always wore some shade of purple, drove a 1956 lavender Thunderbird, and decorated her mansion and both her *Bewitched* dressing rooms in her pet hue. She also appeared in purple often as Endora.

David White (Larry Tate)

David White was born in Denver, Colorado, on April 4, 1916. He received his dramatic training in the 1940s at the Cleveland Playhouse, the Pasadena Playhouse, and Los Angeles City College.

After serving overseas with the Marine Corps for twenty-eight months during World War II, David spent the early postwar era appearing in the stage productions of *Home of the Brave*, *Command Decision*, and *State of the Union*. Shortly thereafter, he landed his first major Broadway role in *Leaf and Bough*. He played a small-town drunk with two sons (Richard Hart and Charlton Heston—who was only eight years younger than David).

David White. *(Columbia Pictures Television.)*

Though the play was a critical failure and ran only two days, David's performance was impressive and he went on to more successful Broadway productions, such as *The Bird Cage*, *Anniversary Waltz*, and *Romeo and Juliet*, among many others.

White's film credits include *Sweet Smell of Success* (1957), *The Apartment* (1960), *Sunrise at Campobello* (1960), *The Great Impostor* (1961), and *Madison Avenue* (1962).

Before *Bewitched*, he appeared in many television dramas, including *Studio One*, *Kraft Theatre*, *Playhouse 90*, and *The Untouchables*. He appeared in the latter in an episode called "The Rusty Heller Story," which featured Elizabeth Montgomery in the lead.

After *Bewitched*, White made numerous guest appearances in series TV, including *The Rockford Files*, *Rhoda*, and *Phyllis*, as well as *The Mary Tyler Moore Show*, *Quincy*, *Remington Steele*, and *Cagney and Lacey*.

He also appeared in such stage productions as *Savages* (at the Mark Taper Forum in Los Angeles), *Enemy of the People* (at the Seattle Repertory), and *Catholics* (at ACT, Seattle).

To pay the rent before his acting career began to flourish, David worked as a farmer, a truck driver, and an executive doorman at the Roxy Theater in New York. He was for a while employed by the J. H. Taylor Management Company, also in New York, and was offered a very prestigious management position but turned it down. "I responded with a very pleasant 'No, thank you, sir,'" he said, "'I'm going to be an actor."

White died on November 26, 1990. He was married to the late actress Mary Welch, who once appeared with her husband on stage in a tour of *Tea and Sympathy*. She also played Charity Hackett in Samuel Fuller's movie version of *Park Row* (1952), and enjoyed a large variety of television credits.

David White, 1989. (Courtesy of David White.)

Marion Lorne (Aunt Clara)

Before *Bewitched,* TV viewers knew Marion Lorne as Mrs. Guerny on *Mr. Peepers,* starring Wally Cox, and as a stooge on *The Gary Moore Show.* Long before that, Lorne had been the reigning star for many years at the Whitehall Theatre in London.

There she appeared in hit after hit, all written especially for her by her late husband, Walter Hackett. "There is no actress on the stage today who can be compared with her," wrote one critic.

Lorne was never a raving beauty, and she knew it, but she didn't care because she also knew her forte was comedy. She told *TV Guide* in 1968, "In my long, long career, I have played everything, but comedy has always been my favorite." Most of the characters her husband created for her seem to have been in the Aunt Clara mold. "People seem to like this vague, silly woman," she said.

When Alfred Hitchcock directed her in *Strangers on a Train,* he was asked what American actress could Lorne be compared to in her London days. Tallulah Bankhead? Helen Hayes? Katherine Cornell? "All of them put together," he replied, "and more. She was more than an actress in England; she was an institution."

Though Lorne's initial theatrical success was in London, she was born in the United States in 1886 in a Pennsylvania mining town called West Pittston, near Wilkes-Barre. Her parents were Scottish and English. She attended the American Academy of Dramatic Arts in New York, played summer stock in Hartford, Connecticut, and finally made it to Broadway, where she was an instant hit. "I've been in a complete and absolute panic ever since," she once said. "I've always wanted to retire, but I could never quit."

Marion Lorne. *(Fredric Tucker collection.)*

She did try to retire after the sudden death of her husband in 1942. But shortly afterward she was offered the part of the potty old lady, Veta Louise Simmons, in the road company of *Harvey*.

Lorne also appeared in several other stage productions as well as on numerous TV shows, including *The Ed Sullivan Show, The Dinah Shore Show,* and *The Jack Paar Show*—all before *Bewitched*. Then, in 1964, she became Aunt Clara; a role, some say, Marion was born to play.

Before she succumbed to heart failure on May 9, 1968, at the age of eighty-two, she had made twenty-eight appearances as Samantha's bumbling, charming relative.

Regular Guest Stars

Paul Lynde (Uncle Arthur)

Broadway, film, and television audiences began their love affair with Paul Lynde at the Number One Fifth Avenue, where Paul received his first break . . . as a stand-up comedian. Then came Leonard Sillman's *New Faces of 1952* on Broadway (which also launched the careers of people like Eartha Kitt, Carol Lawrence,

Paul Lynde. (Nancy Noce.)

and Alice Ghostley, among many others), a two-year run on TV with *The Perry Como Show,* and the Broadway and film versions of *Bye Bye Birdie* (the movie in 1963), which featured Lynde's rousing rendition of the tune "Kids."

Before his untimely death from a heart attack in January 1982, he appeared in the plays *The Impossible Years, Don't Drink the Water, Plaza Suite* (all summer stock productions), and in the movies *New Faces* (1954, with Alice Ghostley), *Send Me No Flowers* (1964), and *Rabbit Test* (1978). Besides playing Uncle Arthur on *Bewitched,* Lynde appeared on TV's *The Dean Martin Show, The Kraft Music Hall, The Donny and Marie Show,* and the daytime and prime-time versions of the game show *Hollywood Squares,* where he occupied the famous center square. He also starred in two series of his own: *The Paul Lynde Show* and *The New Temperatures Rising Show,* both of which were produced by William Asher, who also directed Lynde in the feature *Beach Blanket Bingo* (1965) and, of course, *Bewitched.*

The flamboyant performer made many movie appearances, before and after *Bewitched.* In fact, two of his stage productions were related to *Bewitched.* First, Lynde appeared with Elizabeth Montgomery's mother, Elizabeth Allen, in *Mother Is Engaged,* and then with Alice Ghostley in *Stop, Thief, Stop.* And he handled his success well.

"I always had illusions of grandeur," Lynde told an interviewer in 1974. "As far back as I can remember I was obsessed with being rich and famous."

Lynde was born and raised in Mount Vernon, Ohio, and was a graduate of Northwestern University.

He lived his formative years in the Mount Vernon jail, where his father was sheriff for a two-year elective term. Paul dated his original urge to become an actor from the time he was four or five years old. Shortly after the birth of a younger brother, his mother took him to see the original film version of *Ben Hur* (1926), and as he said in 1974, "I was movie struck then, and I am movie struck now."

Alice Ghostley (Esmeralda)

Alice Ghostley was born in Eve, Missouri, and spent part of her childhood in Arkansas and Oklahoma. It was in a small Oklahoma town that her high school teacher inspired her to pursue a dramatic career. Following graduation from the University of Oklahoma, where she minored in drama, she headed for New Jersey and eventually New York.

"I always wanted to be a movie star like Ruby Keeler, and I was just seventeen, so I thought the big city was the place to begin." She was also inspired by a cousin who was a tightrope walker for the Barnum & Bailey Circus. She later teamed up with her sister, Gladys, and they did an act called the Ghostley Sisters.

"When I first started out," says Ghostley, "I had this natural ability to sing . . . and that was another reason why I picked New York . . . with all the musicals that were happening at the time. But because I looked so different from everybody . . . I was never what you would call an ingenue, I was having difficulty finding jobs. 'Get your eyes straightened,' they would tell me, 'and maybe we could work with you.'"

Alice Ghostley as Esmeralda. (Columbia Pictures Television.)

Alice Ghostley today. (Courtesy of Alice Ghostley.)

For a while, nothing was happening, and to pay for acting and singing lessons, Ghostley worked in a restaurant, a cosmetics factory, a detective agency, and a motion picture theater. Finally, after some assistance from actor/composer/lyricist G. Wood, her big break came: singing "The Boston Beguine" in *New Faces of 1952* with her future *Bewitched* associate, Paul Lynde.

Other Broadway appearances included *The Sign in Sidney Brustein's Window,* for which she earned a Tony Award for Best Actress and the *Saturday Review* Award for Best Performance of 1964–65. She also received a Tony Award nomination for her role in *The Beauty Part* by S. J. Perlman.

She recently appeared in the Broadway production of *Annie* as Miss Hannigan for 907 performances, and in the New York and Vancouver productions of *Nunsense.*

In addition to her stage appearances, Ghostley also has been featured in several films, including *To Kill a Mockingbird* (1962), *The Flim Flam Man* (1967), *Viva Max* (1969), *Gator* (1976), *Rabbit Test* (with Paul Lynde, 1978), and *Grease* (also 1978).

On television today, she can be seen as Bernice Clifton in the popular *Designing Women* sitcom. She is also remembered for her TV performances in such diverse productions as *Twelfth Night*, *The Jackie Gleason Show*, a starring role in the *Captain Nice* series (1966–67), and *The Jonathan Winters Show* (1967–69).

Ghostley lives in Studio City, California, with her husband, actor Felice Orlandi.

Bernard Fox (Dr. Bombay)

Born in South Wales, Bernard Fox is the fifth generation of his family to pursue a career in the theater. During the war he served in the Royal Navy, and on his release he joined the well-known York Repertory Company. In 1952 he appeared with the Whitehall Farce Players in London in *Reluctant Heroes*, *Simple Spymen*, and *Dry Rot.*

Bernard Fox today. (Courtesy of Bernard Fox.)

After leaving the Whitehall, he was seen in other London productions such as G. B. Shaw's *Misalliance, Saturday Night at the Crown,* and a musical version of *The Bells* at the Irving Theatre.

In England, he appeared in such films as *Star of India* (1954), *Blue Murder at St Trinians* (1958), and *The Safecracker* (1958) with Ray Milland. The 1958–59 English television season saw him starring in *Three Live Wires,* a sitcom somewhat similar to America's *Sergeant Bilko* series with Phil Silvers.

Bernard's first appearance in Hollywood was made at the Civic Playhouse in a production of *Write Me a Murder,* which led to numerous television appearances in programs like *The Danny Thomas Show, The Dick Van Dyke Show,* and *The Andy Griffith Show.* Besides his recurring role as Dr. Bombay on *Bewitched,* he was also featured as a semiregular on *Hogan's Heroes,* as Colonel Crittenden. His theatrical films of that time include *Strange Bedfellows* (1964), *Star!* (1968), and *Big Jake* (1971).

After *Bewitched,* he went on to star in the 1972 TV movie *The Hound of the Baskervilles,* in which he played Dr. Watson to Stewart Granger's Sherlock Holmes. Featured roles in films followed in Walt Disney's *Herbie Goes to Monte Carlo* (1977) and *Private Eyes* (1980).

From 1973 to 1979, Bernard was the Victorian chairman (master of ceremonies) in America's only British music hall, the Mayfair Music Hall in Santa Monica, California, which now houses a West Coast troupe of Chicago's Second City comedians. The experience and knowledge gained in those years proved invaluable when he put together his one-man show, *Music Hall Memories,* which plays successfully around colleges, conventions, private groups, and in large gatherings such as the British-American festival in Sante Fe Springs, California.

Fox lives with his wife, Jacqueline, and their two daughters, Amanda and Valerie, in California's San Fernando Valley. He frequently makes guest appearances on shows such as *Murder, She Wrote.*

Erin and Diane Murphy (Tabitha)

Erin and her twin sister Diane Murphy were born on June 17, 1964, at the West Valley Hospital in Encino, California. Diane is five minutes older than Erin. Following their birth, their mother, Stephanie, gave up her job as a teacher to devote her full time to the girls. Wherever she took them, the twins drew attention. When a talent agent wanted to sign up the girls, Stephanie and her husband, Dan, agreed to give it a try.

Erin and Diane made their show business debut when they were a year old in a soap commercial with a man who was to become governor of California and president of the United States—Ronald Reagan.

Today Diane and Erin, age twenty-eight, lead very different lives.

Erin has recently divorced and is a single parent to Jason and Grant. She prefers that they *not* watch her reruns. However, she is now all set to recharge her career.

"I really am excited about getting back into the business," she says. *Bewitched* "was most inspiring in that sense." In fact, Agnes Moorhead organized a fencing and

Erin Murphy today. (Mark Gilman.)

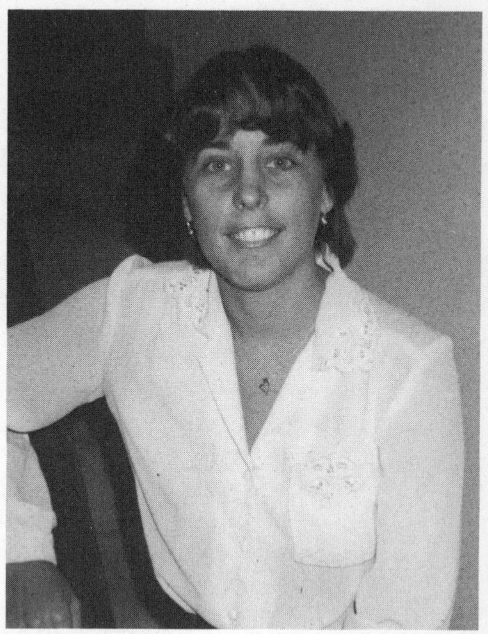

Diane Murphy today. (Mark Gilman.)

acting school at one time, and Erin was to attend after the series ended, but Agnes passed away before that could happen.

Since leaving *Bewitched*, Erin has made only a few appearances on shows like *Lassie* and *Hawaii Five-O*, but she sees an exciting future ahead.

Diane, who is openly gay, has an M.B.A. in management from Golden Gate University, Santa Barbara, and a B.A. in psychology and sociology from the University of California, Santa Barbara.

Currently she is the associate executive director of Shelter Services for Women, a nonprofit organization that operates three shelters for battered women and their children in Santa Barbara. Her primary duties are grant writing, contract management, and budgeting.

She is also a member of the board of directors of the Greater Santa Barbara Community Association, an organization comprised of business, professional, and community members who are gay and lesbian. She served as chairperson of the association's scholarship committee, which gives scholarships to gay and lesbian students based upon their grades and community involvement.

At the moment, she is single and living with her cat, Sugar, in a Santa Barbara condo. "I'm very happy with my life," she says. "I loved working on *Bewitched*, and it gave me some unique and wonderful experiences, but eventually, I wanted to lead a more normal life. So I quit the entertainment business when I was thirteen years old."

Before she left Hollywood, Diane appeared in numerous commercials (including one with Henry Fonda) and other television shows such as the *ABC Afterschool Special* and *The Magical Mystery Trip Through Little Red's Head*.

David and Greg Lawrence (Adam)

Asked what they are doing today, David and Greg Lawrence both respond, "Finding ourselves!" Gifted in both art and writing poetry, they have been in and out of college several times, looking for the ultimate path on which they wish to travel. David looks up from painting Simpson characters on a denim jacket for a

David Lawrence today. (Mark Gilman.)

Greg Lawrence today. (Mark Gilman.)

woman who so admired the one he made for himself that she stopped him on the street and offered to pay him $100 if he would make her one for her grandson. "Who knows," he says. "One of these days I may even return to acting, but for now I prefer to kick back and experiment with a lot of different things."

One of the things the boys experimented with was operating a small pizza and pasta restaurant in Simi Valley, California. Though they developed a happy and faithful clientele, they found themselves bored with the restaurant business after two years and decided to sell.

Greg, an avid water and snow skier, currently works as a waiter at Chin Chin, a popular Chinese restaurant in Studio City, California. Laughing, Greg explains, "I can always say I'm a struggling actor working as a waiter between jobs, but the truth is this gives me time to decide what I want to do when I grow up, which I'm not at all sure I want to do anytime soon!"

David and Greg's mother, while admitting that her boys are typical children of the eighties and she is a parent from the fifties who would prefer to see them well educated, with their feet firmly planted on a path toward a responsible and lucrative future, nevertheless has complete faith in her sons.

"Not only are they gorgeous, bright, and extremely creative young men," she says, "but they are warm, generous, and caring . . . beloved by friends and family alike."

Their mother tells the story of her recent meeting with a psychic, who out of thin air exclaimed, "Stop worrying about your sons. They are slow starters, but once they find themselves, the world better watch out!"

Maurice Evans (Maurice)

Born in the market town of Dorchester, Dorset, England, Maurice Evans was the son of a Welsh druggist and part-time justice of the peace, who also fancied himself a dramatist. Young Maurice began acting in his father's adaptations of Thomas Hardy's novels, making his first appearance on stage in Hardy's *Under the Greenwood Tree*. The boy also had a fair voice and sang in the St. Andrews choir in Stoke Newington after his family moved to London.

He then worked in little theater before making his professional debut in Cambridge in 1926, when he played Orestes in *The Oresteia*. But it was his performance as Lieutenant Raleigh in *Journey's End* that made him a London sensation. As a result he appeared in leading roles in approximately twenty plays between 1930 and 1934.

After numerous other stage performances in Shakespearean roles like Falstaff, Hamlet, and Henry IV, Maurice and wartime friend George Schaefer (former associate dean of theater, film, and television at UCLA) produced *The Teahouse of the August Moon* in 1953. This satire about a U.S. Army unit trying to bring democracy to a Pacific island starred David Wayne and ran on Broadway for 1,027 performances, capturing the 1954 Pulitzer Prize for drama and a Tony Award. Furthermore, while *Teahouse* was still thriving, Evans (this time with Emmett Rogers) produced *No Time for Sergeants*, about a hillbilly draftee who nearly brings the army to its knees. It ran for two years and made a star of Andy

Maurice Evans as Maurice. (Columbia Pictures Television.)

Griffith, who went on to star in the film version (1958), as well as the original television version, which premiered on the *U.S. Steel Hour* on March 15, 1955.

Also in 1955, Maurice established a relationship with television's *Hallmark Hall of Fame*, and went on to bring *Hamlet* (1953), *Macbeth* (1954), *Richard II* (1954), *Dial M for Murder* (1958), *The Tempest* (1960), and *Alice in Wonderland* (1955—in which he served as narrator), among many others, to the small screen. Maurice was enchanted by the possibilities of television. "It is startling to think," he said in 1954, "that the TV audience that will see *Macbeth* probably will be larger than all the combined audiences who have seen the play since Shakespeare wrote it."

Evans's other films include: *Wedding Rehearsal* (1932), *Scrooge* (1935), *Planet of the Apes* (1968) and one of its sequels, *Beneath the Planet of the Apes* (1970), and *Rosemary's Baby* (a film both Endora and Uncle Arthur protest on *Bewitched*).

Evans also appeared in TV's *Batman* (as The Puzzler in two episodes), *I Spy, Name of the Game*, *The Mod Squad*, and *Search*.

After *Bewitched* ended its run in 1972, Evans resurfaced briefly in 1980 in a tour of *Holiday,* Philip Barry's 1928 comedy glorifying nonconformity, and in small parts on television, including a movie of the week, *The Girl, the Gold Watch and Everything* (also in 1980).

Maurice Evans passed away on March 12, 1989, at the age of eighty-seven, in Brighton, England.

Alice Pearce (Gladys Kravitz)

Alice Pearce was born October 16, 1917, the only child of Robert E. Pearce, a National City Bank vice-president, and Margaret Clark Pearce. After attending a series of schools in Belgium, France, and Italy, Alice studied drama at Sarah Lawrence College in Bronxville, New York, and graduated in 1940.

She went on to become one of the stars of *New Faces of 1943* on Broadway, which led to her performance in *Look, Ma, I'm Dancin'!*, a night club act she and her first husband, John Cox (songwriter of such hits as "It's A Big, Wide, Wonderful World"), performed, wrote, and produced for the Blue Angel nightclub in New York.

She also was in *On the Town* with Fred Astaire in 1947. Other stage hits included *Gentlemen Prefer Blondes*, *Bells Are Ringing*, and Noel Coward's *Sail Away* in 1961, her final appearance in the theater.

Her film history includes *On the Town* (1949), *How to Be Very, Very Popular* (with Robert Cummings, 1955), *My Six Loves* (1963), *Kiss Me, Stupid* (1964), *The Disorderly Orderly* (1964), *Dear Brigitte* (with James Stewart, 1965), and *The Glass Bottom Boat* (1966), in which she costarred with fellow *Bewitched* cast-member George Tobias, as his wife.

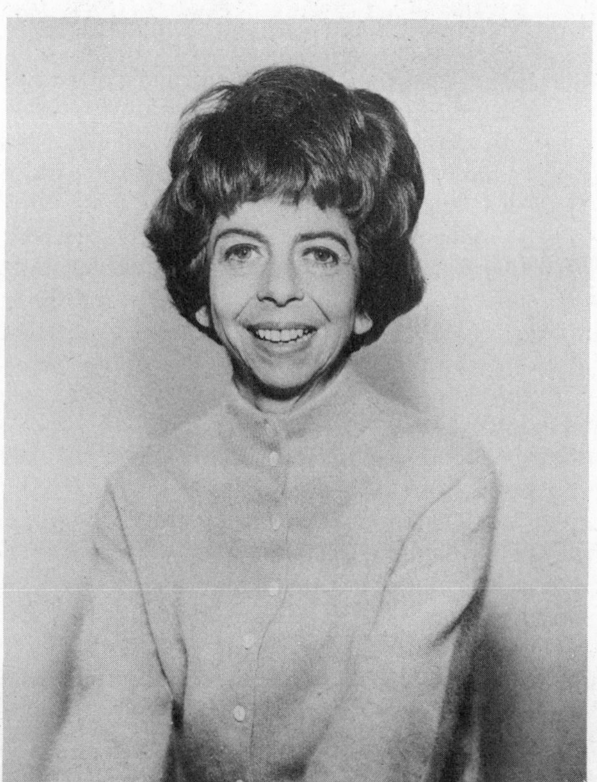

Alice Pearce. (Columbia Pictures Television.)

Her TV work included appearances on *The Milton Berle Show, The Garry Moore Show, The Ed Sullivan Show, The Jack Paar Show,* and *Hazel.* She starred in her own series in 1948, *The Alice Pearce Show,* which she called "fifteen minutes of songs, topical skits, and me."

Her first husband, John Cox, died in 1957 and Pearce married Broadway director Paul Davis in 1964.

Alice Pearce played Gladys Kravitz for two years, knowing that she was ill with cancer. She was forty-eight years old when she passed away on March 3, 1966.

To no one's surprise, there was applause the night her husband, Paul, accepted her Emmy Award for Best Supporting Actress in a Comedy in 1966, as those members of the television academy and the audience recalled Alice's wonderful, wordless squeals as Gladys. She had said that Mrs. Kravitz was her favorite role.

Sandra Gould (Gladys Kravitz)

Sandra Gould made her radio debut at age nine and appeared on radio's *My Friend Irma, The Danny Thomas Show,* and *The Jack Benny Show* (for fifteen years). She spent five years as Mrs. Duffy on *Duffy's Tavern.*

Gould made her Broadway debut when she was eleven years old in *Fly Away Home* with Montgomery Clift and went on to do other Broadway productions like *New Faces, Having a Wonderful Time,* and *Detective Story.*

Married and widowed twice (first to broadcasting executive Larry Berns, then to director Hollingsworth Morse), Gould made numerous guest appearances on TV shows like *December Bride, The Joey Bishop Show, I Love Lucy, The Danny Thomas Show, The Joan Davis Show,* and *I Dream of Jeannie,* before her regular stint on *Bewitched.*

Gould is also a writer; her two books, *Always Say Maybe* and *Sexpots and Pans,* were published by Golden Press. *Always* is a guide for women to find a man, and *Pans* is a cookbook on how to cook for forty-six different types of men.

At the moment Gould is writing a Hollywood-tales type of book and is also working as a features writer for several magazines, including *Sports Illustrated, Los Angeles Magazine, Reader's Digest,* and *Cosmopolitan.* She is an accomplished artist and has sold several hundred paintings.

George Tobias (Abner Kravitz)

George Tobias began a colorful life on July 14, 1901, on New York's Lower East Side. Coming from a theatrical family, he started his own career at the age of fifteen at the Neighborhood Playhouse in New York. At nineteen, he went into a Provincetown Playhouse production of *The Hairy Ape,* a new Eugene O'Neill play that was destined to become an American classic.

Shortly afterward, he was chosen for the original Broadway cast of *What Price Glory,* by Maxwell Anderson and Laurence Stallings. The play was highly successful and George stayed with it from 1924 to 1926.

He later appeared in such plays as *The Road to Rome, The Grey Fox,* and *Elizabeth the Queen,* and then went on to work in summer stock with Jose Ferrer. When he returned to New York, he landed in another new production that was to

Sandra Gould as Gladys Kravitz. (Elizabeth Montgomery/William Asher collection.)

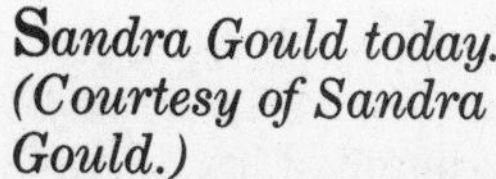

Sandra Gould today. (Courtesy of Sandra Gould.)

George Tobias as Abner Kravitz. (Columbia Pictures Television.)

become one of Broadway's all-time hits, *You Can't Take It with You.* From 1937 to 1939 he played the Russian ballet master in the famous George Kaufman–Moss Hart comedy, then went into the musical *Leave It to Me!* with Mary Martin.

George then came to Hollywood to make movies for MGM, including *Ninotchka* (1939), which years later become a hit on Broadway in a musical version called *Silk Stockings* (1957) with Don Ameche and Hildegarde Neff; this was in turn adapted into another MGM film with Fred Astaire and Cyd Charisse. George was in all three versions.

For many years he was under contract to Warner Brothers, and appeared in *Yankee Doodle Dandy* (1942) and *Air Force* (1943) for the studio, as well as *Mission to Moscow* (1943) and *My Sister Eileen* (1955), which also featured Dick York and was a Columbia release.

George made many other films including *The Set-Up* (1949), *Ten Tall Men* (1951), *The Glenn Miller Story* (1954), *The Seven Little Foys* (1955), *Marjorie Morningstar* (1958), and *The Glass Bottom Boat* (1966, which also featured his *Bewitched* costar Alice Pearce as his wife).

In addition to his regular role as Abner Kravitz, Tobias made several other TV appearances, including a continuing part in *Adventures in Paradise* from 1959 to 1962. And though Abner may have been a softer role for him to play, he was quite an active and rugged man in real life. He was a horseman who owned and trained many horses and loved to play polo. He was also a volunteer mounted policeman.

"He was a sheriff out in Peach Blossum [California] where he lived," recalled David White. "He had a badge and everything. And he was told that if he ever saw something suspicious, he should call it in. I mean, he had a two-way radio in his jeep, and I guess he used to be quite a rambler out there."

Tobias died on February 27, 1980.

Irene Vernon (Louise Tate)

Irene Vernon was born in Mishawaka, Indiana, and she graduated from Mishawaka High School. From there she traveled to New York to become a dancer, performing in many nightclubs, including Ben Martin's Riviera in Fort Lee, New Jersey. After doing a few Broadway shows like the 1943 hit *Artists and Models on Broadway,* which starred Jane Froman and Jackie Gleason, she signed a contract with Metro-Goldwyn-Mayer Studios in California and appeared in bit parts in films like *Till the Clouds Roll By* (1946, her first movie) and *The Pirate* (1948) starring Judy Garland and Gene Kelly.

"I was very excited," says Vernon, "but very dumb and naïve about the business. I was seventeen years old when I left home. And even though I started out as a dancer, acting was really what I wanted to do. And I got lucky later because I was pretty and a received a lot of publicity because of my contract with MGM."

Vernon came to *Bewitched* through her association with Danny Arnold, whom she had acted with in New York. "Danny and I knew each other from the forties,"

Irene Vernon today. (Mark Gilman.)

she recalls, "and we had studied together with a Russian actress named Batani Schneider and her husband Benno Schneider, who had directed Ingrid Bergman on Broadway in *Liliom.*"

Years later, when both Vernon and Arnold resided in Los Angeles, they met again on the lot at Columbia Studios. "I was auditioning for some other show," says Vernon, "and we had bumped into each other and had coffee. And it was then he offered me the part of Louise on *Bewitched*, explaining that it was a very small role, but that it would grow. So I said okay."

On leaving *Bewitched* in 1966, Vernon ventured into a successful career in real estate and presently lives in Beverly Hills.

Kasey Rogers (Louise Tate)

Kasey Rogers was born in Missouri, but lived in California most of her childhood. At two and a half years old, she began taking elocution lessons, and when she was eight she was playing the piano at the Hollywood Bowl and the Shrine Auditorium. She went to Burbank High School in Burbank, California, and became interested in acting while doing school plays.

At nineteen she married, and while she was attending Glendale College, her interest in drama became dominant. She won her first professional job in the entertainment industry as a dancer in an Earl Carroll show. Soon after, she signed with top agency MCA, and received her first film lead in the Paramount Pictures release of *Special Agent* (1949).

Kasey Rogers today. (Courtesy of Kasey Rogers.)

Kasey Rogers and David White as Louise and Larry Tate. (Columbia Pictures Television.)

Kasey's talents were employed in a wide range of roles at Paramount operas with Joel McCrea, heavy drama with the late Robert Walker, com Bob Hope, and adventure with Sterling Hayden.

Other movie credits of Kasey's include C. B. DeMille's *Samson a* (1950), Frank Capra's *Riding High* (1950), *Silver City* (1951), George ed *Place in the Sun* (1951), Alfred Hitchcock's *Strangers on a Train* (195 ork Marion Lorne, in which she says she played ". . . the consummate bi it," *Denver and Rio Grande* (1952), and *Jamaica Run* (1953). All of er 500 was done under the stage name of Laura Elliot. *ossible,*

In addition to her role as Louise on *Bewitched*, Kasey ha wo years television appearances, including guest shots on the classic *M* *The Lucy Show*, and *Flamingo Road*. And she played Julie An *rry Mason,* on *Peyton Place* prior to *Bewitched*.

Kasey also did an episode of *The Lone Ranger*, played a acting. She is and was in two segments of *Wanted: Dead or Alive* in 1959

Now divorced, Kasey has raised four children and currently developing a one-woman show.

Mabel Albertson (Phyllis Stephens)

Mabel Albertson was born in 1901. Her career spanned nearly thirty-five years. Mabel appeared in films like *Mutiny on the Black Hawk* (1938), *My Pal Gus* (1952), *She's Back on Broadway* (1953), *Forever Darling* (1956), *The Long Hot Summer* (1958), *Home Before Dark* (1958), *Don't Give Up the Ship* (1959), *Barefoot in the Park* (1967), and *What's Up, Doc?* (1972).

Besides *Bewitched*, Albertson played similar wise-cracking mothers and mothers-in-law on shows like *That's My Boy, The Whiting Girls* (playing grandma to Tom Ewell), and *That Girl*, in which she played another famous mortal man's mom to Ted Bessell's Don Hollinger, one and only love of Ann Marie, played by Marlo Thomas.

Mabel Albertson died in 1982 of Alzheimer's disease.

Mabel Albertson as Mrs. Stephens. (Elizabeth Montgomery/William Asher collection.)

Mabel Albertson and Roy Roberts as Mrs. and Mr. Stephens. (ABC-Television.)

Robert F. Simon. (Dan Weaver collection.)

Robert F. Simon (Frank Stephens)

Robert F. Simon was born on December 2, 1908, in Mansfield, Ohio. Before he began his acting career, he aspired to be a traveling salesman. In fact, he initially ventured into theater to hone his skills as a commercial traveler. "I was shy," he says, "and I thought acting would help me overcome that. Once I stepped on stage, however, performing came easily to me, and it was then I decided to make a career of it."

Simon's first professional job was in the play *No for an Answer* by Marc Blitzstein, in which he had the opportunity to display his song and dance abilities as well. He also was involved the Cleveland Playhouse, Group Theatre, and Actors Studio, which led to an assignment as understudy to Lee J. Cobb for the lead in *Death of a Salesman.*

As he recalls of the latter: "I never expected Lee to fall ill, but at one point he did, and much to my surprise, I found myself in the production."

From *Salesman* he went on to several other stage performances, as well as many roles in television and film.

Besides Darrin's first father on *Bewitched,* his other TV appearances included regular roles on *The Legend of Custer* (as General Alfred Terry), *Nancy* (as Everett Hudson; on NBC, 1970–71), and *The Amazing Spider-Man* (as J. Jonah Jameson, a role David White portrayed in the *Spider-Man* pilot film).

Simon completed more than fifty films, including *Where the Sidewalk Ends* (1950), *Chief Crazy Horse* (1955), *The Court Martial of Billy Mitchell* (1955, with Elizabeth Montgomery), *The Last Angry Man* (1959), *Captain Newman, M.D.* (1963), *The Reluctant Astronaut* (1967), *Operation Petticoat* (1959) (both *Astronaut* and *Petticoat* also featured Dick Sargent), *The Benny Goodman Story* (1955), and *The Spiral Road* (1962).

Today Simon is retired from acting. He lives in Reseda, California, and has four children.

Roy Roberts (Frank Stephens)

Roy Roberts, Darrin's other father, was born on March 19, 1900, in Tampa, Florida, and passed away on May 28, 1975. As explained by Bill Asher, the role of Frank Stephens was played by Roberts and Simon whenever one or the other was available. Becuase of these two gentlemen's careers, they were called to *Bewitched* at different times.

Roberts played John Cushing from 1964 to 1967 on *The Beverly Hillbillies,* Harrison Cheever on *The Lucy Show* from 1965 to 1968, and Mr. Bodine on *Gunsmoke* from 1965 to 1975. Before his appearances on *Bewitched,* he was Captain Huxley on *The Gale Storm Show* from 1956 to 1960 and Norman Curtis on *Petticoat Junction* from 1963 to 1964. Sometime later, on November 2, 1967, Roberts made his first of thirteen appearances as one of Darrin's two dads.

Roberts film highlights include *The Sullivans* (1944), *It Shouldn't Happen to a Dog* (1946, which was also used as the title for *Bewitched* Episode No. 3), *It's a Mad, Mad, Mad, Mad World* (1963), and *Hotel* (1967).

Parley Baer today. (Courtesy of Parley Baer.)

Dick Wilson today. (Courtesy of Dick Wilson.)

Charles Lane. (Courtesy of J. Carter Gibson Agency.)

Bernie Kopell today. (Courtesy of Bernie Kopell.)

Jane Connell. *(Courtesy of Jane Connell.)*

Sara Seegar. *(Courtesy of Irza Stone.)*

Reta Shaw. *(Fredric Tucker collection.)*

Nancy Kovack Mehta. *(Courtesy of Nancy Mehta.)*

Behind the Scenes

Harry Ackerman (Executive Producer/Creative Consultant)

Though Harry Ackerman began his career in radio, working on programs such as *The Phil Baker Show,* where he was assistant director, when he switched to television he was a power—executive producer for CBS in New York. He supervised the development, writing, and casting of all CBS New York–based shows, including *Studio One* and *Suspense* among others.

And as vice-president for CBS programs in Hollywood, he supervised the production elements on shows like *Gunsmoke* (which he personally developed and cast initially for radio, later recasting it for television), *The Jack Benny Show, Burns and Allen, Amos 'n' Andy* (the radio series and later the TV series), *Our Miss Brooks, The Edgar Bergen Show,* and *I Love Lucy.*

Ackerman was instrumental in developing the concept of *I Love Lucy* with Jess Oppenheimer, Lucille Ball, and Desi Arnaz. He personally supervised its production, and instituted its technical execution.

Martin N. Leeds, once head of business affairs for CBS on the West Coast, wrote in *Emmy Magazine* about Ackerman's contribution to *I Love Lucy:*

> Contrary to popular belief, it was Harry Ackerman—not [Lucille] Ball, Desi Arnaz, or cinematographer Karl Freund—who, on *I Love Lucy,* pioneered the three-camera technique for shows filmed before a live TV audience.
>
> When the series pilot was shot at CBS's Studio A in Hollywood, a kinescope recording was made for sales purposes and sent to the East Coast. Ackerman, then vice-president in charge of programming, went with it.
>
> Arthur Lyons, then head of Philip Morris, the show's sponsor, loved the pilot but balked at getting a kinescope recording other than a live program in the East on a regular basis. It was decided to [shoot the show] on film, but Ackerman was afraid the spontaneity created by a live audience would be lost.
>
> Ackerman phoned me and asked, "Do you know anything about the Fairbanks system of [using] multiple cameras locked into a fixed position?" My answer was "No, other than [the camera] took the picture from the same angled position, but covered a larger area of activity."
>
> Ackerman then asked me to get hold of Al Simon—who had worked with the Fairbanks technique as a production manager—and [ask him] if it would be feasible to place motion picture cameras on the same type of dollies used for live television in order to film in front of a live audience. Simon thought we could, and we hired him to help implement the system.

Ackerman was offered the presidency of CBS-Television by Bill Paley and Frank Stanton after that experiment, but declined in order to remain in production.

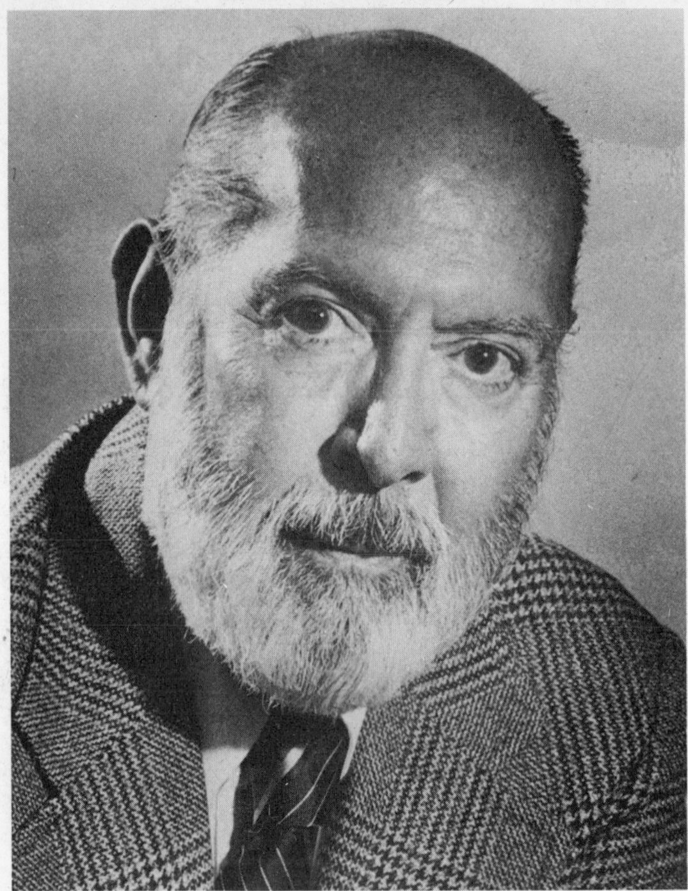

Harry Ackerman in 1988. (Courtesy of Harry Ackerman.)

Other television projects that Ackerman produced included the specials *The Day Lincoln Was Shot,* starring Jack Lemmon and Raymond Massey, *Blithe Spirit,* starring Noel Coward, Laurel Bacall, and Mildred Natwick, and *Twentieth Century,* starring Orson Welles and Betty Grable.

Besides *Bewitched,* Ackerman produced a wealth of TV fare for Screen Gems, including *Dennis the Menace, The Donna Reed Show, Hazel, Gidget, The Flying Nun,* and three Movies of the Week.

Ackerman also independently produced *Bachelor Father* and *Leave It to Beaver,* as well as the 90-minute special, *Paramount Presents,* for Paramount Television.

In 1984 Ackerman produced the TV movie *The Sky's No Limit,* starring Sharon Gless, Dee Wallace, Ann Archer, and Barnard Hughes, and *Welcome Home, Jelly Bean,* a one-hour *Schoolbreak Special* for CBS starring Dana Hill and Christopher Collett.

Ackerman also produced the TV feature *Gidget's Summer Reunion,* a two-hour pilot film for *The New Gidget* series starring Caryn Richman, which he also produced forty-four episodes of for Columbia Pictures Television.

In 1991 Ackerman was honored by the membership of the Caucus for Producers, winning one of the organization's top awards as Member of the Year. The award, presented annually to a Caucus member for his or her body of work in television, was made by producer/writer Gene Reynolds *(M*A*S*H)*, the 1989 winner.

Harry Ackerman died in 1991 of pneumonia contracted while he was in the hospital for cancer treatment.

William Asher (Producer/Director)

Born in New York City, William Asher attended schools there before arriving in Hollywood, California, broke and jobless.

Before World War II, he got a job at Universal Studios as a mail and errand boy. This position, however, was interrupted by service in the army, where he did a four-year stint with the Signal Corps in Astoria, New York, as an army photographer. He was also a photographer at Cushing General Hospital.

Returning to Universal after the war, Asher went to work as an assistant film editor, later becoming an assistant cameraman.

While working behind the camera, Asher wrote the screenplay for the theatrical film *Leather Gloves*, then coscripted, coproduced, and codirected it with Richard Quine (who directed *Bell, Book and Candle*) for Columbia Pictures in 1948.

B*ill Asher. (Courtesy of Bill Asher. Photo by Mark Gilman.)*

Early on in his career, Asher decided to go into the new field of television. He directed *Racket Squad* (which pre-dated the TV version of *Dragnet* and is considered one of the pioneers of television police shows). Though *Racket* was live the first season (it ran in syndication and on CBS from 1951 to 1953), it was filmed for its last two years.

This led to Asher's being hired to direct other filmed TV shows, including *The Pepsi/Schlitz Theater, The Colgate Comedy Hour, The Dinah Shore Show, The Danny Thomas Show, Our Miss Brooks, I Love Lucy,* and *The Jane Wyman Theater,* for which he won an Emmy.

Asher met Elizabeth Montgomery when he directed her in a 1963 film, *Johnny Cool*. Soon afterward, the two were married, and Asher went on to direct the sun-frolicked *Beach Party* (1963), *Muscle Beach Party* (1964), *Beach Blanket Bingo* (1965), *How to Stuff a Wild Bikini* (1965), which featured his wife Elizabeth in a cameo role doing the nose twitch, *Fireball 500* (1966).

Asher's career has been most rewarding. He has won the Sylvania Award and the national *TV Guide* award for *The Danny Thomas Show.* In 1966 he was honored again for *Bewitched.*

After *Bewitched,* Bill Asher worked on many episodes on CBS-TV's popular sitcom *Alice*, which starred Linda Lavin and aired from 1976 to 1985. Shortly following that, he created and coproduced *Kay O'Brien* from 1986 to 1987, also for CBS.

His recent films include *Night Warning* (1982) starring Bo Svenson, and *Movers and Shakers* (1985), with an all-star cast, including Walter Matthau, Charles Grodin (who wrote and produced), Steve Martin, the late Gilda Radner, and Penny Marshall.

Some of Asher's other TV producing/directing assignments include *The Paul Lynde Show, Temperatures Rising*, and *The New Temperatures Rising Show.*

When not working with the Kushner-Locke Entertainment Company (he's producing a new late-night series for CBS), Asher enjoys biking, swimming, surfing, and tennis.

He lives in Beverly Hills with his second wife, actress Joyce Bullifant.

Danny Arnold (Producer)

Bewitched producer Danny Arnold began his career in show business after being discharged from the marines in 1944. He started in the Columbia Studios sound effects department and soon learned music and film editing. His career includes roles as an actor and performances as a stand-up comedian.

Danny is best known for his role as series cocreator, executive producer, frequent director, and script supervisor of *Barney Miller,* one of television's longest running and most innovative situation comedies.

The series has won an Emmy, a George Peabody Award, two Golden Globes, and a Mystery Writers of America Special Award, as well as recognition from police departments around the country, *The Congressional Record,* and city officials across the nation. Danny himself has also been nominated for Emmy Awards as a writer and as a director, and in 1985 he won the Writers' Guild of America Paddy Chayefsky Laurel Award for lifetime achievement in writing excellence.

Danny Arnold. *(Courtesy of Danny Arnold/photo by Rochelle Law.)*

Danny has pioneered several production techniques that have contributed to the quality of excellence of several shows. These include his innovative use of film concepts in videotape production. His four-camera "quad-split" technique has permitted the master, close-ups, and reverse to be shot to a greater degree of perfection while taping simultaneously, thereby allowing maximum control in postproduction.

The use of natural situational lighting has contributed to the excellence of the videotaped picture. It was enough to cause the American Society of Lighting Directors to name Danny its Man of the Year for 1978.

Danny has formed and presided over four companies, including Four D Productions, Inc. (which produced *Barney Miller*), the Mimus Corporation (which produced *Fish*, a spin-off of *Miller*), and the Triseme Corporation (which produced *A.E.S. Hudson Street* and the TV movie, *Don't Look Back: The Story of Satchel Paige*). His most recent company, Tetragram Ltd., has an exclusive arrangement with ABC-TV for the production of three series, the first of which was the highly controversial *Joe Bash* dramedy starring Peter Boyle in 1986.

Some of Danny's other television credits include *The Real McCoys*, *The Wackiest Ship in the Army*, *That Girl*, *The Colgate Comedy Hour*, and *The Tennessee Ernie Ford Show*, where he met his wife, Donna. They have two sons, and they make their home above Hollywood's Sunset Strip, where Danny enjoys photography, gourmet cooking, and collecting paintings.

Richard Michaels (Producer/Director)

Richard Michaels began his career as a script clerk during the first season of *Bewitched.* He went on to become an associate producer and finally a full-fledged director. Michaels acknowledges Bill Asher's role in advancing his career.

"I owe my career to the show and to Bill Asher," he says. "He's the man who gave me my first job. And the show has been the central point of my entire life and career, and I'll never forget the time I spent working on it."

After *Bewitched*, Richard Michaels became one of television's most successful directors. Some of the made-for-TV features he directed include *Leave Yesterday Behind* (1978), starring John Ritter as a paralyzed veterinary student; *Berlin Tunnel 21* (1981), starring Richard Thomas; *Love and Betrayal* (1989), featuring Stefanie Powers and David Birney; and *The Leona Helmsley Story* (1990), starring Suzanne Pleshette.

In series television he has directed episodes of *The Brady Bunch, The Odd Couple,* and *Love, American Style.*

Michaels is married and divides his time between Los Angeles and Hawaii.

Richard Michaels. (Courtesy of Richard Michaels.)

Sol Saks (Pilot Creator)

Born in New York City and raised in Chicago, Sol Saks graduated from the Northwestern University School of Journalism.

Saks arrived in Los Angeles in 1948 and began his career in radio. He had wanted to be a writer since the age of thirteen. Though he is well known for having written the pilot for *Bewitched,* he also gave birth to many other radio and television shows.

A partial list of these programs begins with *Duffy's Tavern* (on radio and featuring Sandra Gould) and *My Favorite Husband*, which was first broadcast on radio, starring Lucille Ball, later featuring Joan Caufield as a scatterbrained wife to Barry Nelson in the television version. Of the latter, Saks comments: "I think that show was the first realistic situation comedy on TV. Both Joan and Barry were actors who did comedy, and not [slapstick] comedians."

Saks also created *Mr. Adams and Eve*, which starred the legendary actress (and guest *Bewitched* director) Ida Lupino and Howard Duff.

In addition, Saks at one time was the supervisor of comedy for CBS, as well as script consultant.

Other writing credits include the theatrical feature *Walk, Don't Run* (1966), starring Cary Grant; the stage plays *The Beginning, Middle and End*, and *Soft Remembrance;* and a book, *The Craft of Comedy Writing*, which was published in 1985 by Writer's Digest Books. Saks has also written numerous short stories and articles, most recently for *Atlantic Monthly.*

Saks is also an associate professor of script writing at California State University and Pepperdine University and has conducted many successful writing workshops.

Saks has never considered himself a comedy writer, per se, but as he explains, "I write mildly humorous scenes for actors." As of June 30, 1991, his stage play *Soft Remembrance* opened in Chicago, with a projected later move to New York.

Saks is widowed with two children, Mary Laurie and Daniel, and he lives in Sherman Oaks, California.

Sol *Saks. (Photo by Stan Levy.)*

ACKNOWLEDGMENTS

Obviously, this book is not the work of one person. Many people have been of great assistance in seeing that it was published. To these people I would very much like to express my sincerest gratitude. I could not have completed this book without the enthusiastic cooperation of those I interviewed, or those who contributed various *Bewitched*-related material, information, photos, and memorabilia.

First, a most sincere thank you to Elizabeth Montgomery and William Asher, both of whom donated much time, effort, and personal recollections to the totality of this book; to Dick York and Dick Sargent, two very special Darrins; and to all the cast and crew who contributed their memories, specifically Harry Ackerman and David White.

A very large thank you must go out to top-notch *Bewitched* and entertainment historian David Keil for his incredible amount of support, knowledge, facts, trivia, and quotations, all of which became a most interconnecting contribution to this book.

I also wish to thank my editors at Dell, Dan Levy and Betsy Bundschuh, for their patience in putting this book together. And I am indebted to the *Bewitched* brigade, including Dan Weaver, Gary Matheson, Steve Randisi, Geoff Davis, Fredric Tucker, George Gallucci, Theodore Bouloukas II, Fred Grandinetti, Bailey Melton, Steve Cox, Laurie Klobas, Bart Andrews, Richard Lamparski, and Professor Arthur Asa Berger.

Thanks also go to photographers Tamara Fowler (of Redhead Photography in Burbank, California), Mark Gilman (of Operator 13 Productions in North Hollywood, California), Marty Jackson (of Los Angeles), Anthony D. Secker (of Loriant Photography of Hawthorne, California), Carmen Grunke (of Woodward, Oklahoma), and Scott Coblio (of Rochester, New York).

To the following TV-movie memorabilia collectors: Larry Edmunds (of Hollywood), Eddie Brandt's Saturday Matinee (of North Hollywood), The Memory Shop (of New York), Photofest, Inc., and Globe Photos, Inc. (both also of New York),

Milton T. Moore, Jr., (of Dallas, Texas), and to E. Ben Emerson, and Rowe Photographic Video and Audio of Rochester, New York, a thousand thank yous for the entire book.

In addition to the permissions information contained elsewhere in this book, further acknowledgment must be given to the following Columbia Pictures Television personnel who gave considerable assistance in the collection of *Bewitched* photos, illustrations, memorabilia, and cover animation: Terence McCluskey, Lisa Krone, Lamont Blake, Allan Press, and Linda Kazynski.

Michael Lipton, Peggy Egan, Ray Biswanger, Helen Gurley, Laurie Britton, and Peter Abel at *TV Guide*, Michael Silverman and Douglas Galloway from *Daily Variety*, Harry Medved at the Screen Actors Guild, George Schaefer, Peter Todd of the British Film Institute in London, Molden Philips of P.R.S. Ltd. (also in London), radio producer Neil L. Midman (of WRC in Boston), and a very special thanks to Marcella Saunders, Helen Lynde, Nancy Noce, Sam Amato, Nora Gianetto, Kathleen O'Brien, and David Hamblin, editors of *DAKA Magazine* of Rochester, New York.

Acknowledgments also must be made to Barbara A. Cyprus, Joseph Janowics (of the Eastman Kodak Company), film director Kevin Konisak, the Santa Monica Library, the Rundell, Charlotte, and Paddy Hill Libraries of Rochester, New York, Bonnie and Bob Marinetti, Marty McClintock, Lele Brown, Anne Hodges, Jonni Hartman, Ethel and Bunny Levert, Louis Herthum, Arnold Patent, the Reverend G. Arthur Hammons, Jim and Melody Rondeau, Paul Wyatte, Lou Tomassetti (president of L.P.I. Consumer Products, Rochester, New York), Marypat Flynn, Denise Brown, Bob Greg, Ken Crosby, Mike Nannini (aka Opie Cunningham), Mr. and Mrs. Sam Picone, Shirley Di Risio, Joanna Whitboone, Jim Pierson, Gina Johnson, and Norman Borisoff.

Further thanks are extended to Bobby Leaf, Ellen Carter, Ellen Kelley, Bob Jacobs, Jim Moorehead, Nancy Spellman, and Dawn Rocha; and Debbie Keil, Gloria Delano, Doug and Margie Staheli, Mario Murcia, Mauricio Lopez, Turie Kontiainen, Nancy Becker, Marcella Lee, Michael Hyler, and Robin Lippincott.

A most beloved thanks must go out to my family: my loving mother and father, Frances and Herb Pilato, who allowed me to return to the room I grew up in to finish this book (and growing up); my sister Pam, her husband Sam, my nephew Sammy, who is a constant inspiration; my cousins Eva and David, Bill, Rita, Fred, Dani, and Wendy; Marie, Angelo, Nicholas, Aunt Antinette, and Uncle Joe; Noreen and Nan D'Agostino, Joanne, Joe, Vincent, Jimmy, and Carl; Aunt Elva, Aunt Amelia, Aunt Parmie, Aunt Anna, and Uncle Tony; Uncle Tony P., Uncle Mac and Aunt Ann (I L-O-V-E You); Aunt Sue, Mary Sue, Jimmy B., and Rose Alice; and to all the departed family souls from the visible world: Aunt Mary, Uncle Carl, Aunt

Alice and Uncle Ange, Uncle Val, Uncle Albert, Uncle Tony F., Uncle Adolph and Aunt Gerdie, Aunt Alice A. and Aunt Fay, Sonny, Grandma and Grandpa Pilato, Nonna and Pappa Turri, and Aunt Rita. I send out all my love to you, knowing you have received it.

But most of all, I thank God whose love and spirit lives within all of our hearts.